CELLS IN INDUSTRY

CELLS IN INDUSTRY

Managing teams for profit

Jim Kirton and Ellen Brooks

McGRAW-HILL BOOK COMPANY

London · New York · St Louis · San Francisco · Auckland
Bogotá · Caracas · Lisbon · Madrid · Mexico · Milan
Montreal · New Delhi · Panama · Paris · San Juan
São Paulo · Singapore · Sydney · Tokyo · Toronto

Published by
McGRAW-HILL Book Company Europe
Shoppenhangers Road, Maidenhead, Berkshire, SL6 2QL, England
Telephone 0628 23432 Fax 0628 770224

British Library Cataloguing in Publication Data

Kirton, J.
  Cells in Industry: Managing Teams for
  Profit
  I. Title II. Brooks, E.
  658.5

  ISBN 0-07-707850-0

Library of Congress Cataloging-in-Publication Data

Kirton, Jim
  Cells in industry: managing teams for profit / Jim Kirton and
Ellen Brooks.
    p. cm.
  Includes index.
  ISBN 0-07-707850-0
  1. Work groups.   2. Management–Employee participation.
  3. Leadership.   4. Organizational behavior.   I. Brooks, Ellen.
  II. Title.
  HD66.K58   1994
  658.4 02–dc20   94-20471
                                               CIP

12345 CUP 987654

Typeset by BookEns Ltd, Baldock, Herts.
and printed and bound in Great Britain at the University Press, Cambridge.

DEDICATION

To Liz

Contents

Acknowledgements

This is the bit, where, within reason, we can say what we like. I (Jim) started my career in manufacturing in the early 1960s as an apprentice with Rose Forgrove at Gainsborough in Lincolnshire and it is fair to say that I was given a good old fashioned initiation into engineering manufacture. My thanks go out to those craftsmen and foremen who gave me such a hard time and taught me so much, particularly what a complicated business manufacturing was.

Since the late 1970s I have worked as a manufacturing consultant in a wide variety of manufacturing industries. In this time it has been my privilege to work closely with some of the pioneers and shapers of team-based cell manufacture. I am honoured that some of these influential people have contributed case studies. My co-author, Ellen, has worked with me in business and industrial journalism for many years. I am particularly grateful for the way she has turned the products of my fevered imagination into well-scripted prose.

During the past 15 years many people have shared their experiences of planning and implementing cell manufacturing with us. We are particularly grateful to those who took time out of their busy schedules to work on the preparation of the case studies: Chris Reed of Alvis Vehicles, Bob Gore and Alan Eldred of Baker Perkins, Mike Hodgson of BAe Airbus and Dick Williams both formerly of BAe Hatfield, Matthew Holmes (who shared the results of his MSc project with us), Ken Jackson and Brian Watson of BNFL, Charles Paterson of GEC Large Machines and Andrew Corcoran of McDonald's Restaurants.

Paul Simon made a substantial contribution in the areas of engineering and logistics. Dick Williams and Margaret Shaw read and commented on the text. Fiona Sperry at McGraw-Hill encouraged us while we tried both to prepare the text and work full-time.

Plenty of others were involved as well. Chris fed us and Liz provided a quiet place where we could write. Our families got used to the idea that we worked evenings and weekends and that it was hard for them to get a turn at a computer. The cats, Claude, Percy, Bilbo and Gobelino, and Titch the dog sat on our laps and interfered whenever they could.

Introduction

I stood on a balcony overlooking the shop floor with Bob Gore, the Manufacturing Director of Baker Perkins Printing Machines Ltd. He turned to me and said, 'Jim, I think we've got it wrong.' My stomach turned to ice, but I managed to reply, 'What do you mean, Bob?' He said, 'Where's all the work? Nothing's happening. All the areas we designed to hold work-in-progress are empty.' Of course, Bob's comment sparked off a thorough investigation and we discovered that far from getting it wrong, by a fortunate combination of circumstances, actually we had got it all right! Our task had been to relocate the assembly of electronic control cabinets for printing machines from dispersed facilities on the old site to a new industrial unit. This allowed us to integrate all of the activities around one team of people. Using common-sense production engineering, we had created a functioning team-based assembly cell, although we didn't know it at the time.

Relocation allowed us to get all the elements right: people, engineering, logistics and accountability. The team of about 8–10 people were all motivated and committed. They had started to communicate extremely well and had developed a lot of unconscious agreement. We were able to co-locate all the processes needed to make the whole assembly and to collaborate with external and internal suppliers to get the logistics right. The goals were very clear because Baker Perkins already had a strong orientation towards accountability at the time, and they were pioneers in component cells, using them to produce shafts, discs, gears, frames and printing rollers. These cells had been implemented under the guidance of Ted Thain, Group Manufacturing Director, and Alan Eldred, the Manufacturing Manager, so people already had an understanding of the potential of cells, and it all came together in the assembly cell.

What actually happened—and the reason why there was no work-in-progress in the set-down areas—was that work was arriving in the morning and by evening it was gone. The day's requirement didn't hang around: it went out on time as planned. The reason why it didn't hang around was because we had created an environment where the easiest, most straightforward thing for people to do was the job in hand. Take logistics, for example. The cell technicians had a good quality work-to list that they could believe in. They knew it represented the *true* requirement to support assembly of the printing machines' electrical cabinets. The logistics train was set up correctly, so the parts were available when they were needed. Wiring provides a good example of what this meant. One technician's job was to prepare all the lengths of wire that would be used inside the electrical cabinet. When he arrived at work in the morning, he would consult his work-to list, find that the correct reels of wire had been delivered, and get on with his work, pulling the wires off the reels. The team had made sure that it was all set up to be straightforward for him to do. He could just roll off the required wires according to guides laid out on his bench, chop them off to length, put on the correct terminations and bundle them together. He found that by 2.30 pm he'd done the day's requirement. So what did he do? He went to see what was required for tomorrow and started to prepare for the following day's work. This was the first step in creating the virtuous spiral. He was able to get ready for what was coming next, instead of just reacting to demands as they were made. This benefit had washed right through the factory. There was no work in the set-down area because it was all done and delivered.

We discovered that something else had also happened. Productivity had gone up by 20 per cent because shortages and quality problems had virtually disappeared. This was in stark contrast to how it used to be, and it was fortuitous. We'd moved electronic cabinet assembly down the road to a new industrial unit, located everything neatly in the space allocated and, incidentally, had created all these improvements without really understanding exactly what we were doing. In the old world, the technician who did the wiring used to arrive in the morning, come to his bench, which was remote from the area where they did the assemblies, and his first question was 'What *can* I do today?' (not 'What *should* I do today?'). He'd have a look to see what was there, identify the shortages and go off to try to assemble all the material he needed to do the job. On the way to the stores he'd divert to the amenities, and then he'd bump into someone who had some questions to ask—work related, or maybe not—and by the time he got back from stores, quite a bit of the morning would be gone before he had started to assemble the wire requirements. He was living in the destructive spiral. The best description of the destructive spiral is a situation where the industrial manager spends all his time just trying to keep the system moving. If he stopped pushing, the whole thing would spiral into the ground and stop. It is a tribute to the ingenuity of production managers that by managing shortages, getting hold of the right tools, etc., they keep production moving as well as they do. And usually by the end of the week they are worn out. Team-based cells work because they change this destructive spiral into a virtuous spiral.

The whole thing takes on a momentum of its own and builds up until it is running like a sewing machine, until, as happened in this case, Mick Douse, the cabinet assembly team leader at Baker Perkins, came to me and said, 'Jim, it runs itself, there's nothing for me to do.' My reply was, 'Oh yes there is, now you can concentrate on doing your *real* job, which is planning ahead and making all this even better.' He protested that he didn't know how to do this kind of planning, so he was able to ask for training, attend some seminars and learn. He was liberated to develop new skills and do what he really should be doing, increasing the contribution he made to the company through what the pundits now call Continuous Improvement, rather than chasing his tail in a destructive spiral.

Having stumbled across team-based cells, I rolled things around in my head and tried to figure out how we could create the same success—regular as clockwork—in companies manufacturing products as diverse as margarine and military vehicles. Over the past 10 years, plenty of companies have tried variations on the theme of cells, with greater or lesser success, and plenty of people have offered advice on how to do it. I have watched, read about and participated in this process, and tried to assess what went right and what went wrong. In this book, I have tried to provide a framework which will help people at all levels in industry to think creatively about using people working in teams to implement change and create team-based cells that will give your business competitive advantage.

1

Evolution of today's manufacturing issues

Manufacturing is a definer for mankind. As long as man has been a reasoning being with a soul, he has been a manufacturer. Ability to fashion tools which make it easier for him to find and process food supplies and make the world a better place for him to live is one of the things that distinguishes man from the higher primates. Archaeologists look for evidence of simple manufactured tools— knapped flint or sharpened bone implements—to help them distinguish the remains of man from those of a transitional anthropoid.

The evolution of manufacture has passed through distinct stages at various periods of history in different parts of the world. The cycle of manufacturing development has taken place at different times in different societies. The stages can be traced in Mesopotamia, South Asia, China, Central and South America and Europe. In some areas the cycle happened twice, for example, in Europe: reaching a peak with the Romans, and then starting again after the Dark Ages.

This chapter examines each stage in the evolutionary cycle (Fig. 1.1) giving examples from specific periods in history, shows how the important manufacturing issues which face us today have developed and looks ahead to what the future might bring.

BONE, FLINT KNAPPING, FIRST METALS

From earliest days, organized manufacture starts to appear.

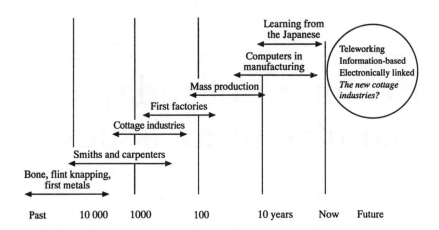

Figure 1.1 Evolution of manufacture

Hunter-gatherers originally formed a simple society that exploited the resources found around it, but did not attempt to process them. Manufacturing as a specialization developed first to provide simple handtools to the hunter-gatherers. Archaeologists have discovered flint quarries and evidence of organized manufacture of flint tools for use by hunter-gatherers: axes for large game, arrowheads for smaller game, knives, etc. This implies the production of a surplus to feed the quarrymen and toolmakers. Early man also manufactured items to help with gathering, such as baskets and containers made from skin. Manufacturing tended to be concentrated within the boundaries of the family, clan or tribe. There is also evidence of trade, because some of these tools have been found many miles away from their sources. Man then made the transition to a pastoral society, following herds of beasts around and managing them. These people developed the manufactured products which helped them with this work, such as containers for milk made of skins, ricks for carrying fodder, etc., and tools to help them erect shelters.

The next transition, from pastoral to agricultural life, first took place in the fertile crescent from Mesopotamia (in modern day Iraq) to the Nile Delta, where the main crop was wheat, in China where rice was grown also and in Central America where the crop was maize. In the fertile crescent, hybrid wheat contributed to the breakthrough because it allowed much bigger yields than grasses. This meant that, not only could people grow enough to feed themselves, they could also produce a surplus. The surplus let them support people who were doing things other than grow food. This had both a positive and a negative side because it enabled the development of a nobility with the potential to oppress the farmers by taking the surplus away.

Mass migrations of entire populations have been regular occurrences throughout history. At first, a nobility may have developed when a nomadic tribe elected a chief or king to lead them during a migration and would donate surplus food to support him. Gradually this role became hereditary and coercive, through evolution of the elected king into an exploitive king, then by conquest, when waves of tribes moved south on horseback to conquer farming communities. These hardy northern people, who were accustomed to living in harsh conditions, easily adapted to the southern climate, were assimilated and became the new nobility. This happened repeatedly in the Middle East and Asia, for example, in China with the Mongols and Manchurians, and in the Middle East where the Hittites, Assyrians and Iranians all moved down in turn from the north to the more hospitable south. The pattern of migration under an elected leader continued across Europe. When the Anglo-Saxons arrived in Britain they elected their king, but this role soon evolved to become hereditary and coercive. The seeds of feudalism in Britain had already been sown, and came to fruition with the Norman Invasion by hardy northern folk who invaded a territory and became the local nobility.

Development of manufacture in the classical world was also based on a local nobility, demanding goods and services and enough surplus food to support the workers who produced them.

With the establishment of a nobility, a two-class society developed. There was no middle class, only nobles and peasants, who were semi-free or slaves. The system which allowed the nobles to take the surplus from the peasant community also created the conditions where leisure was possible and stimulated a demand for products to support this new type of life-style. Demand increased for the manufacture of luxury items, jewellery, books and scrolls, weapons, chariots, suits of armour, all the accoutrements which support the life-style of the nobility. The nobility also wanted to live in dwellings which were superior to hovels and this led to the manufacture of all sorts of products related to building and architecture. Religion was also a powerful force and the production of religious artifacts plays a significant role in the development of manufacturing.

URBANIZATION AND SPECIALIZATION: CARPENTERS AND SMITHS

As people concentrated around the places where surpluses were brought to be traded, towns developed, and this led to the beginnings of a middle class: the independent burgesses who traded in these surpluses, transporting them from where they were produced to where they were wanted. Many of these burgesses became wealthy, participated in local government, became mayors and were looked on as pillars of society. Their houses can still be seen all over Europe in market towns such as Salisbury in England, Bruges in Belgium and Zurich in Switzerland.

Urbanization developed around a local manufacturing base which was grouped into three distinct and easily recognizable activities:

1. Extractive industries: mining, bottle or bell mines, stone quarries, and making the tools associated with these.
2. Local community industries: smithy, carpenter and wheel-wright, making metal and wooden things for community use, e.g. wagons, watermills, windmills. Specialized industries where an individual person had the skill and used it.
3. Textiles, tanneries, potteries: making clothing and shoes, dishes and containers.

The role of the burgesses was that of entrepreneur and trader of goods between craftsmen. It was important for them to promote good relationships between the extractive and manufacturing industries.

Manufacturing also went on in the households of both peasants and aristocrats. Working with textiles was an important task for women who did not labour on the land. The unmarried daughters of the house were all put to work spinning, hence the term 'spinster'.

At the same time, differences developed between town and country manufacturing. Carpenters made hay wagons, buckets, yokes, barrel staves and other wooden implements associated with agriculture. Blacksmiths forged metal structures, gate hinges, barrel hoops, nails, horse shoes, scythes, saws and other tools. As towns developed, these skills were refined to make more ornamental and luxury objects. Located in towns, precious metal smiths worked in silver and gold, making jewellery and church plate, while cabinet-makers produced finely crafted furniture. Later on, metal-workers specialized in clocks and watches, astrolabes and other instruments. The differentiation between blacksmith and silversmith, carpenter and cabinet-maker was very largely country/town.

In towns, the guild system emerged to regulate entry to crafts, setting out qualifications for achieving each grade: apprentice, journeyman, master. Manufacturing was concentrated in a number of discrete specialist areas but it was totally based on the skills of individual artisans; the person who started to make something finished it. The logistics organization made focus on the local area necessary. Methods of transport made the supply of raw materials difficult and expensive, particularly for expensive or rare commodities such as gold and other precious metals.

Basic processes for extracting metals caused the earliest concentration of manufacturing around certain areas. Smelting had to take place where both the raw material and the source of energy needed to convert it were available. Thus, the earliest iron smelting was concentrated in forests growing on top of iron ore deposits, for example, the Weald of Sussex. This meant that plenty of wood was available to make charcoal for fuel. So much iron was smelted there over the ages that the Romans used the slag to pave their local roads.

Techniques for manufacturing pottery were developed by every society in every period of history. In primitive societies there was usually a ready supply of clay, so people made their own pots. Because firing temperatures are low, they were able to design and build effective kilns. In classical times, relatively sophisticated transport allowed the pottery industry to be concentrated in specific areas and this resulted in recognizable styles and levels of quality. In Roman Britain, pottery manufacture was notable in the Peterborough area. Simian ware, dense red terracotta pots from Gaul, were traded all over the world. Amphora for storing oil which had been manufactured in Greece ended up in Britain. During the Dark Ages, the whole evolutionary cycle for manufacturing pottery had to take place again. People again had to manufacture their own pots, and street names still remain to provide evidence of local potteries, e.g. Kiln Lane, Fire Street. Gradually, as transportation improved, pottery manufacture again became focused in specific areas.

The evolution of manufacture was very slow. It took thousands of years to move from farm to town, to craftsmen with specialized skills, to focusing in a specific location. There were no factories. The only concentration of labour took place in the extractive industries and these conditions prevailed for centuries.

COTTAGE INDUSTRIES

The next stage in the evolution of manufacturing was the development of cottage industries. Cottage industries began to develop when peasants who worked on the land began to practice a craft by candlelight in order to earn a little more. This was an early stage of specialization. Mr Webster sat at his loom in his weaving loft, while the entrepreneur trader travelled round from cottage to cottage, co-ordinating activities, delivering raw materials and collecting and paying for the finished work. There had to be a degree of co-operation between spinning, weaving and making up of garments, while materials had to be small in bulk and easily transportable and the craft needed to be relatively high in added value.

Halifax is a good example of a town that depended on a cottage industry. It became the centre of the wool industry in the seventeenth century and weavers' cottages, with big loft windows to let in light, can still be seen in the surrounding countryside. The town regulated the industry. Wool from sheep raised in the surrounding hills was traded at the market. It then passed from cottager to cottager as all the processes needed to turn it into saleable cloth were carried out: washing, carding, combing, spinning, weaving and fulling (cleansing and finishing off). The material was pegged out on lawns, on tenterhooks, to dry, and this provided plenty of opportunity for theft. The law imposed severe penalties for interfering with the textile trade, indicating the value and importance that was placed on this trade. Conviction for offences related to the textile trade such as sheep rustling or stealing cloth could result in execution. An early version of the guillotine stood ready in Gibbet Street. Hence the saying, 'From Hull, hell, and Halifax may the Lord preserve us'. Halifax, Bradford and Leeds later became the focus of the manufacture of woollens in factories. When conditions were right the mill system developed here, but the textile trade remained a cottage industry for generations.

It was the cottage industry entrepreneurs who saw the opportunities of the factory system. However, it was not the skilled cottage industry workers who eventually went into the factories, it was the landless peasants. Manufacture could have remained with artisans in towns for much longer, but several things happened which precipitated emergence of the factory system.

RISE OF THE FACTORY SYSTEM

A factory is a concentration of people and resources in one
locality to specialize in the manufacture of one group of products,
for competitive advantage and superior quality. The rise of
factories was dictated by the need for specialization and
concentration. The four prerequisites which were necessary for
factories to develop all came together in England during the late
eighteenth and early nineteenth centuries. These are shown in Fig.
1.2.

Abundant labour (and the means to feed it)

The creation of an abundant pool of labour was directly related to
the rediscovery and application of the principles of selective
breeding during the Renaissance because this provided the basis
for increased agricultural productivity. When Ferdinand and
Isabella recovered southern Spain from the Moors, classical
information which had been lost to Europe since the decline of
the Roman Empire gradually became available again as Arabic
manuscripts were studied. This process led to the rediscovery of
science, which until then had not been considered as an inquiring

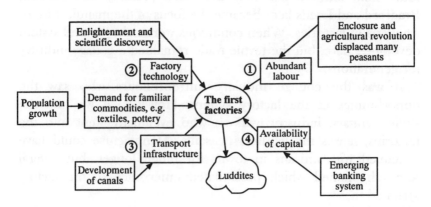

Figure 1.2   Four prerequisites for the development of the factory system

process, but was based on reinterpreting the Aristotelian view of the world. This rediscovered knowledge prompted the inquiring minds of men such as Galileo, Copernicus and Kepler to think again about science. They achieved publicity because they were high-profile and their opinions clashed with religious views. Their efforts paved the way for other thinkers who came later, such as 'Turnip' Townsend, who quietly experimented with plant breeding. He developed a strain of root crops which enabled more cattle to be fed and kept alive over winter, instead of being slaughtered. This prompted cross-breeding of sheep and cattle to produce hardier species with more wool, more beef or more milk. The consequence was an explosion in land productivity, encouraging initial attempts at mechanizing agriculture.

As a result, the nobility wanted to change land use, away from strip farming to pasture for cattle and sheep or large arable fields which would be more profitable. This meant they had to evict many people who were strip farming in order to increase the size of the fields. In Britain, the Enclosures Act of the eighteenth century led to the elimination of strip farming. This was generally a selfish move on the part of the nobility because the more powerful people obtained the best land, while the weaker ones received marginal land. Common land was fenced and farmers with small amounts of land could not afford to enclose it with hedgerows and fences so they were forced to sell to the big estates. The whole process took almost 100 years and created a large pool of unemployed people living in miserable conditions. This concentration of people who were not growing anything needed work and the surge in agricultural productivity meant that it was possible to produce enough surplus to feed them.

As the process of farming consolidation spread from Britain into Europe, peasants were dislodged across the Continent. Victims of highland clearances emigrated to Canada, Nova Scotia, Kentucky and Tennessee. Germans, Swedes, Poles and Italians followed them. The industrial revolution took hold in Britain and spread across Europe and North America, where landless, dispossessed people provided cheap labour for factories. The

American entrepreneurs, the heirs of the original British emigrants, took full advantage of this mass emigration and sucked peasants into the early factories in New England.

Conditions were already in place for the industrial revolution: the landless peasants were milling around jobless, being executed on the gibbet for stealing cloth from the tenterhooks. In the hills of Lancashire and Yorkshire, water power was available, coursing down valleys like Calderdale, Airedale and Ribblesdale. Technological developments provided the catalyst.

Factory technology

The age of enlightenment and scientific discovery also inspired people to think creatively about new ways to apply water power in manufacturing. Cottage industry entrepreneurs began to look at watermills which ground wheat, or powered simple forges, and applied the principles to textile manufacture, which was the focus of the early industrial revolution. A stream of technological innovations followed: Arkwright's water frame, Hargreaves' spinning jenny and Crompton's 'mule' which combined the rollers of the water frame with the moving carriage of the jenny. These all helped to increase productivity a hundredfold, using people with fewer different types of skills. However, they had to be located in a building near the water, with a water wheel. Water powered textile mills appeared throughout the dales, dotted in valleys along rivers. Spinning, weaving, dyeing, fulling and making up the cloth remained separate specializations and transport was still needed to get raw materials to the mill and product to point of sale. Lancashire became the focus for cotton which was imported from America and the West Indies through Liverpool and Manchester, while wool remained the primary product in Yorkshire.

The textile mills started to import dispossessed peasants to feed the machines with raw materials and keep them running. Though the work was hard and the hours long, conditions for the workers were tolerable. The 'dark, satanic mills' did not appear until the coming of steam power fuelled by coal.

Depletion of the forests around the areas where iron ore was smelted led to a significant technological breakthrough. Until this time, iron ore had always been smelted in small quantities using charcoal. The forests in the Weald of Kent and the Forest of Dean had been systematically cleared for this purpose. With the coming of the industrial revolution, demand for iron was increasing just as the wood needed to make the charcoal for smelting it was running out. Pressure was on to find another way of smelting iron. The technological breakthrough occurred in Coalbrookdale, along the Severn Valley in Shropshire where the first attempts were made to use coal, or specifically, coke, to smelt iron. It is significant that the town which grew up here was called Coalbrookdale, not 'Ironbrookdale'. Abraham Derby I, a Quaker, was the first person to produce good quality iron in large quantities using coal. The output of iron increased dramatically as the material started to be used for construction—replacing stone and timber work—for manufacturing tools and machines, and for transport. To prove the usefulness of iron for construction, Thomas Farnolls Pritchard, Abraham Derby III and John Wilkinson conceived the idea of building an Iron Bridge over the Severn, and the project was completed in 1779.

The search for another source of power was prompted by the need to pump water out of coal mines to keep them from flooding. In 1712, Abraham Derby cast an iron cylinder to power a pumping engine developed by Thomas Newcomen. The fuel supply for the pump was guaranteed because the pump was located right next to its source. Refinement of the steam engine came quickly. In 1765 James Watt, in partnership with Matthew Boulton, perfected the separate condenser which produced more power more efficiently using one-third of the fuel. This was enormously successful for draining mines, but to make it useful in a factory, rotary motion was required. One of Watt's assistants, William Murdock, devised a gearing system which enabled steam power to run the same machinery that had been powered by water. James Watt's steam engine became ubiquitous throughout the land as motive power for all factories.

Productivity throughout British manufacturing took a sharp upward turn.

Early steam engines had to be large, with a big boiler and chimney, to get adequate power output. It was difficult to site a factory powered by such an engine high up in a river valley. It made more sense to move down into the towns, where the people lived and where the coal used as fuel could be brought in on barges. Factories mushroomed in the plains at the bottom of valleys, and towns very rapidly built up around them. Trading towns which became the focus for factories rapidly grew much bigger. Bradford sprang up. Leeds, Rochdale, Bolton and Manchester grew from villages into big towns because they were conveniently located at the end of the valley, with suitable land for building houses for the workforce to live in. The steam engine reigned supreme.

Transport infrastructure

For the factory system to work, the added cost of transport had to be less than the benefits of specialization and concentration in one area. Transport costs were a big barrier to specialization. Moving fuel, raw materials and finished products around by mules or horse and cart meant prohibitive transport costs. Transporting coal was incredibly expensive. It was rarely used very far away from where it was mined and so it was a vastly underexploited resource for a long time. Canals provided the answer.

The Romans built canals in Britain and part of the one which ran from Cambridgeshire through the fens to the River Trent is still in use today. It served a dual purpose: to drain the fens and to act as a conduit for trade and transport by connecting the river systems of northern and southern England. Roman canals linked the far north of England to London via Cambridge and Peterborough (an important pottery centre) and to the Midlands via the River Trent. When the Romans left, the canal system gradually disintegrated. It was left for eighteenth century engineers and entrepreneurs to realize the potential of canals and to invest in building them.

In 1759, the Duke of Bridgewater employed James Brindley to build the first modern canal in Britain. This canal halved the cost of taking coal from Worsley to Manchester. Josiah Wedgwood watched with interest because packhorses or wagon loads were not really economical or safe ways of transporting the pottery he was developing in an attempt to reproduce fine Chinese porcelain. In partnership with the Duke of Bridgewater, he conceived a scheme to build a canal 140 miles long which would link the Mersey at Runcorn with the River Trent, and both with the River Severn. His objective was to transport his products by water—with far fewer breakages—to ports for shipment world-wide. The ports of Liverpool, Bristol and Hull would all be linked by water-borne transport. Brindley was again commissioned to engineer the project and the Grand Trunk Canal was completed in 1777. All the elements for the development of the factory system—labour, transport, technology and finance—were then in place at Stoke-on-Trent. Over the next 25 years, Wedgwood precipitated pottery manufacture to such a degree that the population of the area trebled.

Stoke-on-Trent became an example for UK manufacturing industry. Wedgwood achieved competitive advantage through use of resources, transport and product specialization. The little local kilns, and cottage industries in other areas, were forced to wind down as a flood of reasonably priced, high quality earthenware pottery started to come out of Stoke-on-Trent. Canals remained the most convenient method of transporting large and heavy loads until the railway network had spread across the country during the mid-nineteenth century.

The stationary steam engine preceded the mobile steam engine by many decades. First the engineers had to refine steam engine design, use stronger materials which would withstand higher pressures, and make it reliable. Then they were able to think about how to make it smaller and put it on wheels. In the same way, ability to fly did not depend on technology of flight—Leonardo da Vinci had figured that out—but on getting an engine light enough, small enough and powerful enough.

When iron tracks for horse-drawn trams in collieries and ironworks replaced wooden ones, the way was clear to get a steam-powered engine to draw useful loads. In 1814, George Stephenson, employed at Killingworth Colliery near Newcastle, first produced an engine which pulled 30 tons of coal faster than a horse could move it. He and his son made these engines increasingly efficient. When, in 1821, a bill was passed to link Stockton and Darlington by rail, Stephenson successfully advocated the use of a steam engine to pull the carriages, and the 'iron horse' had arrived.

Availability of capital and demand for goods

Establishing mills, erecting factories, digging canals and building railways all cost money. This meant that entrepreneurs had to be prepared to make a considerable investment and needed access to surplus cash. They had to be articulate, mobile and to have access to a variety of people who might be persuaded to provide funds. Canals were financed by surplus money from colonial trading profits made in tobacco, tea and cotton, and by landowners who found mineral deposits on their estates. Private individuals also funded projects. For example, Richard Arkwright persuaded a friend who was a liquor merchant to finance his water frame and John Roebuck, who subsequently went bankrupt, provided funds for Watt to develop an experimental engine with a separate condenser. Industrial growth was encouraged by the development of the banking system. The number of banks in London and in the provinces rose steadily after 1750. Banks were prepared to provide loans, usually to landowners, at a fixed rate of interest for one year. Many of the bankers and entrepreneurs who financed the developing industrial base were Nonconformists, particularly Quakers, who were unable to participate in government, the civil services, or universities because of their beliefs, but were permitted to engage in trade and thrived in the world of industry and finance.

Throughout the eighteenth and nineteenth centuries, the

population grew steadily. The increasing prosperity which came through the growth of the factory system meant that many more people could afford to buy goods which improved their standard of living, and demand for manufactured products increased steadily.

Social issues

When factories first began to provide employment for displaced agricultural workers, entrepreneurs employed masses of low paid labour not to use their brains but to do repetitive tasks for long hours. To earn enough to live, entire families, including women and children, worked in factories and mines. Exploitative bosses tended to brutalize workers as the easiest way of achieving competitive advantage (and this is still true today in some places in the world). More enlightened bosses, such as the Quakers, found themselves under real economic pressures. There were no precedents for management or organization and no accepted standards of behaviour on either side, bosses or workers. Timekeeping was an alien concept to farm labourers. They did not work to the clock, but had always gone to work when the sun came up and quit when it got dark. If it rained they did something else. Managers believed that unless they were strict, people would fail to turn up for work. Organization was very authoritarian, with harsh penalties for failure to conform and the roots of hierarchical management were laid here. Workers who were promoted and paid a little bit more to act as overseers very often became the most brutal. People could be dismissed without reason, and parents sometimes had to punish their own children for fear of losing their jobs. In the mid-nineteenth century powerful people became aware of the difficulties of exploited factory workers and tried to ameliorate their lot. Lord Shaftesbury and Elisabeth Fry were instrumental in getting legislation passed which made the worst abuses illegal.

MASS PRODUCTION AND INTERCHANGEABLE PARTS

The factory system first revolutionized the production of textiles and pottery. Then new technology and steam power transformed the production of metal products. Increased prosperity meant that mass ownership of tools and other products made of metal became possible. With the coming of steam and the railways, factories organized and run on the principles we would still recognize today started to appear. However, there was a price to pay for increased prosperity, the 'dark satanic mills', with factory chimneys belching smoke, smog and pollution hanging like a pall over industrial centres.

The Great Exhibition of 1851 was held to extol Britain's prowess in the industrial world (and by doing this seemed to sow the seeds of its own eclipse). At about the same time, the industrial revolution in Germany produced the first steel cannon. Cannon had previously been made of cast iron or bronze, but in London, the German Krupp, a basic steelmaker, exhibited a revolutionary steel cannon which changed the whole art of artillery design. Rifled, breech loading, steel cannon were much more accurate and had an improved firing rate.

As metal took over from wood, and steam power moved pistons, gears and cylinders at previously unthinkable speeds, accurate tolerances became vital and micrometers were developed for accurate calibration. Early machine tools, bores and drop hammers were very crude until the time of Joseph Bramah and Henry Maudslay, who designed and produced lathes, hydraulic presses, and planing, drilling and milling machines. Maudslay was an extremely practical man whose manufacturing philosophy we would do well to emulate today. In the early nineteenth century he exhorted engineers, 'Keep a sharp look-out upon your material, get rid of every pound of material you can do without; put yourself the question "What business has it to be there?" Avoid complexities, and make everything as simple as possible.' Maudslay developed the slide rest, which clamped the cutting tool on a lathe in a mobile rest. Previously, the operator had held the tool in his hand while operating the lathe using a pole treadle. Maudslay's screw cutting lathe was accurate, simple to operate and eliminated the need to fit an individual nut to its individual screw, as long as the screws and nuts were made by the same lathe. Maudslay also devised a screw micrometer accurate to one ten-thousandth of an inch. Joseph Whitworth, who finally standard-ized screw threads during the 1840s, used a micrometer capable of measuring to one millionth of an inch. Greater accuracy made machines steadily more efficient, with fewer breakdowns.

Marc Isambard Brunel's tooling for producing blocks, installed in a factory at Portsmouth, is an example of the early use of machine tools for mass production of identical items. At a time when the Royal Navy was completely under sail, over 100 000 wooden blocks for handling ships' rigging were consumed every year. All these wooden blocks were shaped, drilled and grooved by hand, employing some 200 people in a thriving cottage industry. Marc Brunel devised a series of machines which were prototypes for machinery later used in mass production. Each machine held the wooden block and moved the tool along it with absolute precision. Maudslay built the cutting machines, and a factory was established in Portsmouth in the 1850s, where 10 men manufactured 160 000 blocks a year. The market peaked in the 1880s and gradually diminished as sailing ships were replaced by steam, but the factory remained in production until the 1930s and is now a museum.

The industrial revolution spread from Britain and started to take hold in Europe and North America. In the latter part of the nineteenth century, focus on innovative manufacturing develop-ments shifted across the Atlantic to the United States where the population was growing at a phenomenal rate through immigra-tion, doubling every few years. There had been a population explosion in Britain in the nineteenth century, when the population had gone from being less than that of France to being significantly greater, but this was nothing like the one seen in North America. In a few decades after gaining independence from

Britain, the former colonies zoomed past her in size, power and influence, owing to this remarkable influx of people who were welcomed from all over Europe. This influx was able to exploit the vast land resources of the United States and homesteads were planted so rapidly that the frontier moved west at about 10 miles a day. Such rapid growth created an insatiable demand for goods and services. America was a huge market, even in the late nineteenth and early twentieth centuries, and everyone wanted a gun, a pair of boots, a pair of jeans and eventually a motor car. Europe's 'huddled masses yearning to be free' did not have, nor did they need, the skills the cottage industry workers had. They were sucked into a factory system which only required them to do a few tasks repetitively.

Demand for everything was on a grand scale in America and manufacturers who could satisfy it were sure of a profit. Whereas UK railways ordered two engines at a time, American companies needed six, so the Americans took British designs and modified them to suit the conditions. They couldn't afford to manufacture in the same way because they did not have the time. British engines were carefully made out of cast iron, rigid and polished, designed to run on a well-aligned gravelled track bed. However, Americans had to lay hundreds of miles of track in a hurry, so their track and engines needed to be flexible, able to function under conditions which would derail a British engine. They had to do more with less so they made their engines thin and light. Steam engines to power paddle-boats were also more pragmatically made and used local materials.

Once factories had begun to develop, manufacturers on both sides of the Atlantic needed steam engines and all sorts of machines to manufacture their products. Subsequently the machine tool industry prospered. Tools developed to aid manufacturing had an additional benefit: it became possible to make identical items. The first true machine tool was the boring machine invented by the French during the Napoleonic wars. Until then, cannon had been cast in molten metal, and no adjustments had been made to the bore. The new machine tool made the bore true. In the same way, when a gunsmith made the entire gun himself, every piece was unique. In theory there may have been a pattern, like the Brown Bess musket for the British army but, in fact, every piece was individually made and each gunsmith interpreted the pattern in his own way. Only the calibre and the barrel length were about the same, which allowed weapons to share lead balls. After developing the cotton gin, Eli Whitney took on a contract from the US government to supply 10 000 muskets in 15 months. To achieve this, he developed the concept of interchangeable parts and demonstrated his achievement in front of amazed officials in Washington. The result was a steady supply of guns for soldiers and homesteaders.

Machine tools for the mass production of shoes were developed in America, but the thing which people most associate with mass production in the USA is Henry Ford's Model T. Ford's first car powered by an internal combustion engine was running in 1896, and he had built an improved version three years later. He founded the Ford Motor Company in 1903, where he built on the concept of interchangeable parts by breaking down the process of making each part into small pieces and creating a production line. Between 1908 and 1927 more than 15 million Model T Fords were built. The design was so successful that no major changes were needed during that period. This was an all-time record for the production of a single model, beaten only recently by the VW Beetle.

The rise of the automobile as a major form of transport straddles the First World War. This period gave a tremendous boost to both the automobile and the aircraft industries, because there was an insatiable demand for vehicles. The manufacturing processes for early road vehicles and aircraft were much the same. Both products comprised an engine and a body of roughly the same dimensions. They were manufactured on a moving track which brought the work to the man, using similar technology, and needed much the same amount of effort and man hours. The dramatic increase in the complexity of aircraft did not take place until towards the end of the Second World War.

With the beginning of mass production the social organization of labour was forced to change. Division of labour meant breaking down the job into specialized, repetitive tasks and setting up a track which brought the job to the man, instead of letting the man go to the job. Mass production and division of labour made it necessary to invent the concept of work measurement. Management determined the standard number of hours it ought to take to do a job, then measured productivity in man-hours, or by piece-work. Attention was focused on refining ways of measuring the completion of small pieces of repetitive work. Two famous experiments influenced these developments.

F.W. Taylor who originated the principles of *Scientific Management* (Harper & Brothers, New York, 1911), was one of the first to experiment with ways of increasing productivity in factories organized around mass production. Taylor worked at the Bethlehem steel works in Bethlehem, Pennsylvania. At the end of the nineteenth century, the price of pig iron rose during the Spanish-American war, and the company decided to sell surplus stock. Iron pigs each weighing 92 pounds were loaded onto rail wagons by men carrying them up a ramp. Each man was loading two and a half tons a day. Taylor and his colleagues observed that one employee, Schmidt, a Dutchman, ran to and from work every day. Further investigation revealed that he was also building his own house during evenings and weekends. They reasoned that if he could still run home in the evening, and then work some more, he must have some energy left so they designed an experiment to find out how to get the maximum output from him. Schmidt was offered a 60 per cent increase in wages to participate in the experiment. His job was to do exactly as he was told. They told him when to carry pigs and at what rate, and when to rest. After observing results at different lengths of time and different rates for several weeks, they redesigned the task and Schmidt's productivity went up to 47.5 tons per day. However, he probably no longer had enough energy left to run home, let alone build his house in the evenings. This leads to the question, at what point does getting the maximum amount of effort from the workforce turn into unreasonable exploitation?

Another experiment, carried out at the Hawthorne Electrical Works, attempted to determine what effect the working environment had on the level of output in the factory. When the lighting in the electrical assembly shop was increased, productivity went up. A further increase in lighting resulted in further improvements in productivity. After a third increase in light, output went up again. But by then, everyone was getting headaches and eyestrain from the bright light so the experimenters decided to decrease the lighting level, but *output still went up.* The productivity improvements had taken place because the researchers were paying attention to the people. If people are being observed at their work, productivity goes up, never mind the lighting.

These and other studies based on mass production, division of labour and careful task design set the scene for much manufacturing practice in the West from the 1920s right up to the present. Everybody went rushing out trying to design a job to get the maximum amount of energy from a person. The results of time and motion study and careful job measurement washed right back through all of manufacturing industry from the assembly track to jobbing batch work. Every job was allocated a standard time and workers were paid according to how long it took them to do the job, compared to standard time. The process of chopping a job into highly specialized tasks washed back through the system too. The application of these techniques spread throughout manufacturing industry in the USA and Europe, and began to reach industrial centres world-wide. The end result was a highly productive, low cost manufacturing system which increased prosperity in Europe and gave every American a car, a gun and a pair of Levis. The guns were all Winchester repeaters, the cars were all black, and the Levis were all blue, but everyone had them. This was the apogee of mass production, which opened up trade throughout the world.

2

Understanding what went wrong and why we have to change

To understand why the factory system, which developed so successfully for so many years, started to run into difficulties, we have to go right back and take a look at what had been happening with world trade. First let's look at the price of commodities. A commodity is a product which is undifferentiated, that is, no matter where you buy it, it is essentially the same. Iron ore, coal, oil, minerals, steel, wool, cotton, linen, and food staples such as wheat, rice, oats, etc., are examples. Decisions on buying commodities are based on price and availability, provided basic quality thresholds are achieved. Commodity prices rise and fall, crudely related to availability and demand. If we look back through the centuries, we find that prices rose and fell based on supply versus demand. When the population is rising quickly, and demand for goods is high, commodity prices rise and this encourages people to produce more and find new sources. One of the features of the industrial revolution was the search for new ways of satisfying demand for raw materials. Many of the alternative sources were much more productive and cheaper to exploit than original sources. For example, the search for alternative sources of tin led to development of the Malaysian tin mines, and the decline and eventual closure of the Cornish mines, which had formerly been the source of most of the world's supply.

In a world of growing population and increasing demand, one would expect commodity prices to rise steadily and people to search for new sources. An interesting consequence is that when demand is increasing, companies or governments which can monopolize the sources of raw materials will ensure the security of their supply and suppress competitors' access. From the start of the industrial revolution to the end of the Second World War (with a few minor blips), world population, and with it the demand for goods increased many times, and real commodity prices rose steadily (Fig. 2.1).

COMMODITIES AND COLONIAL CONFLICT

Monopolizing the source of supply gave a country strong leverage. The need to find and monopolize new sources of raw material encouraged political control and colonization. Britain did very well from this strategy; at one time over 50 per cent of the world's supply of gold and 70 per cent of the tin and rubber came from British controlled sources: South Africa, Australia, Malaysia. Trade in these commodities was free, but politically controlled.

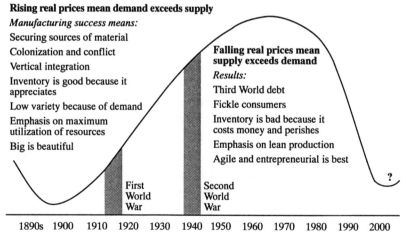

Figure 2.1   The commodity price theory of manufacturing

Many of the conflicts of the eighteenth, nineteenth and early twentieth centuries were fought over control of resources. I would argue that even the First and Second World Wars were in part a continuation of the colonial squabbles between Britain, France and Russia, on the one hand, and emergent nations (Germany and Japan), on the other. As industrialization proceeded, emergent nations became resentful of being denied control of their own sources of materials. European countries with mature colonies, notably Britain and France, had control of raw materials, but others, notably Germany (and also Japan) did not. An important objective for both Germany and Japan was prising control of raw material supplies out of British and French hands. At the end of the First World War, Germany was deprived of what little access to raw materials she had, Namibia, Tanzania and Togoland, thereby helping to sow the seeds of the Second World War. In both wars, the need for commodities in a period of rising prices and growing demand for manufactured goods, helped to precipitate the conflict.

COMMODITIES AND VERTICAL INTEGRATION IN MANUFACTURING

The need to ensure access to commodities also encouraged vertical integration in manufacturing. Henry Ford eventually had his own forests and his own iron mines to make sure he had access to raw materials. In a period of rising prices it was a Good Thing to have plentiful stocks of raw materials, because they would be continually increasing in value. With ever-rising demand, companies had a ready market and could sell all they made. Securing a supply of raw material became an attractive economic policy. Also, in a period of high demand, everything that could be produced was sold; there was little pressure to produce a wide variety of products. Ford's customers could have any colour they liked as long as it was black. The problem was not selling, but making enough. Accounting methods made a virtue of having stocks, because it looked like profit on paper. If you bought 1000 tonnes of tin at £6 per tonne, and later tin went up to £10 per tonne, you made a profit (on paper) of £4000.

MASS PRODUCTION AND LOSS OF ACCOUNTABILITY

Chapter 1 described how mass production came about as a consequence of the economic and technological developments that resulted from rising demand and how the benefits of mass production reshaped the lives of people world-wide. However, mass production put focus onto managing tiny slices of the job. Managing the whole was not an issue; as long as the product came off the end of the assembly line, the factory worker did not know, nor did he need to know, about the entire process. Who were the customers? Workers had no idea who used the thousands of identical parts they turned out. As long as individuals were kept busy on their special tasks, management knew that something to sell would fall out at the end. This was the guiding principle of the manufacturing age, and it affected every type of industry.

The first signs that this bubble was going to burst came just after the Second World War. The assembly line for building cars was just as good an idea as it had ever been and innovative technology was making mass production even slicker. The emergence of television and TV advertising increased the demand for mass-produced goods. Consumers were introduced to a whole new world of variety that came into their homes via that tiny screen and their horizons were broadened by a cornucopia of the latest ideas and products. People began to realize that they didn't always have to have black. Only people who were brought up during the 1930s, 1940s and early 1950s will be able to remember how limited horizons were. In Britain, some of us remember that the Co-op was typical of what was available. Everything—sugar, flour, butter, biscuits—was sold by weight and wrapped in front of you. How many of us can remember the blue cartridge paper bags for

sugar and flour? Prepackaged meats were restricted to products
such as spam and corned beef. Some prepackaged food reached
Europe during the Second World War because the only way to
get food to starving Europe was to dry, can, powder or condense it.
However, this fulfilled the need at the time, and set the wheels in
motion for a food revolution after the war. Demand for branded
and packaged consumer goods exploded with TV advertising. The
same thing happened with clothing. We could buy good quality
tweeds and leather shoes in the High Street, but choice was
limited and there was no distinction in fashion between different
generations. Television and mass media advertising reached the
United States first and created insatiable demand for variety. The
Second World War had stimulated the US economy: Americans
came out of it twice as rich as they went in. They could afford to
satisfy their wish for two-tone convertibles or shocking pink
Chevrolets with enormous fins. It took a little longer for the trend
to reach Britain, but a bit more prosperity, plus rising expectations
of the welfare state, led people to demand a much wider choice of
food, clothing, and household goods than they had before the war.
Just having a washing machine was no longer enough. The
housewife wanted to choose between six different models, with a
variety of features, in different sizes and colours. Manufacturers
were confronted with the need to offer variety or lose market
share. In a world of variety, product life cycle also became much
shorter, giving a company less time to make a profit from a
product. This meant that companies had to find ways to react
quickly to market trends, develop products with unique selling
features, and look for niches.

COMMODITIES AND TRANSPORT

Ready availability of bulk transport has influenced the availability
of commodities. Today, many varieties of rice from different parts
of the world are available in supermarkets. Advertising has
introduced us to a variety of foods from all over the world and

readily available transport brings them to us. In Britain we now take pizza, wine, bananas, melons, and peanuts for granted. Americans also have access to a wider variety of foods imported from all over the world than ever before.

FALLING COMMODITY PRICES AND THE END OF THE OLD CONSTRAINTS

In the late 1960s and throughout the 1970s, economic forces started to have a severe impact on the long-held perceptions of manufacturing industry world-wide. Then the unthinkable happened. Commodity prices, which had risen steadily for decades, peaked and then started to drop. Metal prices dropped, the steel industry suffered, the price of crude oil peaked and dropped. Timber, coffee, groundnuts, rice and wool all became cheaper in real terms than they had been for 30 or 40 years. There are four main reasons why this started to happen:

1. Population growth in developed countries started to flatten out.
2. Technology has introduced cheap, readily available substitutes for traditional raw materials. Plastic is a cheap substitute for both timber and metal. For example, radio cases used to be made out of wood, and the raw material put restrictions on size and style. Now, radio cases are injection moulded and a quarter of their previous size. Technology has also enabled us to discover and exploit new sources of supply, for example, North Sea oil and gas.
3. Developing countries have contributed to the widespread availability of cheap commodities. Every developing country wants its own steel works because this is a mark of progress. As a result, the market has been flooded with low priced steel produced in developing countries.
4. Government economic policies have stimulated excess food production: Europe now has a butter mountain, an egg mountain and a wine lake because supply has got ahead of

demand. When supply gets ahead of demand, commodity prices fall.

Technology, expectations, aspirations and exploitation have made all sorts of products widely available. Suddenly, it is possible to buy commodities cheaper than we can produce them, and it will be cheaper to buy them next month than this month. Why own a forest to secure a supply of wood? Inventory becomes a liability when commodity prices are falling. Why buy 10 tonnes at £6 per tonne today, when next year the price per tonne may be £5.70 in real terms? Vertical integration and plenty of stock begin to lose their appeal as manufacturing policies in this environment.

NEW DEMANDS ON MANUFACTURING

The results of rising expectations and insatiable demand for variety placed new demands on the manufacturing industry. The need to superimpose flexibility and variety on a system based on mass production and economies of scale began to cause problems. Now we can begin to look at the last three decades to see how the manufacturing industry world-wide has tried to cope with these problems. The first evidence that all was not well started to appear in the 1950s in smokestack industries in the West when they started to feel the effects of their markets slipping away. One cause was increasing competition, and a good example is the ship-building industry, as the emerging Far Eastern countries started to enter the market.

Confronted with these circumstances, manufacturers first started to look around to see how they could improve their flexibility and responsiveness. Table 2.1 shows how this search for solutions progressed over the next 30 to 40 years and still continues.

Group technology
Factories in the 1950s were productive but very rigid—*dirigiste*—

Table 2.1   The search for solutions

1950s/1960s	1970s	1980s	1990s
Group technology Coding systems Planned maintenance	Numerical control	Flexible manufacturing systems Statistical process control	
Production control	Bills of material Planning and scheduling End of post-war steady growth and low unemployment Consolidate	Material requirements planning II Just-in-Time Profit centres Total quality management Reorganization	Cell manufacture
Big is beautiful Mergers, conglomerates	High unemploy- ment Adversarial relationships	Employee involvement	

and unsteerable. It was difficult for them to change direction. New ideas emerged as the first attempts were made to build on the theories of scientific management developed before the war by Taylor and Bedeaux. One of these was Group Technology. This idea proposed breaking away from the notion that machine tools had to be organized functionally by department, locating all the lathes together, all the milling machines together, etc. Instead, it suggested looking at the components of a product in terms of geometry and grouping the machines together according to component shape. Defining families of parts by geometry made it possible to group together all the machine tools needed to make those parts. Coding systems for classifying parts by geometry grew out of group technology. The concepts behind group technology and coding systems for parts were excellent, really breaking new ground and showing the way forward. But on its own, group technology was unable to fulfil its promise because it was an island of solution being applied in a sea of indifference or misunderstanding. Both supporting technologies and a ground swell of belief from the people were lacking. This is characteristic of many solutions which were generated throughout a 30 year period and it is relevant because, later, cell manufacturing was able to draw on group technology along with other pathfinding ideas and help them to realize their full potential.

Planned maintenance

Planned maintenance was another good idea which failed to yield benefits in the 1960s because it was not suitable in the environment of the big machine shop. The machine shop manager was looking at hundreds of machine tools and trying to develop a planned maintenance programme for them. No one really knew what the individual requirements of each machine tool were. The job of finding out and drawing up the plan was passed down the hierarchy to a junior engineer and, of course, what he did was play it safe. He decided to change bearings, lubricant, etc., on a strict timetable, regardless of whether the machine actually needed it. Planned maintenance ended up getting a bad name because in the traditional machine shop environment it was expensive and the machines didn't perform any better as their real needs were rarely addressed.

Old solutions for new problems

During the 1950s and 1960s companies were still applying the old solutions of 'big is beautiful' in an effort to solve their problems. They knew they were hurting, so their reaction was to do more of what they understood and were familiar with. Ways of coping with rising commodity prices built around vertical integration and economies of scale were taken as panaceas. So when the signs of undertow started to appear and UK manufacturing came under pressure, the solution offered was 'big is beautiful' and resulted in conglomerates and mergers. In the UK we rushed to consolidate the aircraft and the motor industries, which made the situation worse. Failure to spot the underlying causes led to repetitive application of useless remedies.

Numerical Control (NC) and Computer Numerical Control (CNC)

The first fruits of the electronics revolution started to be seen in the late 1960s and early 1970s. Electronic processing was applied to machine tools and the first Numerically Controlled (NC) machine tools appeared. Until this time, machine tools in factories based on batch production were mechanical, operated by handles and wheels which the operator used to set up and control the process. All machine tools had to be designed as a compromise between function and the need for manual operation, and we often felt that the ideal lathe operator needed the height and arm span of a gorilla. There were some power aids but quality and precision were really down to the skill of the man operating the machine. Numerically controlled machine tools used electronics to determine the position of the tool in the work piece. So in simple NC drilling and boring machines, the position of the hole was decided by a simple electronic processor, and in NC controlled lathes, the position of the turning tool was decided by the processor. NC tools were programmed using punch paper tape and this created a new band of bureaucrats who planned how the work would be done, what tool would be used, and what path the tool should take, and then wrote codes so that key punch operators could produce the paper tapes which ran the NC machine tools.

The next development in the 1970s was CNC control, which is

variously interpreted as either Computer Numerical Control or Continuous Numerical Control. This was a major leap forward in productivity and engineering quality, but again it was slow to catch on because it did not fully deliver what it promised. Early NC machines operated point-to-point. This meant that we could control the location of each point where the tool touched the work, but not the path in between. With CNC we could describe the path between two points numerically and code it, allowing us to produce profiles and shapes. This led to purpose designed CNC lathes (rather than ordinary machine tools with the NC bit tacked on) and to the emergence of machining centres which could perform several tasks. This radically changed the shape and appearance of machine tools because human intervention now took place through a control panel and reduced or eliminated the need for handles and dials. CNC machining required a new sort of infrastructure and until people became aware of its possibilities and developed appropriate skills and knowledge support was not there. As a result, it really took quite a long time for CNC tools to catch on and take over. It was not until the 1970s that more CNC machine tools were being manufactured than manual ones, and this was another pointer to the future.

Production control systems

The need for manufacturing to be more agile also prompted the development of production control systems. Until the development of suitable computers, these were manual and paper-based. An enormous amount of space was needed to house early computers, which had the capacity of today's desktop, so initial users tended to be utilities companies, local government and banks, who used them for accounts processing. Paper-based production control systems were developed to track the parts through the manufacturing process. People who started work in the 1950s and 1960s will remember the thousands of job cards describing the processes used to manufacture parts stored in rows of filing cabinets which were reproduced on a Roneo machine (no photocopiers yet!) and stacked together to make a set of manufacturing instructions for issue to the shop floor.

The failure of MRP

The electronics revolution of the 1970s also led to the development of a production control application known as MRP. Again there is debate about what MRP really stands for. It could mean Manufacturing Requirements Planning, Material Requirements Planning, Material Resource Planning or Manufacturing Resource Planning, depending on who you are, what question you are asking and why you want to know. What we were really talking about is taking the coding systems developed in the 1950s and 1960s and applying the power of the computer to them. The second generation of computers—using transistors rather than valves—started to emerge during the 1970s and when magnetic data recording replaced punched cards, computers really came into their own. They were a great improvement on the first generation, but were still large, bulky mainframes requiring an air-conditioned room and a systems department plus a data processing department to run them. These specialists looked upon themselves as a race apart, and created a mystique about systems, the value of the information and their unique expertise, that some companies are still trying to dispel! Nevertheless, they developed some of the first MRP scheduling systems to help manage and schedule production.

There is a significant difference between MRP and ideas such as group technology and CNC machine tools. Group technology benefits may have been constrained, but improvements were genuine, and CNC was slow to be accepted but was a definite improvement. MRP was peddled by computer software and hardware manufacturers as the be-all and end-all of management: 'Let the computer control your factory for you!' and it was disastrous. Many MRP systems failed badly and damaged the organizations that installed them.

All this went on against the background of industrial strife in the

1970s, particularly in the UK. As the 'big is beautiful' solutions were failing we were starting to see the consequences. Real pain and heartache attended the end of the old industrial relations practices which were built around the concept of division of labour, and skills-based unions became anomalies. We can see with hindsight that these conglomerates were industrial dinosaurs and their days were numbered, but we couldn't see this at the time. Even as we are writing this book in the summer of 1993 IBM are suffering record losses and facing possible breakup. This has led to a painful downsizing with first-ever large scale compulsory redundancies. They are attempting to respond by breaking up into accountable, focused business units but are facing heavy opposition from some areas within the company.

Effects of government intervention

When we were in the last throes of socialism and interventionism, we lived in a world where manufacturing management had plenty of people to blame for their own failures. They could blame the government for not backing their projects; they could blame exchange rates or interest rates for being either too high or too low. There was a general tendency for manufacturing industry to attribute its own failures to some outside cause. For example, the UK aerospace industry demanded huge subsidies before launching an aircraft, then complained when British Airways bought from Boeing. During the 1980s, the government suggested that aerospace should raise the money on the private capital market, and when private funds were not forthcoming, private investors were accused of being short-sighted. Private investors wanted to see a proven track record of profitable projects, but the aerospace industry claimed that they were unable to provide this because previous projects had suffered from too much government interference.

People had become used to being feather-bedded, being told what to do, when and how they could trade, who they could export to, when they could export. They got used to exchange controls, used to having to buy dollars on the controlled dollar market. Now that freedom has come to manufacturing, and companies can trade with anyone they want, in any way they like, offering what they think are the most appropriate products, they find they no longer have anybody to blame but themselves. Cell manufacturing reflects this, because it makes businesses visibly accountable for their own performance. There is no longer any place to hide. Successful businesses in the 1990s will be truly accountable and will be seen to stand or fall by their own efforts.

Maggie's Purge

When Margaret Thatcher became Prime Minister of the UK in 1979, she immediately accelerated and encouraged the clearing out of all these industrial dinosaurs. In 'Maggie's Purge', industries which were no longer appropriate for the way the world would be in the future were allowed to die. This toppled the last legacy of socialism. Industries were no longer propped up by government money if they were in difficulties, but were forced to sink or swim on their own merits. This cleared out huge sectors of industry in parts of the Midlands, Wales and the North. Many well-known firms simply disappeared: Rubery Owen—gone! Alfred Herbert—gone! BSA—gone! Archdale—gone! Wolseley, Riley, Standard Triumph, Morris and Austin are memories in the car industry and their demise caused great pain and misery to many people. What it did, though, was make the companies which survived much tougher, leaner, fitter and able to remain alive in the new conditions. However, by the end of the 1980s the screw was as tight as it would go; so to get better, companies had to be different, not just tighter, but *different*. And companies were not quite sure what this 'different' meant.

The technology dream ticket

In the 1970s and even while Maggie's Purge was going in the early 1980s, we saw the attempts of manufacturing managers to abandon their responsibility for solving problems. They saw that change was inevitable but cast around for ways of achieving it without really grasping the nettle, which requires effective management and real understanding of what managers need to do to reform the business. It was never much publicized but there was a deep-down feeling in the early 1980s that many industrial managers were woefully inadequate for the task that faced them. Of course this statement would be challenged, but nevertheless, what we saw was the attempt of many to abandon their responsibilities and use the 'dream technology' ticket to try to spend their way out of trouble. 'Let technology manage our factories so we don't have to take unpalatable actions to introduce change.' The attempt to cure everything with technology led to FMS, MRP and MRP II, Robots, CIM. All these technological solutions now have a bad name because they have failed to deliver the promised benefits. By computerizing what was already there, rather than simplifying the whole system, all they did was add complexity to methods that were already unmanageable and failed utterly to take people into account. General Motors' attempt to wire up the factory with MAP (Manufacturing Automation Protocol) is a prime example of spending millions of dollars going down a blind alley.

Re-emergence of previously abandoned ideas
Against this background an interesting thing happened because, throughout the first four decades of the twentieth century, some good ideas were being developed by voices in the wilderness. Walter Shewhart, W. Edwards Deming, Joseph Juran and Professor J. Burbage contributed good ideas based around statistical process control (SPC), group technology and total quality. Some of these ideas were developed in the West before or just after the war, and then disappeared for decades before their true value was realized. Shewhart developed SPC in 1931 and I studied it at polytechnic in 1968, but I never found a good reason for using it until I began to explore the possibilities of team-based cell manufacture. It was a good theoretical exercise but meant

nothing to the operator on the Ward 7 Capstan Lathe in an average batch machining company in 1962.

We had tried these ideas in the West, concluded that they were not relevant to the prevailing manufacturing conditions, and abandoned them. But the Japanese latched on to the techniques, took them up and made them work. Deming made several trips to Japan to lecture and promote his ideas, but he was unable to get a hearing in the United States. When we in the West began to observe what an outstanding success the Japanese had made of these techniques, we changed our tune and decided, 'Oh, it does work! It is applicable!' So we tried again, but what happened? Kanban, JIT, Quality Circles: didn't work. SPC: didn't work! Why not?

JIT (Just-in-Time) delivery is an example. The Japanese made it work but we failed because we tried to take traditional western manufacturing and apply JIT signals to it. Demand-based triggers only allow manufacturing to take place on demand. When the job is split into too many pieces, it can pass through the hands of 10 or 15 'owners' and we were trying to superimpose JIT on this complexity. The trouble was, we had moved so far back from our customer that we didn't know what his demand was. By the time an operator received the 15th demand signal it was too late anyway. Putting demand signals on 15 separate ownerships was like playing Chinese whispers. 'Send reinforcements, we're going to advance,' becomes 'Send three and fourpence, we're going to a dance.' JIT only works well with a handful of accountabilities. However, this time we couldn't say that the techniques were at fault because the Japanese had made them succeed. So everyone trooped off on study tours to Japan, to try to find out the secrets of their success. The issue became, 'We know that these techniques work, so how do we make them work in our environment?'

THERE IS ANOTHER WAY: TEAMING IN CELLS

It seems that team-based cell manufacturing has evolved as the response. The Japanese don't necessarily use what we define as cells, so it may be that cells and teaming are a way of satisfying Western cultural needs. Teaming means different things to different people in different societies and we may need cell team organization, whereas perhaps with the Japanese teaming is different. Team-based cell manufacturing—bringing people together in teams where they are expected to apply all their intellectual capabilities to bring about continuous improvement in the way they do their jobs—helps to fulfil the promise of many of the good ideas developed in manufacturing over the last 50 years. Cell teams are able to apply SPC, make the best use of CNC machines, carry out planned maintenance, organize around group technology and coded parts, in an environment which allows people to use these tools naturally and unselfconsciously in a human-sized environment.

Now we are beginning to see what 'different' means. Companies that are going to succeed in the 1990s cannot afford to ignore any of the skills and abilities of all the people in the business. Businesses are relying more and more on intellectual content. At Baker Perkins Printing Machines Ltd, I saw the shift in the technology of printing machines from working with knobs and dials to making use of information technology to determine the correct settings. The printing machine changed from being a purely mechanical device to containing significant elements of electro-mechanical and information processing. So companies are shifting much more to depend on knowledge of how to manage and process information, and are including more information programming in the actual products. Highly developed car engine management systems provide a good example of this change.

To handle processes and products with this high intellectual content, businesses in the 1990s need all the capabilities of all the people. It is no longer acceptable to ask people to leave their brains at the gate when they come to work in the morning. It was not very long ago that people were actually told that it was not their job to think, just to do the task they were given. If you analyse a cross-section of people working in industry today, you will find that in their personal lives they undertake highly demanding, highly responsible tasks, such as justices of the peace, lay preachers, councillors, secretaries to local dramatic societies, scout and guide leaders, all demonstrating that they have capabilities that we just have not taken advantage of or have even actively discouraged them from using. From now on, successful companies will be differentiated by their ability to develop and use all the skills of their people.

Cell manufacturing is a significant step in this direction. It takes some of the good things like group technology, SPC, total quality and planned maintenance, and brings them together within this idea of building teams of people who use all their abilities, and it has been shown to be an approach which really does give significant new direction to manufacturing businesses. Who knows how this will develop or what will happen beyond the 1990s. That is another story.

3

What's different about team-based cells?

- Cells make one team responsible for all the processes needed to produce the product.
- Cells cut down serial accountabilities from more than 10 to 4 or 5.
- Cells collapse lead times and allow manufacture to true customer demand.
- Cells create conditions where shortages disappear and quality improves dramatically.
- Cells relate performance measures to business needs.

Let us start by comparing a factory with a traditional manufacturing environment to a man who has a headache and takes some aspirin. The headache gets worse, so he takes more aspirin. Finally, his headache gets so bad that he realizes he ought to do something different, because the aspirin isn't working. Only when he goes for an X-ray does he discover that he actually has a fractured skull and the aspirin was never going to cure it. The same thing happened with the manufacturing industry in the 1950s and 1960s. We have already described how economic conditions changed and commodity prices dropped, but people in manufacturing were so conditioned by previous experience that they were unable to accept this. Managers looked back on their previous experience and said, 'I have made these decisions during my career and my track record proves that I have been successful. What I've done has resulted in progress for my company, so don't tell me that suddenly I'm doing something wrong.' Traditional methods have been very deeply ingrained in people's behaviour patterns and the way they react to circumstances, causing—as we have seen—repetitive application of the wrong solutions to the problems besetting manufacturing industry. We have all inherited the results of this ingrained behaviour. So what is it about cell manufacturing based around teams that makes the big shift away from the conditions of the first half of the twentieth century which still form part of the mindset of many people? Team-based cells provide the framework for actually curing the diseases plaguing Western manufacturing industry in the 1990s, instead of just treating the symptoms.

In Chapter 2 we looked at all the separate attempts that have been made to reduce long lead times and high costs, and saw why they did not quite succeed. The underlying principles of team-based cells started to be understood when major industries spotted how flexible, responsive and competitive small businesses could be. Managers began to analyse the characteristics of small businesses and to look for ways to transplant them into large organizations riddled with inertia, waste and inefficiency. Gradually, some fundamental principles began to crystallize, based around the issues of people and organization, engineering, logistics and accountability. Many of the ideas were sparked off by Japanese techniques. However, I don't believe team-based cells are wholly a Japanese idea, and the Japanese do not use cell manufacture as we define it in the West. The 'cells' concept takes a number of Japanese methods and welds them together to suit western culture. Successful cell manufacture depends on understanding what motivates people so we can align what the business needs with what the people want. What the Japanese (or the Indian, Malaysian, Taiwanese or Chinese) workforce wants varies significantly from the desires and aspirations of people in the EEC or North America. The single most important factor allowing us to align business needs with the aspirations of the workforce has been reducing the number of serial accountabilities.

THE BIG CHANGE: REDUCING SERIAL ACCOUNTABILITY

We have seen how focus on division of labour and skills specialization developed to meet the ever-increasing demand for manufactured goods. However, this meant that factories had to be functionally organized. All like skills and processes were grouped together and managed as a unit. The consequence of this was the creation of many, many serial accountabilities in an engineering company. The product or process had to be 'owned' by many different people during the process of supplying the material, making the product, and getting it into the hands of the customer. The reason why team-based cells allow us to make the big shift away from these conditions is that, by putting all of the processes we need to make a complete component together in one location, we do not need more than four or at most five serial accountabilities:

- Get the material
- Make a component
- Make a sub-assembly ⎫
- Make a final assembly ⎭
- Deliver to the customer

We do this by creating teams that focus on product groups rather than processes (Fig. 3.1). The teams are accountable for all the operations and processes required to complete a product or group of products, recreating the entrepreneurial flair of the small business unit. Some business units can operate with three accountabilities, and none should need more than five. In this world, everyone is much closer to the action, and no one is more than three or four steps away from the customer, and they can relate what they are doing to the precise needs of the customer. This allows us to plan through 4 or 5 steps instead of 15 to 30, so we can start thinking about planning to meet actual customer demand.

In some businesses I have experienced, there are as many as 30

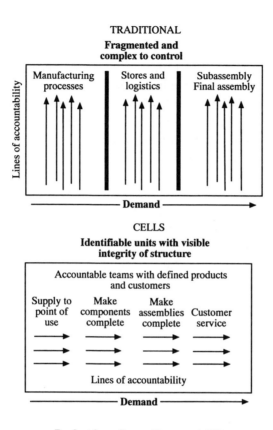

Figure 3.1 The shift from functional to product-focused organization

'owners', and there are seldom fewer than 10. In this environment, the 'fog of manufacturing' very soon closes in. I have asked a foreman on the shop floor, 'Who had this component before you did?' He would reply, 'Fred, in Grinding.' The foreman may also have known that George in Paint got it next. 'Who gets it after that . . . without looking at the paperwork?' 'Don't know.' Not only that, the foreman doesn't care either. The customer is someone he occasionally sees walking past the end of the gangway with the managing director. The foreman on the shop floor finds it very difficult to relate what he's doing to the needs of the customer. In this environment, the fog of manufacturing and remoteness from the customer make it almost impossible to talk about manufacturing to customer demand. Cells and JIT manufacturing got a bad name at first because people tried to apply them in the old style 'make to forecast' factory with long lead times. There were so many serial accountabilities that it didn't take long to lose track of who the customer was and what he wanted. Many businesses have tried to implement cells in this environment, and of course have failed. I often give the 'Weaver Bird syndrome' as one example of why cells can go wrong. The story goes:

> Once upon a time, the weaver bird, who builds the finest nest in the bird kingdom (actually sewing leaves together with grass stems), called all the birds together to show them how to do it. After five minutes the crow shouted 'I know how to do it' and rushed off before the seminar was over. The weaver bird shouted, 'Come back, come back, I've hardly started.' But the crow didn't listen and the result is the crow's nest.

There are plenty of cells in place which are like crows' nests. I call them 'white line cells'; paint a white line around some machines, and, hey presto!, 'we've got cells'. They have only been perceived superficially and have no depth. These are not really cells and don't work as expected. The trouble with this approach is that the technique gets a bad name: 'Ugh, we tried cells and they didn't work.' Too many companies have perceived cells, as, say, group technology, without addressing any of the other issues. Team-based cells are a combination of elements—people and organization, engineering, logistics, accountability and performance measures—and they all have to be in place for cells to be effective. Teams have strong agreement on goals, and on the role of each member towards achieving that goal. When all these elements are in place, if a component going through a cell has a total process time of 5 hours, the cell is managed as a single unit, and the cell team has all the resources that are available to do the job, it ought to be reasonable to expect them to complete the whole process in 1 week, *not* 20 weeks. This makes dramatic collapse in lead time a reality and starts to change the destructive spiral into the virtuous spiral.

When all the processes in a cell are being managed as a single entity, we might as well consider them as a single operation. From the viewpoint of logistics, having one cell equal one operation radically simplifies all the paperwork and monitoring that has to go with production. When manufacturing has been organized around cells, the overall lead time from launch to customer receipt collapses. Compressing the lead time taken to complete the four or five serial accountabilities makes it possible to start thinking about running the business based on real customer demand.

COLLAPSING LEAD TIMES

One of the characteristics of a functional organization is that the many serial accountabilities make long lead times absolutely inevitable. When I started my career, I did a manufacturing apprenticeship. I must have been about 19 years old when I began to work in the manufacturing planning section of an engineering company. My job was to assign dates to activities by working through a job book full of cards. Each card represented an operation (and a serial accountability) and I was required to put the week number when the job should be completed onto each job card. I said to the supervisor of the department, Mr Fox (who inevitably had the sobriquet 'Cubby') 'Cubby, how do I do this?' He said, 'It's fairly straightforward, lad. You go back from the required completion date for the product and allow one week per operation.' I protested long and loud. 'Surely, Cubby, that can't be right, because the time allowed for this drilling operation is less than an hour for the whole batch. Why should it take a whole week?' Whereupon Cubby cuffed me benignly round the back of the head and said in a gruff tone, 'Don't be silly, lad.

Manufacturing is a complicated business. You'll soon understand.'

In fact, I soon found out that it got even worse. The more time we allowed for production, the more time we had to add on to compensate for the uncertainty factor. When doing the planning, with 10 operations and 1 week per operation, we ended up with a situation where the only thing we could be sure of was that we would not complete the product on the date scheduled. So what did we do? We added *even more time* onto the build programme to allow for this. One company I worked for had a 'kitting allowance' of 8 weeks. That's a euphemism for another 8 weeks—2 months!—added onto the lead time to compensate for uncertainty about when the job would actually be complete. There was so much work-in-progress that we couldn't see the wood for the trees, and needed several expediters running around looking for the bits of wood we needed.

All this made a deep impression on me. For ages I believed that manufacturing was a complicated business and that it was unreasonable to expect a relationship between the amount of time it took to do a job, and the time allowed in the schedule. It took a long time for me to shake off this conviction. But of course, there is no one more self-righteous than the convert, so now I preach the point that there absolutely must be a relationship between process time and lead time.

MANUFACTURE TO CUSTOMER DEMAND

Reducing the number of serial accountabilities and reducing lead time make Just-in-Time (JIT) supply very effective. It puts us close to the customer organizationally, in terms of accountability, and with regard to time, immediacy. With four serial accountabilities we ought to be able to work direct to customer demand.

There should be no need to launch a product to a 'guess' and modify it to suit customer requirements after it has been ordered, or to stop when we reach a certain point in the build programme to see if anybody will order it. We can't start manufacturing to customer demand overnight. Instead we have to gradually shift the balance from launching to forecast with excessively long lead times, to launching to customer demand with confidence that we can complete the product in time.

ELIMINATION OF SHORTAGES

Short lead times and working to customer demand mean much less work-in-progress, and shortages start to disappear. Shortages have always plagued medium to high complexity engineering businesses. Work-to lists are gazzumped by shortage lists, and this creates even more shortages in the future:

> 'Here is the red-hot three star shortage list. These items *must* be produced first. Absolutely nothing must take precedence over them ... except this one, ... oh, and this one over here.'

So nothing really ever gets done until it finally becomes a shortage. One of the things that starts to happen, once a factory begins to organize around teams working in cells, with few serial accountabilities and appropriate performance measures in place, is that shortages begin to melt away. Each team is directly accountable to its customer, knows what its requirements are and keeps its supplier informed of exactly what is needed in order to meet customer demand, so the work-to list becomes believable. When shortages go away, you are actually working to the customer's requirements.

EMPHASIS ON RIGHT-FIRST-TIME QUALITY

Quality has traditionally been associated with conformance to a specification for an operation. The technician living in the 'fog of manufacturing' could not relate what he did to what happened in the next process. Trying to draw up a quality specification for a component was extremely difficult because there were so many unwritten things which could not be put on a specification. The drawing could specify dimensions and surface finishes using mechanistic and scientific criteria, but at the end of the line the customer was still saying, 'It's no good, it has to be like this!' The customer has subjective, visual criteria for what the product should be like, but the technician in the machine shop still says, 'Don't tell me, I just follow the drawing.' Also, sometimes it's hard to realize the consequences of diverging from the specification, so the technician believes he is manufacturing to standard when he's not. As an example, let's look at the manufacture of spars, the big alloy girders for aircraft wings. In one machine shop, the inspectors insisted that the spars were finished off by sandpapering or polishing with an abrasive cloth. Later it was discovered that this actually degraded the surface of the spar and the customer would have preferred the 'as machined' finish. Cell manufacturing puts the supplier in touch with the customer so this type of occurrence can be avoided. When team-based cells are organized, many of the techniques first tried and discarded in the 1940s, 1950s and 1960s suddenly become viable. Statistical Process Control (SPC) starts to work in a small team environment. In the old world, a technician would accept a quality defect and 'bodge' it, or perhaps not even realize it was a defect. In a small team, people discuss and compare quality problems and work out joint solutions for eliminating them. The relationship between quality, planned maintenance and production engineering becomes clearer and easier to handle as all the people are involved. Cells create the conditions where defect levels can come down from 5 or 6 per cent to virtually nil. When shortages disappear, and quality problems drop, all the time that people used to spend waiting for shortages and reworking defects becomes available for useful work and productivity goes up dramatically. The people in the team have created the situation where the most logical, appropriate, rewarding thing is to do the job that needs to be done.

RELATING PERFORMANCE MEASURES TO BUSINESS NEEDS

When you cannot manufacture to true demand, you cannot measure the performance of your business according to how well you satisfy the customer's needs. In the manufacturing environment we have inherited, where rising commodity prices meant that inventory was good and demand always exceeded supply, it was appropriate to say that—if we couldn't measure how well we satisfied true customer demand—at least keeping the machines and people busy would ensure the production of saleable products. This meant a very strong focus on labour and machine utilization. In today's world, the inevitable consequences of keeping machines and people busy are:

1. Excessive inventories of parts, whether they are needed or not.
2. The production manager (who is usually appointed because of his ability to focus strongly on tasks and goals) will very rapidly come to understand what he gets his backside kicked for at the Monday morning production meeting. Although he will give intellectual acknowledgement to overall issues of customer satisfaction and service, he will actually respond to what he gets measured on, which is generally labour and machine utilization.

I can personally give examples of where these measures actually run counter to the needs of the customer and the business. At one company where I worked many years ago as a very green and naive production engineer, I was approached by the machine shop manager and the purchasing manager. They came to me with a die casting which eventually ended up in a DIY product. They pointed out that every die casting was being supplied with a lump of unwanted metal on the end, and the machine shop had to remove it before the assembly department could use the part. They asked me to make the process of removing this piece of metal a standard operation. At that time, they had to charge the removal of this piece of metal as an overhead because it was a nonstandard operation. The machine shop manager was upset because this degraded his machine and labour utilization figures and the purchasing manager was upset because he had to pay for it out of his budget. I asked them why they didn't get the supplier to provide the die casting without the unwanted bit of metal. They said they had been trying to do that for a long time, but the supplier 'didn't want to know'. So—in my innocence—I said, 'If I make it part of the standard hours, the cost of removing it will always be there, it's just that we'll never know about it.' 'Right', they said. 'So the incentive to remove the defect will be gone forever, won't it?' 'Well', they waffled, 'you know what we mean', and leant on me rather severely. It is to my eternal shame that I caved in and accommodated them initially. They persuaded me to undertake an action which went against the business needs, because the current situation was making them look bad with respect to how their performance was measured. I didn't sleep well that night and the following morning swallowing hard, undid my misdeed and went and told the two managers what I had done. Never again, I promised myself. I remembered this lesson.

Team-based cells create a series of small entrepreneurial activities inside the business where the things team members consider important, and the things they measure themselves by, are the same things the overall business considers important and measures itself by (Fig. 3.2).

It allows us to define what we need from the cell in terms of business needs, then to measure the cell's performance in terms of

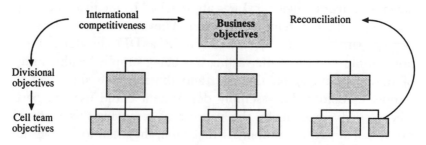

Figure 3.2   Aligning cell team objectives with business objectives

meeting the business needs, so we close the loop backwards and forwards. We can define the competitiveness of the whole business as the sum of the performance of the individual team-based cells. This is in sharp contrast to the old world where it was very difficult to relate labour and machine utilization directly to the overall health and profitability of the business. Many an accountant's career was based on the ability to interpret these figures, but cell manufacturing makes the organization of the business easier to understand and measure.

APPROPRIATE EMPHASIS ON ALL THE ELEMENTS OF TEAM-BASED CELLS

We have seen that team-based cells offer a unique and practical alternative to traditional manufacturing techniques. They allow companies to achieve the flexibility and responsiveness of a small business, which is vital to maintaining competitive advantage in today's economic conditions. In the next section we are going to look in more detail at how to put in place the four essential elements of team-based cells:

- People and organization
- Engineering
- Logistics and control
- Accountability and performance measures

To deliver the benefits, team-based cells need to have appropriate emphasis on all of these areas. In the early days, I believed cells were all about engineering issues: how to arrange machines. Plenty of companies today still believe that is all they have to do to make cells work. Many benefits come from the group technology aspects of cells, but there is a measure of disappointment because some of the other benefits are not being realized. For me, the next step was realizing that the new cell layout had to be supported by logistics and systems which were radically different from traditional methods. Then for me came the damascene conversion (which

I had in about 1985) that cells were really all about making the most of all the skills of our people, that is, creating conditions where instead of asking them to leave their brains at the gate, we started asking them to contribute their ideas. This meant creating an environment where the new patterns of behaviour required for the business could grow and blossom. Finally, came the realization that we could not operate in a demand-driven world using the old way of measuring performance and accounting. When all four pieces of this jigsaw are in place then we start to see the real benefits and fulfilment of the promise of team-based cells.

4

What is a team-based cell?

If I am only allowed to use one illustration to show what team-based cells are all about, Fig. 4.1 is the one I use. It really puts across the essence of what teaming in cells is all about. It gives the most concise definition of a team-based cell that I know.

> A cell is a multi-skilled, multi-process production unit small enough to be managed by one person, which is accountable for output of a finished quality product. It is run by flexible team members working and communicating as a unit with a single goal. To fulfil its obligation—output of finished quality products—the team has a right to expect two things: believable work-to lists and workable work; plus teaming with identified people in engineering, quality, logistics, etc.

With such a team we are able to recreate the entrepreneurial flair of a small business within a large organization. I want to examine each element of this definition in a bit more detail.

A MULTI-SKILLED, MULTI-PROCESS PRODUCTION UNIT

Cell manufacturing brings together in one location all the skills (people) and processes (machinery and equipment) needed to produce a defined product or family of parts (Fig. 4.1). The team

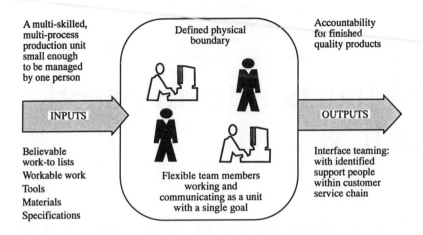

Figure 4.1   A multi-skilled, multi-process production unit

members have access to all the processes required to produce the product and the people have the breadth of skills needed to carry out those processes. This does not mean that every team member has to be able to do every task, but each team member should be able to undertake more than one task. The ultimate aim might be to achieve a situation where 70 per cent of the people have 70 per cent of the skills. In that sort of environment you really start to see flexibility. The team can handle everything that is thrown at it, one way or another.

MANAGED PRODUCTION UNIT

There are two issues involved in sizing the production unit so that it is small enough to be managed by one person: span of vision and number of people. The production unit needs to be arranged so that the team leader can see everything he is accountable for in one span of vision. What we are trying to do with team-based cells is create an environment where the team leader can actually manage the whole unit without having to have recourse to fancy aids or tools. When the team leader can see all that he is accountable for by standing up and looking around, he can rely on 'visible' management. Most people who have worked in an industrial environment would probably agree that the human brain is the best parallel processor there is around. It is very good at what can be called 'fuzzy logic'. The team leader doesn't need complex accounting tools to provide him with statistics on inventory to know that there is too much lying around. He can tell by looking. He gets a 'feel' for what is right and can judge intuitively when something seems odd. (This is something computers have not achieved. They need 'numbers' logic.) He can equate the amount of inventory to the level of activity and the demands that he knows he has to meet and balance these all in his head, just like someone running their own business.

For example, some time ago at home, I wanted the chimney breast in the dining room taken out, because it was getting in the way. I called a builder and asked him to do the job, and I was fascinated watching the way he worked. He came along, looked at the chimney breast, and gave me an on the spot quote of £300, an awful sum in those days. He came back on the appointed day, all ready with what he had decided he would need in order to get the job started. When he'd removed the chimney breast and reached the point where he needed to make good, he sized up what he'd need for that job: plaster board, plaster, skirting board, etc., and went off to the builder's merchant to get just enough. Once satisfied with the quality of his work, he tidied up, did his reckoning and brought me his invoice. I could see exactly how much material he'd used, and I could see the quality, so I was happy to pay him on the spot. 'Wow', I thought, 'wouldn't it be wonderful if we could make things that simple in industry. No middle men, no computers, no delays.' Creating units small enough to be managed by one person is one of the things that brings this sort of flexibility into a large company.

The number of people in the team is the other issue involved in creating a unit small enough to be managed by one person. Most of you would agree that it is really only possible for one person to manage an absolute maximum of 20 people. There is plenty of precedence for this. Most sports teams have between 11 and 15 players (OK, hockey teams have 8). The smallest unit or division in most nations' armies is a section or squad of 8 to 10 people. Jesus had 12 disciples. There are 12 members on a jury. If someone tells you they've got a cell with 150 people in it, then it is not the kind of cell we are talking about here. You'll probably find when you look closer that there are a number of different teams of people inside the unit they've called a cell, because people naturally break themselves into units of about 12.

Figure 4.2 shows that for up to about 12 people the output from an effective team is greater than the sum of the individuals, contribution; this is due to the high levels of unconscious agreement on goals, tasks and roles. A 12 by 12 communication network is about the limit for a team to be able to unconsciously share goals, tasks and roles. Adding more team members will start to degrade overall team performance to the point where, at about 20 people, the team will start to break into smaller units.

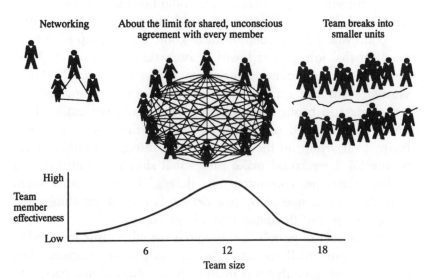

Figure 4.2   Team size

ACCOUNTABLE FOR PRODUCING FINISHED QUALITY PRODUCTS

Another thing that really delivers results in team-based cells is that the people have accountability for output of a finished quality product. In a typical manufacturing business a finished product can be a family of components defined by geometry, or an assembly defined by the nature of the assembled product. The way that the product of each cell is defined will affect planning activities and this has to be taken into account. Product definition for teams does not apply only to the shop-floor. Other teams working in sales, design or engineering also have a finished product, with a defined customer. For sales, this product will be an order with the complete specification for that order delivered to engineering. For engineering, the product is the interpretation of the customer's requirement into an engineered product design and specification delivered to manufacturing. In each case there is a clear product and a clear delivery point.

The exception is the service cell, where the team is required to provide a service to the group, i.e., maintenance or treatments, painting, shot blasting. These services usually require expensive special equipment, and business can't afford the luxury of providing it for every cell, so they have to share. Equivalent small businesses are hairdressers, plumbers, small toolmakers, or suppliers of dental appliances. They provide a specialized service to a number of different individuals or companies based on their specific capabilities. Their product is less easily defined, because they apply their expertise across a wide range of other people's products. Nevertheless there is a clearly defined deliverable service.

Giving team members access to all the processes required to produce the product and making sure they have the breadth of skills needed to complete the task means that you can put accountability where the action is: at cell level. The cell team can carry out operator approval, can set and monitor achievement of targets for quality and output, because they know they have the authority to take action on these issues. Don't forget that the objective is to get 100 per cent quality, not to inspect parts and tell the technician whether they are good or not, after it's too late.

Putting accountability for quality with the operator brings out the issue of operator approval and this means that the operator has to be trained and then given real responsibility to inspect and sign off his own work. This is how you start to get improved quality. When people work as a team, and are responsible for inspecting their own work, they no longer tolerate defects. Initially there is an apparent increase in defects, because people are reporting things that once they would have bodged or let slip by them. At BAe Hatfield, with the agreement of team members and the support staff, people asked, 'Should we be tolerating this? No we shouldn't. Report it.' So defects temporarily rose. As a team, they decided what they were going to do about it, and then defects plummeted and melted away.

Making the team members responsible for quality and output leads to interesting questions of how to reward them for their efforts. Cells and piecework do not go together, but piecework is a powerful motivator and has to be replaced with something. This issue will come up again in the chapter on accountability and performance measures and is also a significant factor in motivating people while implementing culture change.

To fulfil its obligation—output of finished quality products—the team has a right to expect two things: believable work-to lists and workable work; plus teaming with identified people in engineering, quality, logistics, materials management, etc.

BELIEVABLE WORK-TO LISTS AND WORKABLE WORK

In some businesses, there is a computer-printed work-to list which everybody ignores in favour of the scruffy handwritten list which the foreman prepares in the morning and is considered to be the real 'hot list'. The work-to list is discredited and nothing ever gets finished until it finally gets onto the handwritten 'hot list'. In cell manufacturing the work-to list *is* the hot list. To make cells work, you make sure the team members know they are making what is actually needed, and you don't ask them to undertake a task unless you know they will have workable work: all the tools, materials and specifications when they are needed in order to finish the job. Many's the time, right to this day, I have seen work being stuffed into the factory when there was no expectation of finishing it, just to make sure that people had plenty to go at. If they couldn't work on one job because of a shortage or lack of tooling, maybe there was a chance they could work on another part-finished job. In cell manufacturing, the team has the authority not to accept work unless it's workable. Now we need to pause for a minute, while all the old sweats who are reading this complain. You'll be saying sarcastically, 'Of course, if we'd got all that in place, everything we needed right there, we could do the job dead easy.' What I say to you is, '*Yes, yes*, of course it would be easy. So let's use common sense and do it like that.' That's our objective: to make it simple and straightforward.

LEVELS OF INTERFACE TEAMING

Interface teaming with identified support people

The team members will need to be able to draw on the expertise of people in design, engineering, quality, logistics, materials management, maintenance, etc. Until now these activities have been provided by centres of professionalism, but in successful cell manufacture we assign them right down into the cells. This does not mean that each cell has its own production engineer, quality engineer, materials manager and maintenance team. What happens is that a group of cells representing a family of products will have a production engineer and quality engineer working with the team leaders to identify the real needs of the cells. A group of specialists can work very effectively with a specified group of cells, getting to know the people in each team, their tasks, their problems and the idiosyncrasies of their machinery and equipment.

When a cell is set up it brings together several previously isolated processes, e.g. milling, drilling, turning, plus all the interface activities. As the people with expertise in these areas interact they start to realize the effect their process has on other operations, both in the cell and downstream. A powerful effect of teaming is that people begin to see the quality implications of what's going on in the cell. For example, the team leader might watch one process and come to the conclusion that it is not really under control. He can see that only the skill of the operator is getting the process right. He's driving it by the seat of his pants, twitching it here, making a micro-adjustment there, sticking a bit of cigarette paper underneath the tooling. When 'interface' teaming really gets going, the team leader has a personal relationship with the quality engineer, and can ask him to look at the process. The quality engineer might decide to do a capability study on the process to check it out. He will probably do a statistical analysis of its output and prepare a Shewhart chart of the results. This is the Shewhart chart we were all taught to use in technical college but never found a reason to apply in our jobs. (Shewhart, Walter A., *Economic Control of Quality of Manufactured Product,* Van Nostrand Co., Princeton, NJ, 1931; reprinted 1981 by the American Society for Quality Control). At this point it may dawn on the team members that what they are doing is statistical process control (SPC), only it seems so simple.

If the results of the study show that the machine is fundamentally unable to meet the quality requirements of the process, the operator and team leader have a chat with the production engineer and the maintenance engineer to see if they can find the cause. When the maintenance engineer has a look, he immediately spots that the seals on a slide are causing the problem. He points out that those seals need to be changed about every 3 months and promises to keep an eye on them and change them when they get worn. Isn't this planned maintenance? Yes, of course, and it's so much less trouble than people think. While the maintenance engineer is looking at the seals the production engineer has been studying the jig arrangement and has had an idea! He shows the team leader how rearranging the jigs slightly will make the process easier, and suggests asking the design engineer if a small change in the product design would help even more. They are applying 'design for manufacture' almost without knowing it. SPC, planned maintenance, production engineering and design for manufacture, all taking place in one cell: the *people* are doing it and not making a big deal out of it. That is the magic of cells. Cells take many of the excellent techniques which were developed in the first half of the century and give them human dimensions.

There is still a role for centres of professional excellence, however. People who work in the cells could get a little short-sighted, and businesses always need people who are able to stand away from day-to-day tasks and look ahead, so there is a role for planning. Cell interface people can be drawn from centres of excellence, and at the same time interface teaming draws centres of excellence closer to the real world of manufacturing (Fig. 4.3). This way of organizing interface activities opens out career opportunities. Because team members are not leaving their brains at the gate but using them in the cell, they discover new skills and reveal hidden talents. These talents are spotted and developed for the benefit of the company. A team member could move from the

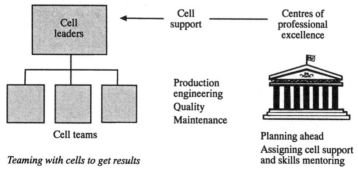

Figure 4.3   Interface teaming with centres of professional excellence

cell to the interface team, then into the centre of excellence, then back into operations as a team leader.

Interface teaming with the customer service chain

Interface teaming between the sections of the customer service chain is just as vital as interface teaming between team-based cells and centres of excellence. One level out from the cell team is the teaming of the activities required to make the mainstream business function. Companies that will survive in the 1990s are agile and good at interpreting the requirements of the customer service chain. Taking away the brick walls between these activities needs special interface teaming within each activity and at the boundaries (Fig. 4.4).

Any business which creates or handles a physical product has a customer service chain. For a product in manufacturing engineering this will typically consist of:

- *Selling* Understanding customer requirements and demonstrating that your product can fulfil them economically, reliably, and add value to the customer's business.

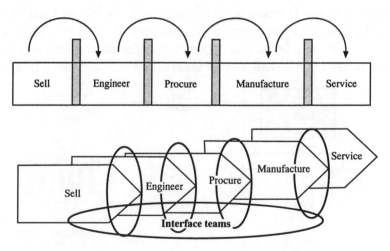

Figure 4.4   Interface teaming with the customer service chain

- *Engineering* Interpreting the customer's requirement into an engineered product design and specification.
- *Procurement* Getting into place all the elements you need from outside the company.
- *Manufacturing* Doing the physical conversion work of creating the product.
- *Service* Getting the product into the hands of the customer at the right time and at the right price and making sure it continues to add value to his business.

In many businesses today, the sections of the customer service chain live in compartments with brick walls in between. People from one department toss their bit over the brick wall into the next department. To be really successful, businesses have to break down these barriers that are focused around serial account-abilities.

People in the customer service chain may in the broadest sense be considered direct workers because they are the people who actually add value to the product. But I use the word 'direct' very loosely because I think the definition is going to disappear very soon. The issue of success is making the customer service chain sing. Businesses need people to support that customer service chain just as much as they need direct workers. These people are absolutely essential to the business, but they tend to add cost rather than value, so the issue here is making their contribution as efficient and cost-effective as possible.

Team-based cells play a significant role in the customer service chain, not only in manufacturing, but also in sales, engineering, procurement and service. Interface teaming at this level involves the people responsible for leadership and co-ordination of teams in each department, who form an interface team which goes across the boundaries. These must be true teams where the people know each other and have developed unconscious agreement of goals and roles. Successful businesses have built teams at cell level first, and have gone on to develop interface teams with support people, and finally with leaders and co-ordinators (Fig. 4.5).

TEAMS NEED	CELLS PROVIDE
Visible, meaningful targets	Clear, logical targets
Local monitors	Ease of monitoring
Relevant information	Simple, local information
Visible benefits from efforts	Focus on cell performance
Control of resources	Control of resources
Relevant training	Easy to identify training needs
CELLS NEED	**TEAMS PROVIDE**
Autonomous working	Local control
Clear communication	Clear communication
Focused goals	Common goals
Motivation to achieve goals	Motivation to achieve goals
People who can manage their own tasks	Empowerment

Figure 4.5 Cells and teams are complementary

For example, within manufacturing operations, all the team-based cells form a customer service chain and have supplier–customer relationships. Team leaders need to form a higher level team to understand supplier-customer relationships within manufacturing. At the next level up, representatives from sales, engineering, procurement, manufacturing and service need to form an interface team to understand supplier–customer relationships at the highest level. Interface teaming ensures that the rights and obligations of suppliers and customers throughout the business are communicated, acknowledged and fulfilled. The same principles can be applied to create team-based cells which provide information for service and support and this leads on to the subject of simultaneous engineering which will be covered in the next chapter.

Vision-mission interface teaming

Interface teaming needs to stretch out to the highest levels of the company, because all the directors need to lift themselves above their individual areas of responsibility and become involved in creating the vision and mission which will be used to prepare the business strategy. Interface teaming at all levels opens up avenues for developing the skills of people and starts to give real meaning to continuous improvement.

5

Harnessing the power of your people

The people element of team-based cell manufacturing is the one I talk about most. That's because I believe it's the most important. Unless the people *want* to make cells work, they won't work. This chapter looks at the issues around organizing people in team-based cells, and the things that have to be done to motivate them and make sure they realize their full potential. I've already described in the introduction how I stumbled across team-based cells when working with Baker Perkins. The performance improvements from this project (see Case Study, page 198) were so astonishing that I was left groping to find out what had happened to bring about this dramatic improvement. You could say that was my damascene conversion, when I realized that team-based cells are really all about people and the key to success is creating the environment in manufacturing where the simplest, most straightforward, most logical, most obvious, most enjoyable thing to do is the job that needs to be done. This was the event that sent me scurrying off to textbooks and articles to try to find out what had happened, and this was also the point where I evolved from being a 'manufacturing person' into being a 'people person'. The other aspects of team-based cells—engineering, logistics and accountability—are very important; their function is to help create an environment where people can give of their best.

WHAT IS A TEAM?

We have examined the definition of team-based cells in some detail, and have found that their success largely depends on the ability of individuals to come together and function as a team. Now we had better spend some time understanding what teams are, how they work, and what it takes to convince individuals that they will be better off working in a team.

Little team and big team: squad solidarity and regimental pride

When a team is working well, each member networks with every other member, implicitly acknowledging the others' roles and unconsciously sharing what the goals of the team are. If you were to ask each member of the team what they were doing, they might have a great deal of difficulty articulating this because it is so deeply ingrained in all behaviour and communication. To get to the stage of unconscious sharing of goals and roles takes time, and it also sets an upper limit on the number of people who can really share that type of teaming. As with the number of people one person can manage effectively, this is round about 12 to 15 people. Get above 20 and you're struggling. To make a useful analogy, I tend to call this little team 'Squad Solidarity': personal bonding at an individual level with fellow team members.

Most people who work in companies will recognize that there also has to be a bigger team, usually with about 100 members, and perhaps peaking at a maximum of about 300 to 400. Everyone feels an identity with this larger group of people, who tend to share a more intellectualized idea of the company's vision and mission: why it is in business and what it wants to achieve. This bigger team, for which I use the label 'Regimental Pride' tends to focus on being best at doing something, such as getting their products to market better, faster, cheaper. In the big team people are not forming unconscious links of networking with every individual, because there are too many people to do that, but they do share the corporate symbols of identity, such as company logos, regimental ties, flags, badges, pins, uniforms, colours. Each person probably knows most other big team members by sight, maybe by name, but they have their own 'little team' with whom to share squad solidarity. If a company becomes very big the symbol becomes too diffuse and people don't identify with it as readily. Individual employees don't think 'it's *my* company', but tend to identify with their location instead. When this happens 'sub-symbols' start to appear in sections of the company.

At the regimental pride level, teaming is proprietal, ownership is more externally expressed rather than implicitly shared. This is evidenced by competition, like that between the Paras and the Commandos. Paras may squabble among themselves, but soon close ranks if they are pitted against the Commandos in any type of competition. The Oxford and Cambridge boat race is another symbol of big teams staging a competition for the purpose of displaying regimental pride. The next step beyond regimental pride is tribal (or national) loyalty, in which thousands of people identify with the same goal or symbol. Football teams have thousands of fans, and national identification is felt by millions.

THE FOUR STAGES OF TEAM FORMATION

When teams are performing well, all the members have that unconscious agreement about roles and objectives. Take musicians as an analogy: any group of musicians, a string quartet or a rock band. 'You're on guitar, we're on keyboards: together we are going to play this piece.' Another example is a successful soccer team. When things are going well, it's almost as if they read each other's minds. How did he know to kick the ball there? Casual observers may claim it's just luck, but actually it's the unconscious sharing of strategy and tactics that comes from successful teaming. To get people working as a team doesn't happen overnight. You can group a number of people together and call them a team, but they won't behave like a team unless they go through the process of teambuilding. My favourite description of this process is 'Forming, Storming, Norming and Performing'. I don't know who created this phrase to describe teambuilding (if you are out there, get in touch) but I am eternally grateful to you, because it is extremely apt.

Forming Finding out about the other team members: who they are, where they come from, their track record, what baggage have they brought with them into the team, and giving them this information about yourself. If we think of our musical analogy, this is the time when the musicians get to know each other's personality and capabilities.

Storming A stage of conflict, working out what team role each individual is going to fulfil. (This is where team typing is useful: see pages 84 and 85.) Who is going to be team leader? Who is best suited to be shaper, resource investigator, etc.? Before the team can actually say they are a team, they've got to shed a lot of baggage they've brought with them and get negative issues off their chests. It helps just to be able to voice their concerns to other team members, without necessarily resolving them. As soon as that's out of the way, they get on with something serious. In our musical analogy, the musicians start to rehearse and this leads to differences of opinion over tempo, volume, emphasis and who plays what.

Norming After the storming, people start to compromise and reach agreement, setting out the role of each individual and the rules and guidelines by which the team will operate, defining acceptable performance standards and what will be needed to achieve them. The musicians decide on how they are going to play the music and focus rehearsals on achieving the agreed standards.

Performing Everyone understands what they have to do and has unconscious agreement with the other team members. The musicians present a well-rehearsed performance in line with defined roles.

Team-based cells do not really deliver all the promised benefits until both the cell teams and the interface teams have gone through the forming, storming, norming and performing phases (Fig. 5.1). Companies often get some good improvements as a result of the physical changes involved in cell implementation, but then reach a plateau. Once this plateau is hit, the business won't move forward until the people issues are sorted out and the interface teams are working. Otherwise, we only create little teams that view other little teams as 'that bloody supplier' and 'that bloody customer'. You are trying to create a chain of suppliers and customers inside the business, and it is important to form partnerships with internal suppliers and customers, in the same way that you want to form partnerships with external suppliers, as part of the logistics effort (see Chapter 7).

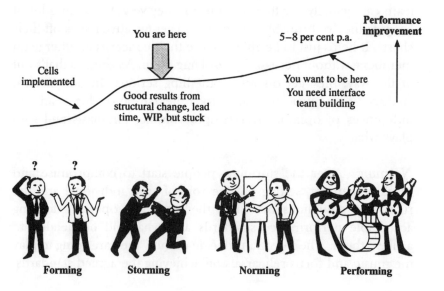

Figure 5.1 Stages of team formation: forming, storming, norming and performing

CONVERGENCE OF GOALS AND OBJECTIVES OF THE TEAM AND THE BUSINESS

Vision mission values

Successful team-based cells take into account both the needs of the business and its goals, i.e. the big team, and the needs of the individuals in the teams, the little team. Business objectives tend to be expressed intellectually in terms of vision and mission. The mission is developed from the vision statement, and leads to the preparation of the business strategy which describes the methods the company will use to achieve the mission. The culture of every company is based on a set of values which govern the behaviour of employees. These values and beliefs have a strong influence on the attitudes and objectives of the little team. Values lead to behaviour patterns necessary to implement the strategy which will achieve the mission. Definitions and examples of vision, mission and values are given below.

- *Vision: why the business exists*
  - A guiding philosophy which sets high sights: Disney, 'To make people happy'.
  - Tends to be qualitative and enduring.
  - It has no finish line (employees can strive for it even after achieving the mission).
- *Mission: a clear statement of objective*
  - Has a finish line so you know when you have achieved it, then set a new mission.
  - Is risky, attainable, but only with effort.
  - Time based—within reach of present employees, i.e. 4–5 years—and quantifiable.
- *Values: deeply ingrained beliefs that underpin behaviour*
  - Beliefs and moral principles that lie behind the company's culture: e.g. quality, communication, innovation, excellence, sensitivity, etc.
  - What constitutes acceptable or unacceptable behaviour.

British Airways
   Vision To be the world's favourite airline.
   Mission To have better in-flight service, comfort, punctuality, and more friendly and helpful ground services than competitors.
   Strategy To translate service, comfort, punctuality, etc., into actionable, measurable policies and train staff to adhere to them.
   Values Quality, service (20 000 trained to 'put people first').

Body Shop
   Vision To develop cosmetics that do not harm animals or the environment.
   Mission To be more environmentally conscious than competitors, thus attracting green consumers and green employees.
   Values Train employees in what can be recycled (each has two waste bins).

NASA mission To land a man on the moon and return him safely to earth by 1970.
Pepsi mission Beat Coke.
Honda mission We will crush, squash, slaughter Yamaha.

(The trouble with NASA was that it had no ultimate vision, so it could not set the next mission properly, and look what happened in the 1970s and early 1980s.)
   Successful teaming in manufacturing business makes sure the goals of that corporate body, which are set intellectually, and the implicit goals of each team member, which are based on value judgements, are aligned. The whole system of values and beliefs is based on shared knowledge of the team roles and goals, which—be warned—may not necessarily be what you think they are. There is plenty of evidence which shows when company and individual goals are not aligned, and most of it means trouble. When the little team's goals are more aligned with the objectives of the union to which they belong than to the company's objectives, you start to see real industrial relations problems. When the little team's goals are aligned with their own interpretation of what survival means,

rather than that of the business, you get dissension and subversion. A good example of this comes from the Vietnam war, when the enlisted US soldiers formed very strong 'squad solidarity' based on survival in the face of the enemy, to the point where they would throw grenades at their own officers if they were seen to threaten survival. This is a prime example of negative alignment of goals and objectives. One of the key things we are trying to do in team-based cells is get big team and little team goals in alignment because the results are very powerful (Fig. 5.2). When you get it right, stand out of the way, because things will go so fast and so well you won't know what's hit you.

Cells work when the goals and objectives of the business and the individuals within it converge. But how do we start to bring in line the business vision and mission and the little team goals and roles? I grew up in a world where practicality and pragmatism were virtues. I was given a technical education and was encouraged to think only in tangibles. My generation (and several since then) was taught to define the strategy of the business and to base business decisions on things that were mechanistic, financial, competitive. We kept busy writing out a financial justification for the purchase of new capital equipment or preparing capital

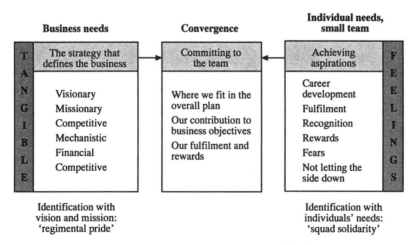

Business needs	Convergence	Individual needs, small team	
The strategy that defines the business	**Committing to the team**	**Achieving aspirations**	F
			E
Visionary	Where we fit in the overall plan	Career development	E
Missionary		Fulfilment	L
Competitive	Our contribution to business objectives	Recognition	I
Mechanistic		Rewards	
Financial	Our fulfilment and rewards	Fears	N
Competitive		Not letting the side down	G
			S

T A N G I B L E

Identification with vision and mission: 'regimental pride'

Identification with individuals' needs: 'squad solidarity'

Figure 5.2   Achieving convergence of goals and objectives

expenditure proposals. All our decisions were made for pragmatic, documented reasons. Then off we went to implement them on the basis that whatever we said was right, because we'd done the calculations, and the people would just have to come along with us ... *but sometimes they didn't.* What often happened was that the benefits which justified decisions on expenditure were not fully realized, and we knew it! We had justified the purchase of equipment by saying that it was going to achieve certain levels of utilization, productivity improvement, or lead time reduction and then this wouldn't quite happen. However not many companies bothered to do a thorough post-investment analysis of benefits achieved: they just bought in the equipment and tried to make it work.

At the same time, the profit and loss and balance sheet benefits were often not as good as expected. So it was no wonder that the accountants in the business set such stringent targets for investment benefits: 'This investment must have a simple pay-back period of 18 months', knowing that if they said this, there was a slight chance that they might get a 3-year pay back. We used to pay lip-service to training: 'Oh, let's put another 5 per cent on for training.' Very often this was never even spent. Personnel departments said we ought to do a bit of training, but then set about it without really understanding what it was supposed to achieve.

We now realize that the tangible things which define the strategy of the business are only part of the equation. On the other side are all the soft issues which affect people personally, and they are a bit difficult for people grounded in technology, facts and measurements to get hold of, define and pin down. But it can be done, and unless these things are taken into consideration, business won't realize its full potential. All these issues centre around urges, feelings and desires. For example, why did I write this book? It wasn't anything to do with competitive, tangible, financial, measurable things. It was about aspiration, something I wanted to achieve, very much based on an issue of feelings. The things that motivate people as individuals, or interactive members of small teams, are career development, achieving fulfilment, getting rewards and recognition, and not wanting to let the side down. Companies which have implemented really successful team-based cells are those which have recognized and made an effort to satisfy these needs as well as the business needs. They have shown people that they cared about personal issues by developing a plan which converges these needs, shows where individuals fit into the plan, identifies what job each person will do, asks whether they want to do it (or feel capable of doing it), and shows how they are to be rewarded.

All the issues discussed in the remainder of this chapter—communication, involvement, assessment, selection and training—help to converge big team and little team goals and objectives. At the end of the day, the business needs will drive decisions, but you will have more chance of achieving the benefits if you achieve convergence of business and individual needs.

HOW TO MAKE IT ALL HAPPEN

What steps do you have to go through with a group of individuals to get their goals and objectives in line with the business objectives? That is the way you will get them to perform. If you want them to perform, you have to make sure they are competent. If you want them to be competent, you have to provide the right training. If you want them to get the most from training they have to be committed. If you want their commitment, you have to make sure they understand what's going on. The step-by-step plan illustrated in Fig. 5.3 shows how to take people through all these stages of development.

C^3—Consistent, caring communication
The starting point in bringing about a dramatic culture change has usually got a fairly broad base to it. With luck, you will start with a group of people who are already fairly positive about the business

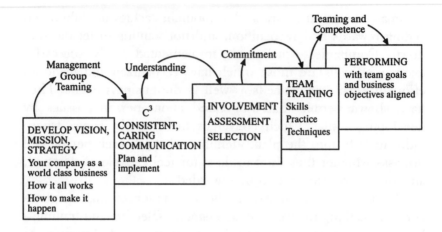

Figure 5.3　The process of culture change

and you want to give them a boost so that they really lift their performance. Most often, you have a group of people who feel that they've been knocked about a bit. They've usually had a wide range of experiences which has reduced their morale and made them doubt the company management. People's feelings about a company can be very patchy when they have lived through stringent measures intended to improve competitiveness, often including a series of painful redundancies. When confronted with yet another plan, some people will say, 'OK, I hear what you are saying about team-based cells, and I'd like to be positive, but I need to understand more of what it's about.' At the other end of the spectrum, others will be saying, 'We've heard this all before. You tried it in 1979. It didn't work then and it won't work now.' Suspicion of motives is a big hurdle that has to be overcome. The problem is, you often get management piling straight in at the deep end, telling people what the changes are, sending them on a training course, and expecting them to start performing at their full potential without allowing them an opportunity to understand, absorb and contribute to the change.

The issue of gaining understanding of, and commitment to, change is vital. I remember working with BNFL at Workington, on a project to plan and implement a new factory on a greenfield site. This was an early and primitive foray into cell manufacture. We put in state-of-the-art equipment and the operators who were to transfer to the new factory had extensive off-site training courses in how to use it. On the day when the operators were to begin work at the new site, we arrived at 7.30 am to see how things went. I stood there with my colleagues open-mouthed, as we watched an employee turn up for work and totally ignore the smart new equipment around him (and for the early 1980s it was smart, including computers, TV screens, bar code readers). Instead, he started to do his old job. He went in search of raw material, found some in cardboard boxes, dragged them to the line and emptied them. He'd brought an old hacksaw blade taped up at one end and sharpened at the other and he used this to open the boxes so that he could manually heave large, heavy cylinders out of them. We were absolutely aghast. We finally decided we had to intervene and show him how the system worked and what he was supposed to do.

He had been given quite a lot of off-site training, but it was only as we started to walk him through the job that he began to connect that training with an actual job that he was expected to do and was able to do. We were lucky with him, and the others in that area. Quite soon the old way of working became a rapidly fading memory, because we'd created the right physical environment in a cell, so that the most logical thing for them to do was the job in hand; but at the beginning the new way of working had taken them by surprise, when with planning, it need not have done.

The first stage you want to reach in any process of culture change is what I call 'benign neutrality', where the people involved say, 'I understand what you're trying to do and I'm prepared to go along with you for now.' I think it is unfair to ask more than that of any group at first. To get to this point you need what I call 'C^3': consistent, caring communication.

Consistent means that the information people receive has basically the same core content, regardless of the source it comes from, and this consistent message has to make sense from whatever perspective people look at it. One of the techniques which all employees use—from MD to shop-floor operator—is checking out a complex issue by asking several different people the same question from a number of different viewpoints and angles, then comparing the answers for consistency. If the answers are consistent (including the messages received from eyes and their body language) then probably the message is right. The MD uses this method because he is accountable for a vast range of skills and technologies, and he cannot be expected to have an in-depth understanding of all of them, but he needs information to be able to plan and manage the business. Operators on the shop-floor use the same technique, asking different managers the same question and checking for consistency. Watch out, because you can be floored by unexpected questions from operators, what I call 'bike shed' questions. 'Where's the bike shed?' they ask, looking at the proposed new layout. And you wonder, 'Why on earth is he asking that?' But little by little you begin to see what is in their minds. No bike shed means no bikes. No bikes means not many people coming to work on bikes. If so few people come on bikes that they can't be bothered to build a bike shed, maybe the place is really going to close. This example is deliberately exaggerated, but it provides an indication of the kind of logic people will use to check out the consistency of your message.

The second point is that the message must be *caring*. This is where people watch your body language. It's not just 'read my lips', but 'watch my feet' as well. And the messages you speak and convey by body language must be the same. If you shuffle your feet and turn your shoulder, they'll think you're fibbing. People have to know you care about their future, and that it's your future as well. You have to believe in what you are saying so that they can feel your belief and know that you are not just passing on all massage parrot fashion from a higher authority.

Communication, and plenty of it, is needed to reinforce the message. It may be possible to overdo communication, but I haven't seen it happen yet. You have a whole range of communication media available, from keynote briefings of all employees by the MD or general manager, to presentations to small groups, which give employees an opportunity to ask 'bike shed' questions.

A model of the new layout, showing machinery grouped into cells, is a useful communication tool. It uses the physical changes as an introduction to the cultural and organizational changes that will accompany the new layout. Getting the people involved in planning and building the model is an excellent way of gaining their commitment to change. BAe Hatfield used a detailed model as a focal point for communication. The entire workforce of several thousand people was invited to view the model in groups at lunchtime over several days. Each group was taken through a briefing process which explained why things had to change, what was going to happen, provided an opportunity for questions and allowed people to examine the model. They were able to say, 'Oh, look. There's my machine,' or even more significantly, 'Where's *my* machine?' In this way, people began to get a feeling for the real magnitude and significance of the proposed changes. Afterwards the model was installed as a permanent display in an information centre which employees could visit.

The process of communication also forces managers to come to terms with some tough issues. If a person's machine is not there, the manager making the presentation has to be prepared to explain why not, openly and clearly. The objective of the communication is to make sure people understand why the changes are taking place, and that they are necessary to achieve the company's business strategy: the big team goal. Though it may be hard for people individually to swallow, the whole workforce will respect honesty and consistency, but resent floundering and flannelling.

The control room, war room or change room (whatever name seems appropriate in the circumstances) is another key feature of a communication plan. Very early in the project, you will need to allocate a good sized, centrally located room to act as the nerve centre for the project, and furnish it with a flip chart, overhead projector and screen, and adequate tables and chairs for group meetings. There should be plenty of wall space: you may want to cover the walls with cork to make it easy to pin up displays. In this room, you use wall displays to make a visible statement of your intention to change and to highlight the things you are going to do. It very rapidly becomes the focal point for meetings which are concerned with bringing about the changes. The room must be open at reasonable times for everyone to visit and no one must be refused entry or rumours will soon spread.

The information displayed in the war room evolves during the process of change, but usually comprises two elements. The first is a statement of intent: what it is you are actually going to do. This might be a plan showing the new layout of the shop-floor, with the team-based cells defined, statements of your vision and mission, a bar chart showing the various activities, the timescales for doing them, milestone dates for completion, and the various plans for people development, logistics, systems, quality, inventory control, machinery and equipment moves, and cell start-up. This element, the statement of intent, needs to have a feeling of permanence about it. Details might change, but the basic plan should remain consistent throughout the project. It is useful to divide the wall space with a dado rail—or even a piece of tape—at about waist height. The information on your statement of intent is displayed above the line, and slightly less permanent information on day-to-day activities and progress is displayed below the line, such as computer printouts and minutes of recent meetings, with action lists and complete-by dates highlighted. This information answers the questions: 'How are we getting on? Are we achieving these goals and objectives that you see displayed?'. The war room will represent the work of quite a number of people in the business who are involved in implementing the change, and they will want to keep the information relating to their activities up to date. As soon as the war room is up and running, the MD won't be able to resist bringing visitors to look round, to impress them with the progress the company is making towards improving competitive performance.

These are the main communication tools you have available to help people understand what you are trying to do and to gain their commitment. Naturally, it will probably take a little while until you get a critical mass of people who reach the stage of 'benign neutrality' where they are prepared to go along with you. Then you get to the next stage, where you actually start to involve them in the process of change.

Involvement: building commitment

Once you have gained people's understanding of where you are going, it's time to start building their commitment. To do this you need to involve them in the process of planning and implementing the changes. What happens next is that, despite themselves, they begin to get interested. Once they get involved they discover for themselves that there is a different way of doing things. Enjoyment of this process of self-discovery leads to ownership of the change and retention of new knowledge and skills. A useful formula to remember when implementing change is:

Involvement + Enjoyment = Ownership + Retention = Commitment

Ownership of the new way of working is what you want to bring about, because when people feel that the new methods are theirs, it builds their commitment. In any group of ten people, when you have communicated a clear, consistent message, eight out of ten are probably pretty much with you, and are prepared to make a commitment to the change. Then you are left with another two who, because of their past experience, are still not convinced. They've heard what you're saying but they don't like it, and don't agree and don't want to do it. As you start to involve people, these two start to see that this is the way it's going to go, whether they like it or not. You get a situation that is a bit like a train pulling out of the station, with eight of the people on board. The other two are going to look at the train pulling out, look at each other, weigh up what's likely to happen if they don't get on, and the chances are, one of them is going to dash down the platform shouting: 'Wait for me, I'm coming,' and jump on the train. Out of any group of ten, you are usually left with one person who will not make a commitment to the process of change and, whatever happens, people must see that his redeployment is managed firmly but fairly.

Assessment, selection and training

Don't even start to think about training until you have actually got commitment. People must be saying, 'Look, I've been involved. I like it! I want more. What happens next?' In team-based cells that work, the key roles in the cell team and interface teams must be filled by people you *know* have the commitment and competence to do the job. In the old world, foremen were very good at running their own functional departments. They generally rose up through the craft they were trained in, and were skilled at understanding the needs of the craft. They became adept at maximizing labour and machine utilization, because that is how their performance was measured. To be competent at their job, they needed a particular blend of skills, knowledge and experience. In team-based cells, the roles, goals and responsibilities are completely different. The qualities a team leader needs are not the same as those of a foreman, but are more like those of a small businessman. This is the time to get people involved in defining job roles, preparing job descriptions for team leaders, interface team members and operators, and participating in assessment centres, so that you don't get any square pegs in round holes.

The assessment centre is a technique which has been extremely successful in making the transition to team-based cells. It serves several purposes:

1. It helps to ensure that you appoint people with the right competence to key jobs.
2. The actual process of conducting the assessment centre involves people and convinces them that you are serious about change.

3. People see that everyone is being given a chance and appointments are being made objectively, and this encourages them to give the team leaders their support.

Personal interviews are currently most often used as the basis of selection for a post. The problem with personal interviews is that they rely on one person's judgement of another and people tend to be drawn towards employing others like themselves. 'If he thinks like me, speaks like me, acts like me, agrees with me, then he must be OK.' This is very subjective and full of dangers because you are not likely to get a proper spread of people capable of fulfilling different team roles. This did not matter too much in a structured environment, but now we are talking about a world where we need to be much more agile and responsive. In addition, conducting a whole series of personal interviews just to appoint one person is very time-consuming and unproductive. Managers spend hours interviewing, and more hours discussing candidates with their colleagues, and in the end, they make an inspired guess about who is the best candidate to appoint.

Assessment centres were originally developed for military use during the Second World War so that officer candidates could be processed quickly and objectively. They combine a number of structured activities to allow systematic observation and measurement of the characteristics required for the job, for example:

- Group discussion role play exercises.
- Individual exercises such as scheduling, planning or problem solving.
- Structured interviews.
- Numeracy, literacy and spatial awareness tests.
- Psychometric tests.
- Team role type assessments.

Because every candidate participates in the same exercises and takes the same numeracy, literacy, personality and team-type tests, assessors are able to compare like to like when analysing the results.

Psychometric tests assess candidates to see whether they possess a fair balance of the type of personality factors that will make them competent to undertake a particular job. They do *not* test qualifications or experience, which are covered by other activities in the assessment centre. Psychometric tests require people to answer a variety of subjective questions, allowing measurement of some criteria not easily explored in an interview.

Belbin Associates have described nine personality types or roles which should be present in every team for it to function effectively (Dr Meredith Belbin, *Team Role Theory Psychometrics*, Belbin Associates, Cambridge). This does not mean that every team needs nine members, because an individual can fulfil more than one team role at a time. People usually have two or possibly three roles to which they are very well suited, and two or three to which they are not at all suited, and should avoid. Belbin and other psychometric tests will identify a person's preferred team roles. The team roles are:

Plant	Creative, innovative and inventive, independent, clever and original
	Prefer to work alone, perhaps using unorthodox methods
	Introverts, react strongly to praise or criticism
	May lack practical constraints and have trouble communicating
Resource investigators	Enthusiastic, inquisitive, quick off the mark, extroverts
	Adept at exploring new opportunities and developing contacts
	Skilled at finding out what is available and what can be done
	Good communicators
	Need constant stimulation to keep enthusiasm from fading
Monitor evaluators	Serious minded, prudent, able to think critically
	Slow in making decisions

	Capacity for shrewd judgements, taking all factors into account
	May appear dry, boring or over-critical
Co-ordinators (chairmen)	Mature, trusting, confident
	Able to delegate readily and tackle problems calmly
	Recognize and harness individual talents towards group objectives
	Work better with colleagues of equal rank than when directing juniors
	Inclined to clash with Shapers because of different management styles
Shapers	Aggressive extroverts with a great need for achievement
	Highly motivated with lots of nervous energy
	Strong desire to win
	Headstrong and assertive, single minded and argumentative
	Able to rise above problems, generate action and thrive under pressure
	Don't mind taking unpopular decisions
Implementers (company workers)	Practical common sense, self-controlled and disciplined
	Work hard and tackle problems systematically
	Reliable, efficient, with a capacity for application
	May lack spontaneity and flexibility
Team workers	Mild, sociable, supportive, concerned about others
	Flexible, able to adapt to different situations and people
	Perceptive, diplomatic, good listeners
	May be indecisive in a crisis
Completer finishers	Capacity for precision, follow through and attention to detail
	Able to concentrate, work accurately and meet schedules
	Introverted, need little external stimulus or incentive

Anxious internally, yet outwardly unruffled
Not keen on delegating, prefer to do everything
themselves
Specialists   Keen to acquire technical skills and specialist
knowledge
Take pride in their own subject but lack interest in
those of other people
Single minded, dedicated to maintaining
professional standards

Assessment centres are organized to give every candidate several
opportunities to impress several different assessors. This provides
an unbiased technique for judging a candidate's suitability for a
role. Assessment centres are usually three or four times more
accurate than any other type of selection process. A view of the
effectiveness of different methods is shown in Table 5.1.

Table 5.1   Effectiveness of different types of selection process (Source:
Andy and Irene Moon, Pacer Consulting Group)

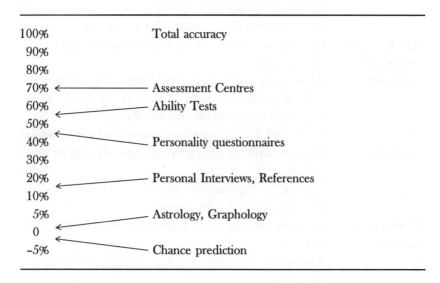

Many competent and well-qualified companies specialize in running assessment centres, creating individual and role play exercises, and administering and interpreting psychometric tests. Don't hesitate to seek help in this specialist area.

The assessment centre process

A typical process for preparing and running an assessment centre tailored to suit the requirements of the vacant position(s) is as follows:

1. Agree on the job description for the position.
2. Interview a cross-section of managers to establish what competences and characteristics they believe a candidate needs to do the job well. Collate the results and select the 10 most frequently mentioned competences and characteristics for assessment. In this way, you ensure that all the relevant managers agree on the type of person required for the job.
3. Advertise the position internally, stating the number of vacancies to be filled and informing applicants that they will be asked to participate in an assessment centre.
4. Work with a specialist to design an assessment centre incorporating activities which will assess the required competences and personality characteristics objectively.
5. Arrange the venue, schedule the activities and decide how many assessors you need.
6. Select and train the managers who will act as assessors so that they understand how to observe, record, classify and evaluate the behaviour of the applicants. Help them to recognize signs of positive and negative behaviour.
7. Run the assessment centre, making sure that all assessors complete their evaluation forms immediately after each exercise. Arrange to have the results of ability tests and personality questionnaires available by the end of the day.
8. Average the scores awarded to each candidate by each assessor for all the exercises and prepare a matrix for comparison.

9. Discuss details of each candidate, including their favoured team roles, asking assessors to give evidence from the exercises to support their decisions.
10. Make appointments based on unanimous group decisions.

Assessment centres have at least four significant benefits:

- They can be incredibly productive. I have been involved in sessions where 6 assessors have assessed 48 candidates over 2 days and reached a group decision on appointing 20 people. Imagine how long this would have taken if 3 managers had each interviewed all 48 applicants.
- When managers all agree on the capabilities and qualities of the people, and know their skills, they can capitalize on people's strengths and compensate for their weaknesses.
- Assessment centres are good at finding lights hiding under bushels. The process of inviting candidates to participate, reveals capabilities they didn't even know they possessed.
- You identify any gaps in skills that you need to fill, and get a clear idea of where people need training.

Training in knowledge and skills

Only when you have identified people with the right qualities to fulfil key roles, such as team leaders, and understood the preferred team roles of the team members, can you talk sensibly about team training, identifying and developing the specific skills and techniques that the people in each team need to complete their tasks and accountabilities. One way to achieve this is to get the team members to draw up a matrix of all the skills needed in the team, indicating the skills each team member has or might need to acquire. All the people will not need all of the skills, but looking at the matrix soon highlights where there is a skills shortage and allows you to concentrate on training the right people in those skills first. This will also be useful when deciding how to reward the team as a whole, and will come up again in Chapter 8 which considers accountability and performance measures.

6

Engineering

When we talk about engineering as one of the four key elements of team-based cells, what kind of engineering do we mean? The engineering aspects of cells (Table 6.1) cover two separate but related issues:

- How manufacturing cells are engineered; selection, layout and maintenance of the machinery and equipment.
- The design, production and quality engineering of the products manufactured by the cells.

Table 6.1   Engineering characteristics of a team-based cell

Product	Equipment	Workflow
Defined product families	Capacity	Simple, direct routing between operations
	Minimum set-up	
Minimum batch size		Close spacing and
	Reliability	clear line of sight to reduce
Design for manufacture		WIP
	Flexible fixturing and handling	

I use manufactured products as a model for the engineering of team-based cells, but it is important to realize that some of the concepts are equally applicable to basic forming and extractive industries. In the same way, the concepts relating to teaming and people are valid in non-manufacturing sectors of industry such as banking, insurance, health care, administration and local government. All these service activities could use most of the principles of team-based cells, with plenty of opportunity to bring about significant benefits.

HOW MANUFACTURING CELLS ARE ENGINEERED

Our definition of a team-based cell groups all the processes to manufacture a clearly defined product together in the cell. When this criterion is met, it acts as an enabler, getting the team to think about manufacturing much smaller batches with much shorter lead times. In the old world of manufacturing with functional organization, milling machines were in one shop and turning machines were in another, maybe a quarter of a mile away. There was no point in transporting just a few parts between those machines and monitoring their movements. Clearly, this was inefficient use of resources, so the demand for large batch sizes grew and, as we've already seen, large stocks and plenty of WIP were good things, weren't they?! There was no incentive for short set-up times or flexibility when making large batches because it didn't matter. The whole history of machine tool development up to the 1960s was predicated on the assumption that set-up times were not important.

As the world started to change and set-up times began to matter, emphasis started to be placed on group technology and NC machines as a solution to the problems of flexibility. The use of NC machines and group technology have an important role to play in planning the layout of team-based cells. They are big enablers for reducing set-up times and batch sizes. When you have all the processes and equipment necessary to make a family of parts located together in one cell, there is no reason why you shouldn't be able to make batch sizes of 1—or 4, or 8—but the need to make 200 or 2000 at a time has been eliminated. This has put pressure on machine tool technology to introduce changes which enable industry to do quick set ups and small batch sizes. We have already seen how interface teaming enables the design engineer, production engineer, quality engineer and team leader to get together and decide how to design the process inside the cell for maximum flexibility and efficiency. They work with the cell team members to design the cell so that it will manufacture what the customer wants, when he wants it.

Before looking in detail at calculating the size, capacity and machinery requirements of an individual cell, it is important to understand characteristics of the three main types of cells most frequently used in manufacturing business. They are all different, but they all have one underlying theme which makes them work, which is how they bring together the manufacturing and interface activities to create this thing we call the virtuous spiral of continuous improvement.

Types of cells

In deciding how to break down manufacturing activities into cells, we have to deal with the following two types of variable.

1. Type of activity.
   (a) Component manufacturing: machining, drilling, milling, turning, pressing, forging. (There is some overlap from basic forming processes, e.g. die casting and injection moulding fit in both areas, but most extruding, rolling, etc., belong in basic forming industries.
   (b) Assembly: putting things together.
   (c) Process: painting, plating, heat treating, surface treatment.
2. Volume and complexity (see Fig. 6.1).

Figure 6.1 shows the appropriate method for dealing with variable volumes and complexities to make sure real demand exists from customer cells before allowing the next lot of material to be manufactured and moved. A Kanban system will deal with high

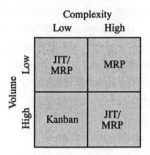

Figure 6.1   Methods for dealing with variable volumes and complexities

volume, low complexity items, while a combination of JIT and MRP will be needed for low volume, low complexity items and high volume, high complexity items; MRP alone should be adequate for low volume, high complexity parts.

Component manufacturing cells   These cells are defined by co-locating and managing as a single unit all the equipment needed to manufacture a family of geometrically related components, or process related components. They are responsible for the output of a finished family of components and all the processes required—machining, drilling, milling, turning, pressing, etc.—are located in the cell. Component cells have a series of customers in the assembly business whose requirements they have to fulfil. They get to know their customers and the products and become familiar with the tempo of supply. Typical examples of component cells are shown in Table 6.2.

One of the issues of managing cells and making them work properly is being very clear on cell definition so that decisions about assigning products to cells are easy and straightforward. In the precision machining environment, some components are 'oddballs' and the expenditure of setting up a cell just for them cannot be justified. In these cases a 'we do everything' cell or a 'we do everything the other cells can't do' cell becomes a viable option. This type of cell appears in different guises in different

Table 6.2 Typical component cells

Round parts		
Shafts/spindles	Small	Large
Discs/cones		
Gears		
Prismatic parts		
Cases	Small	Large
Frames/plates		
Links/arms		

industries. In aerospace, it appears as a manufacturing services cell, incorporating skills which are not core to the business but are necessary in order to fulfil obligations to customers, for example, coppersmiths and woodworking.

There is usually one defining process which adds more than 50 per cent of the value to the component. Taking a round parts cell as an example, the definer would be the turning operation, which would probably account for 50 per cent or more of the total workload. This defining process would probably require a couple of NC lathes. There will also be some finishing operations around drilling, milling, and grinding but the essential characteristic for that cell would be turning.

Similar logic is used for defining processes for round components, using NC chucking lathes and some finishing operations. For frame components, the defining operation will be a machining centre and some finishing operations, etc. This logic is used to define all the component cells in the batch manufacturing environment. Using the principles of group technology will help to define the component cells. Working out how to define product families for cell manufacture is one of the key engineering tasks.

Assembly cells The defining characteristic of assembly cells is that they are organized around a family of assembled products rather than a family of components. They are planned around the hierarchy of component subassembly and final assembly. The complexity of the product determines whether you need both a subassembly and a final assembly cell. Subassembly cells draw parts from one or more of the component cells and from external suppliers who provide bought-out components. Figures 6.2, 6.3 and 6.4 show some different types of assembly cell structures. In all of these examples it is the understanding and creating of the correct assembly cells and the relationship and location of the cells that help to create the environment to get the people issues right. Excellent cell design and engineering act as enablers for teaming and team-based manufacture which provide significant, durable benefits in productivity, lead time and quality.

Process cells

These cells are defined by the process they carry out: heat treat, surface treat, paint, etc. They are built round a core process which they provide as a service to other areas of manufacturing, selling this service to the other team leaders in the business who bring their work to it. The team leader in the process cell will form

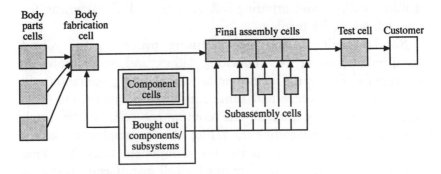

Figure 6.2   Assembly cell: automotive type

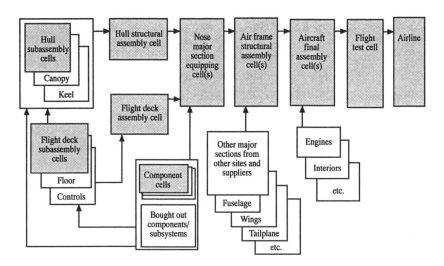

Figure 6.3   Assembly cell: airframe type

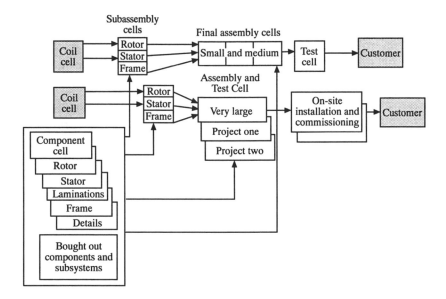

Figure 6.4   Assembly cell: industrial goods type, e.g. rotating electrical machines

working relationships with the people in the cells, start to understand the working patterns of the cells, and understand what they have to do to provide each cell with the service it needs.

I have yet to see a circumstance where it has been economically viable to incorporate a dedicated process facility within a component cell. Process facilities tend to be big, expensive, and immobile; just look at a typical heat treatment or surface treatment plant. Therefore, a single process facility in a fixed location will provide its service to a number of cells. Component manufacturing cells bring their product to that process. It is important to plan carefully to minimize out-of-cell work. Maybe this can be achieved by designing the cell process so that all the cell's operations are complete before it passes to a process cell. Critical success factors of a process cell will be determined by how well they provide the service. They need to build up a reputation for quality, service and value for money.

Process cells will be organized differently in the context of volume, size and complexity. In low volume manufacture, and in high volume with lower size and less complexity, the process cell will be able to provide a service to several cells. Consider manufacturers of consumer durables such as electric drills. The heat-treating cell has to provide a service for all heat-treated parts (gears, spindles, etc.) for the whole set of products, and the same is true of the paint plant. However, in a high volume environment manufacturing large, complex products, i.e. a car plant, the process becomes part of the manufacturing line. For example, the Ford Mondeo production line has its own treatment and paint areas as part of the process. Nevertheless, the issues of teaming are just as necessary in a high volume process as in a low volume cell.

MAKING IT HAPPEN: CONVERTING A FUNCTIONAL SHOP LAYOUT INTO TEAM-BASED CELLS

In order to convert the functional shop into a layout focused around team-based cells, we have to define product families for cell manufacture. This means arranging parts in groups requiring similar series of operations. When deciding on these groups or families many of the things we have to take into account will be specific to an individual organization's culture, so it is difficult to describe an optimum solution, because this depends on a company's business objectives. Generally, with a large number of parts, the first task is to classify each part and give it an identity so that a computer can be used to help create possible groupings into families of parts. The usual way of classifying or coding parts is by giving each part a number code relating to its shape and dimensions. In addition, a supplementary code can be added to describe the machining operations it needs, how it is used, the nature of the metallic finish, and any other aspects of the part which are relevant to the company. When all this data has been entered, the computer can be used to help sort the parts into families and that will help to group the machines into cells.

Coding systems were introduced in the 1950s and 1960s, partly as an aid to group technology. They were intensively developed and intended to be the basis for comprehensive renumbering of the complete parts list in a manufacturing business. The cell environment allows us to use the principles of coding for the parts in a simple way, tailored to suit each specific set of circumstances, without getting bogged down in redesigning the entire parts list. What's this? We've done it again: taken a system that was developed in the 1950s or 1960s and brought it down to human dimensions.

The feasibility of the resulting structures and the characteristics of the cells will depend on the equipment available within the business. The number of cells in a business unit is as likely to be a consequence of team size as of products or equipment. I have never come across any norm for the number of cells in a business unit manufacturing a family of products or number of parts in a family. However, too large a family will mean a large number of machines and too many people in the cell, while too small a product group will result in costly duplication of machinery. Also, when planning a cell, we need to remember that as the number of machines increases, so too do the material handling problems. In my experience, the number of machines per cell tends to be between 3 and 15. Each cell should only be expected to produce the family of parts that it was designed to make. If the cell has been designed correctly, it would be unlikely that parts could be transferred from one cell to another.

When the cells have been defined, each one needs to have its own dedicated core team. These people remain together as a team and are not asked to move about between cells too much. The advantage of this is that the team will learn to understand the unique problems associated with manufacturing the product group.

The machines in a cell are typically arranged in a U shape as shown in Fig. 6.5. This allows team members to work in close proximity and to pass material from one process to the next easily. When output requirements are low, one or two team members can operate the complete process with a minimum of movement.

The goal of team-based cells is to seek continuous improvement. Therefore, as production requirements change, it must be possible to move machines from one place to another, so it is better not to fix them permanently to the floor or otherwise make them immobile.

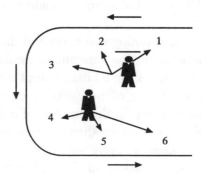

Figure 6.5   Typical cell layout

Workable level scheduling in the cells

Another key engineering task is calculating the capacity of each manufacturing cell. This can be done manually using one or two representative parts selected from a family of similar parts. The selected parts should have all of the processes in the cell and the operations and set-up times should be typical of, or the average of, the whole family. Broad brush capacity planning calculations may be carried out based on these parts as representative of the whole family. It is also possible to use one of the excellent capacity planning software packages available for PCs. Or you may prefer to create your own spreadsheet to set up a matrix of the products you want to make, the operation times, set-up times and expected volumes.

Once the capacity of each cell has been established, successful implementation will depend on 'levelled cell scheduling' to smooth the production process. One way to do this is to add up all the demand for products in the master production schedule, and then reconcile the total to the demand in the production plan. However, in the process of preparing the master production schedule, the product mix in the production plan has to be defined. Since product mix is often critical in varying the impact on key work centres, merely reconciling the master production schedule to the production plan may not guarantee that the schedule will be workable. The planners and schedulers need the capability to convert the quantities on the master schedule into a detailed load profile for each cell. The process of conversion is called 'rough-cut capacity planning'. Figure 6.6 shows the output of such a conversion, and indicates the profile of capacity required, which can then be compared to the capacity available.

Two steps are required to obtain a workable level schedule:

1. Determine the line speed or cycle time, using production schedule figures.
2. Balance the load in each cell.

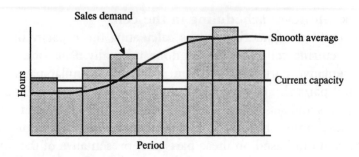

Figure 6.6   Load profile/bottleneck cell

To be successful, team-based manufacture requires a steady production rate during the master production period (typically one month), depending on the natural tempo of the business. The cycle time (a steady rate) is the time available to make a representative group of products, which has a mix corresponding to the total production period. The first task is to find the constituents of this group from the total product requirements over the master scheduling period. For example, let us assume that the demand for three products is as follows:

Product	Demand	Process time minutes/unit	Elapsed time minutes/unit
A	3	2.5	7.5
B	6	1.0	6.0
C	9	3.0	27.0
Total			40.5

A conventional batch production system would suggest producing the product in the following way.

Production with conventional system

Product A	AAA	Production sequence
Product B	BBBBBB	AAABBBBBBCCCCCCCCC
Product C	CCCCCCCCC	

There will be a standard elapsed time of 13.5 minutes before the shipping department receives the first of product C to make up an order. Since the total production is to be manufactured over 3 days, working 1 shift of 8 hours per day, the cycle time is the proportion of this time that it takes to make a six unit mix.

Cycle time = 6/40 × (3 × 8 × 60) minutes = 213.3 minutes

This reduces, on division, to a cycle group as follows:

Product A	1	2.5	2.5
Product B	2	1	2
Product C	3	3	9

The customer's orders are for every combination of product and type of product in a random manner. Therefore it is best to produce some of each type on each day, as shown below.

Production with levelled scheduling

Product A	AAA	Day 1	Day 2	Day 3
Product B	BBBBBB	ABBCCC/ABBCCC/ABBCCC		
Product C	CCCCCCCCC			

The purpose of load levelling is to plan production based as nearly as possible on the consecutive manufacture of cycle groups over the cycle time. For example, to make the pattern shown above, we need to repeat every cycle time. A production plan which follows the pattern shown above will create an even demand on components which are needed to make A, B and C. However, this is only practical and economic if set-up times have been reduced to a few seconds and materials flow like water.

Once level scheduling is in place, the sales department will be able to provide a whole range of products that customers want to buy, without holding large stocks, with consequent benefits to sales and profitability. The business can reduce the waste of resources and absorb the variation in cycle time between models, resulting in a better labour balance and reduced cycle time. Inventory and shortages both go down, while flexibility and productivity go up.

Ignoring the 'spare capacity' myth

People often say that a downside of team-based cells is the need for spare capacity in order to have the flexibility and adaptability to make lots of small batches. We need to qualify this statement and put it into context. Let's use a typical component cell as a model, but the logic applies equally to an assembly or process cell. In an assembly cell, capacity is usually dictated by human resource and assembly fixtures, but in a component cell it is dictated by machinery and equipment. Process cells tend not to be a problem, because the process tends to be generic: plating, painting, etc. There may be a few processes where special set up is necessary, but usually capacity is dictated by the size of the facility.

In a typical component cell, a defining process creates the main features of the family of products being manufactured. For a cell making a family of round components within a certain dimensional envelope, the cell would need all the elements to complete that family: turning, milling, drilling, keyway milling, grinding, etc. The defining process will generate most of the quality parameters, where there is metal and where there isn't metal, and will usually add more than half the value. Typically, in a round component cell, you will need a couple of NC lathes to complete this defining process. For a defining process, because quality is critical, it is usual practice to use state-of-the-art machine tools. State-of-the-art NC machine tools are not cheap. An NC lathe can cost anywhere between £100 000 and £1M. When you are setting up the cell and designing the processes, if your capacity plan shows that you need two and a quarter NC machines, you are going to have to make do with two. You are not going to have spare capacity, so it will be the team's task, with the team leader, to balance priorities according to the capacity requirements and the capabilities of these machines. Plan the cell around the defining process and the rest of the finishing processes fall in behind.

I often see quite elderly existing equipment being used for the secondary operations required to finish the product, i.e. drilling holes, milling flats, milling keyways, grinding. This equipment is perfectly satisfactory for the job, but long since written off the books, or with very low residual value. The team members use their ingenuity to set up these machines so that they can carry out all the operations required. For example, I have seen special machines created from standard machine tools, via ingenious tooling, enabling operators to complete all the family of parts with almost zero set up. For the finishing processes, using the older equipment, there probably will be some spare capacity, but this is not a significant issue. Some downstream machines may only have 15 per cent or 20 per cent utilization, but they are left set up to do a particular operation on a family of components and are always ready when needed. The team members generally have the flexibility to be able to work all the different machines in the downstream operations, as well as the defining operation. Managing the expensive defining processes enables industrial managers to save hundreds of thousands of pounds by not providing excess capacity.

Equipment layout and workflow

When the family of products for the cell has been defined, the capacity plan calculated, processes and equipment assigned, the issue of cell layout can become the responsibility of the team, with the help of a competent production engineer. When cell team members get involved in doing their own layout, they take responsibility for making it work. If there is one person in the business who knows more about the detail of doing the job than anyone else, it's the person who does it. So if you can mobilize these skills and knowledge and enable them to be expressed, an excellent job can be achieved. Cell layout is totally a matter of common sense. At BAe Hatfield, the pilot cell team produced several alternative layouts and the engineering support team helped them to choose the most effective. At Baker Perkins, the

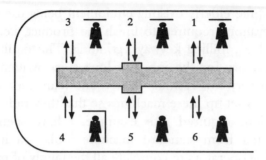

Figure 6.7   Baker Perkins shaft cell layout

shaft cell team arranged their machines in a simple horseshoe around a spine of material handling equipment, hand-operated carts that ran on tracks (Fig. 6.7). All the shafts could sit on these carts in Vs, and move up and down the cell. The parts could be side shifted to the workstation, then shifted back onto the cart when that workstation had completed its task. This was a case of visible management. I remember asking them, 'Is this all the work in progress there is?' and they answered, '*Yes*'. I said, 'But what about all the rest?', and they said, 'There is no "rest". This is it. All the work you can see is all that there is, and it's there down the central spine.'

Getting the team members involved in cell layout encourages them to think about materials handling and logistics issues, how they are going to control the amount of inventory and WIP in the cell. This leads to the issues of Just-in-Time (JIT) and compensators, which are covered in Chapter 7.

DESIGN, PRODUCTION AND QUALITY ENGINEERING OF THE CELLS' PRODUCTS

Design for manufacture
Cells allow manufacturing businesses to cope with variety. They also act as enablers for design for manufacture. If you are going to get your batch sizes right down, one thing that really helps is to

design the product so that it is simple to manufacture. This was brought home to me when I was invited to visit IBM's factories at Greenock, where they made PCs, and nearby Spango Valley, where they made a number of computer-related items such as monitors, keyboards, processors, etc. This was in 1984, the era of FMS (flexible manufacturing systems) and CIM (computer integrated manufacturing). I was very impressed with what I saw. At the Spango Valley factory, where an FMS system was operating, the bar-coded parts arrived, were placed on a conveyor and routed automatically to the manufacturing cell. They went right through the manufacturing process without being touched by human hand. (I don't know if it is still working today.) IBM had set this assembly line up as a shop window for their factory automation technology and were using IBM SCARA robots with swing joints and a vertical placing capability. What really interested me was the robot line for assembling a power supply: or was it a processor? All the materials came in by conveyor at high level, so they didn't interfere with people who were working, then came down in a lift to the line. The plastic moulded case of the product, in that anonymous beige colour of most computers, arrived in an oversize cardboard shoebox about 18 inches (45 cm) square and 8 inches (20 cm) deep, with the top half fitted over the bottom half. One of the robots removed the packaging and top half of the case. These were placed on a conveyor which ran below the assembly process and they moved along the line with the product. The bottom half of the case, still inside its cardboard packaging with polystyrene dunnage to keep it in place, moved along the line where robots sequentially inserted no more than half a dozen major modules. When it arrived at the end of the line, a robot picked up the top half of the case and refitted it with one screw as a fastener, and the completed product went for automatic testing. When it had completed the functional test, a final robot put the cardboard lid back onto the packaging.

This was impressive, but there was a niggling question in the back of my mind. I turned to the person from IBM who was showing me around and said, 'You've clearly redesigned the product to make it suitable for robot assembly.' 'That's right, we've done a lot of design to make sure it could all be assembled from one direction, and we could keep it in the packaging and keep the top half of the case and the packaging lid together.' 'Tell me,' I said, 'How much of the ultimate benefit was in the design for manufacture, and how much in the robots?' It seemed to me that when they had redesigned the product for the benefit of robots they had made it easy to assemble anyway, so that even a *person* could do it quickly. 'Funny you should ask that: I have to tell you the design for manufacture was so beneficial that it made the additional expenditure on robots much harder to justify.' I hope this illustrates what a powerful tool design for manufacture is; just how valuable it can be. Working in a team-based cell environment, where design, production and quality engineers are all involved, can help achieve these benefits.

Simultaneous engineering

Cells both place demands for minimum batch size, low set-up times and design for manufacture, and actually enable businesses to achieve these objectives. The demands of the market are driving the need for businesses to be more agile and responsive, and forcing us to move away from all those years when equipment was designed for lowest cycle time, with set-up time taking a much lower priority. I am reminded of a visit I made to Japan in 1982. This was an early lesson and moved me along the road towards understanding the need for team-based cells. Our visit to a car body press shop was extremely instructive. It is important to stress that Western automotive industry has moved a long way in this direction now, but in those days it took European car manufacturers up to 8 hours to change a press tool, so it was significant to see that the Japanese were doing it in a few minutes. When we looked closely at what they were doing, it was so simple you couldn't imagine ever wanting to do it any other way. When something is done right, it's hard to see what's special about it. All the press tools were predesigned to standard shut height. Most of the engineering that controlled the up and down movement of the top half was actually designed into the tool, rather than the press. The press tools were preproven away from the production process, and they sat on railway lines like wagons waiting for their turn to go into the press. The open-sided press allowed the current tool to be wheeled out easily and the new tool inserted with a minimum of effort.

In Western manufacturing, most of the set-up time was in adjusting the press, not in the tool. A fork truck had to be used to lever the tool into the space, then the two halves of the tool each had to be bolted onto the press, and the fit would never be quite right at the first attempt, so time-consuming adjustments were needed. Seeing this quick tool change was one of the things that started me thinking about how we could get the same flexibility into UK manufacturing. It has meant a big investment in press tools, but that was worth it, because it eliminated the need to have huge stores of pressed panels. Now we can make each one quickly, as it's needed.

At that period, we all thought that flexible manufacturing systems (FMS) were the route to flexibility: let the computer have all the agility and do all the thinking. Many FMS installations failed to deliver the benefits that had justified the investment and, as a result, FMS has been largely discredited. FMS tried to computerize all the complexity of the old way of manufacturing. It was only later that we realized the human brain was the best parallel processor available, and that we had to harness the power of the team, and use the computer as an enabler. Moving away from designing machine tools with more regard to unit cycle time than set-up time, and getting a more appropriate balance, has brought measurable benefits.

One of the pressures in the modern world where the old certainties have gone—commodity prices no longer increase, customers demand every colour, not only black—is that you can't plan on making a product for 5 years, let alone 35 years. Businesses only succeed when they are able to get new products to market faster than their competitors. The pressure to innovate is becoming more and more intense and the companies that are succeeding are the ones that are innovating and getting new products through the factory quickly.

Simultaneous engineering extends the principles of teaming beyond manufacturing operations and into the area of new product introduction. In the old world, the salesman sold the product and threw what he'd done over the brick wall to the design engineer. The designer did his bit without reference to anyone else, passed it to the production engineer, and said, 'Here you go, figure out how to make that!' At the same time, design created a bill of materials, rarely giving much thought to the cost or availability of the items specified. Then production engineering had to work out what to make and what to buy, and pass on bought-out requirements to purchasing. It was so bad that I've seen cases where all the design work done to support the salesperson, so that he could provide a tender, would be scrapped by the design engineers when the job was confirmed, and they would start all over again, right from scratch. Why? Because there had been one design department working for sales, and another one working for engineering! Inevitably, this whole process took a long time. By the time a new product reached manufacturing, especially if it was a one-off design, up to three-quarters of the allocated lead time had been used up. Getting the product to the customer has become more and more a critical success factor, both for companies that make one-off products where design is part of the lead time, and for companies that make high volume products where getting a new product with new design features into the hands of the customer more quickly than the competition is an order winning criterion.

Competition between Britain and France in the nineteenth century illustrates the benefits of getting new ideas into production quickly. The French were often very innovative in developing new military technology. The British did not generate as many new ideas themselves but were able to copy French innovation and get the finished product into service very quickly, sometimes more quickly than the French. For example, when France started to build the first ironclad battleship of the line, *La Gloire*, the British watched and then adopted the same strategy and were able to launch *Warrior*, their own ironclad, first. A short product development lead time actually allows companies to overtake their competitors and get their product to market first. This provides a definite strategic advantage. Examples of winning competitive advantage by getting the product to market quickly are legion. It's hard to buy a video recorder that isn't made in Japan. The key component of most video cassettes, no matter what label is on the outside, has been made by the Japanese company which first developed it. This is called hollowing out the competition, that is, making sure that the core of the competition's product is yours, so that you are in control.

There has been plenty of pressure on businesses to gain strategic advantage by getting products developed and into the market quickly. The motor industry provides a good example of shortening the product development cycle. It used to take 4 to 5 years to develop a new car. Now it has to be done in half that time if a company wants to stay competitive. The companies succeeding now in the motor industry are the ones that can develop new products quickly. Rover, for example, have had a metamorphosis. They have defined what their customer service chain is, organized their operations around it, and put all their efforts into developing new products that fulfil customer needs.

There is an issue here for high technology companies such as aerospace, which should take heed of events in the car industry. Car companies lead the way in being able to design and produce high variety, low volume vehicles and the Japanese are masters at this. A real problem in aerospace is new product development. It takes forever: and for a totally new aircraft it takes even longer than that. Look at EFA (European Fighter Aircraft now called Eurofighter 2000). How long has it been in development? The demonstrator flew in 1986/87, but the aircraft is still being designed and the first prototype which was scheduled to fly in late 1993, finally got off the ground in spring 1994. In-service entry won't be until the end of the millennium and by then it will already be obsolete. This is appallingly bad and commercial aircraft development cycles are not much better. Western aircraft industry has to take note, because they saw what the Japanese did with the car industry, and how this really shook up western car manufacturers; in fact it is only collaboration with the Japanese that kept some of them going.

On my visit to Japan in 1982, I toured a company that made fluid control valves. What they were actually making when I visited was a common or garden variety domestic stopcock. It did not look at all exciting, but when we started to talk to the designer we found out that they had all sorts of plans for 'whizzo' fluid control devices for hydraulics. In design, we saw all sorts of future projects for advanced hydraulic parts. We asked, 'Where are these things going to be used?' They looked at us oddly and replied, 'In aircraft, of course.' When we asked what cash flow their current products generated, they told us that was not so important as the design support they received. So we asked:

'Who supports the design?'
'Ministry of International Trade in Industry.'
'Why are they doing this?'
'Because Japan wants to get into aerospace.'

Way back in 1982, the Japanese were already planning how to create the infrastructure which would allow them to get into aerospace at some future time. On that trip we saw fluid control devices. What else might we have seen? Avionics? Microelectronics? Composite processing technology? We now know, years later, how successful their forward planning has been. They are emerging as big players in the aerospace industry. If they achieve in aerospace what they accomplished in the automotive industry, the West had better watch out. However, I think that Western aerospace industry is taking heed of this message, and working hard to shorten product development lead time, so the next generation of aircraft will be developed much more quickly, partly because of collaboration with the Japanese.

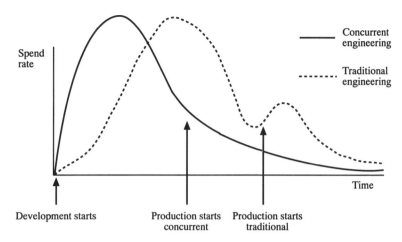

Figure 6.8 Spend curves for simultaneous and traditional engineering compared

This is where the issue of simultaneous engineering comes in. No longer can we afford to do sales, design, quality, production engineering and procurement sequentially. They must all be done with significant overlap. Simultaneous engineering means more activity and higher spend sooner, but reduces the amount spent later on design changes (Fig. 6.8).

Interface teaming is a fundamental issue in simultaneous engineering. The task is bringing multi-functional teams together to create an engineering product, and to get that product to market quickly. People regularly work like this in emergencies, or when they have a special project. You don't have to cast your mind back very far to the Falklands War. Britain urgently needed airborne early warning radar. A project team was assembled to kit out Sea King helicopters, and they completed the design and implementation so quickly that the helicopters were able to join the UK task force. During the Gulf War, the British Army urgently needed a scatterable mine system. Alvis designed and manufactured a batch of vehicles to carry the scatter mine launch system in 14 weeks, using teams working simultaneously. These are only two examples of how well industry can respond when the need is imperative.

The question is, how do you make this a permanent feature of your business?

The cultural issues associated with simultaneous engineering go very deep, because people believe that if they work this way all the time, it will be a threat to their main line job. Putting these effective project teams together also threatens the management which is not part of the special project team. That's why, as soon as the emergency is over, people rush right back to doing their perceived job in the old way, saying, 'Devolving control to teams is OK to get an urgent job out, but we could never run the business this way.' *Why not?* Of course you can, and the key is team-based cells.

LEAD TIME REDUCTION

What is the result of all the engineering changes we have discussed? We have physically co-located all the means of production for a family of parts. We've minimized the set-up times, and used design for manufacture to make the production process as simple as possible (Fig. 6.9). Remember the old world where we had to allow 1 week per operation, resulting in a 15-week lead time for a product that probably only took 5 hours to make. The main components of lead time are set-up time and queuing. By engineering the cells so that all the equipment needed is located in one place, and empowering the people to find ways of reducing set-up time, surely it is reasonable to propose that a job with 5 hours of work content can be completed in a week. This would allow plenty of time to balance conflicting priorities in a cell making a family of products. *This method has cut lead time down from weeks to days.* Once again we see how cells act as enablers to achieve dramatic production improvements. For cells to work, you need this dramatic collapse in lead time, and at the same time, cells enable you to achieve it.

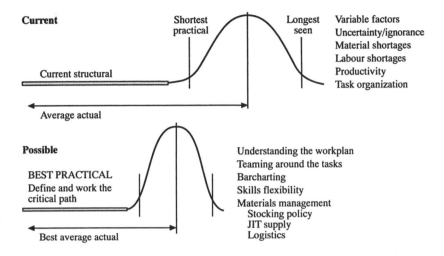

Figure 6.9   Factors influencing lead time reduction

The benefits of engineering: one cell equals one operation

Once you have set up team-based cells, or a pilot cell, and have demonstrated their benefits and potential, you are able to say to the teams:

> 'Right, here you are now, you are accountable for quality and output and we trust you to achieve it. We give you the authority, the accountability and responsibility to run your own cell and deliver the product required.'

Then you really don't need to be too concerned at the micro-management level about what is going on inside the cell on a day-to-day basis. This is significant because it means that you don't need to monitor output and progress process by process. You can monitor it cell by cell. This means that, for the purpose of managing the business, you can consider that *one cell equals one operation.* Go back to the old world where you have to manage all that material through all those operations across the shop. Remember that thick book of operation cards I had? That is all in the past. All you really need to monitor is *input to* and *output from* each cell. This simplifies the management of manufacturing and cuts out piles of paperwork. Cells both enable this and need it to operate successfully. To really fulfil the vision of collapsed lead time, vastly simplified management is essential. You still need technical information at an operation-by-operation level; you still need to know technically what you want on each process and how long it will take, but all this is planning information, to design and implement cell manufacture. It is *not* monitoring and management information. It can be dealt with inside the cell to allow the leader and team to manage their work effectively, or used at the highest level to set targets for improvement.

Once the engineering aspects of a team-based cell are in place, it is time for the cell team to take a serious look at material supply, logistics and work in progress.

7

Logistics and systems

Peter Gettings, a member of the BAe team who was involved in the team-based cells project at Hatfield, told me what happened once when he was showing visitors from a BAe military site what was going on in the implementation of cell manufacturing. After the extensive tour, one of the visitors stopped, thought deeply for a moment, and then said, 'I see what you've done. You've designed the manufacturing system to be so simple to run that you don't need computer systems, and then you've put them back in where they are clearly seen to add value.' This was such a simple and profound statement that I asked Peter to repeat it so that I could write it down. It defines exactly what we are trying to achieve with cell logistics and systems.

Team-based cells reduce production lead time by pulling material from one process to another so rhythmically that it 'flows like water'. Ideally the shipping rate, which is the rate at which the

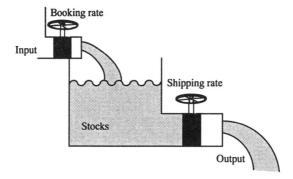

Figure 7.1   Let products flow like water

customer requires the product, and the booking rate, which is the rate at which suppliers should deliver bought-in materials, should be perfectly synchronized (Fig. 7.1).

JUST-IN-TIME MANUFACTURE

One of the objectives of team-based cells, as discussed in Chapter 6, is to create an environment where one cell is considered one operation. This radically simplifies manufacturing planning and control and takes layers and layers of complication out of the manufacturing system, so we really can start to think about planning a manufacturing system with few enough control points to allow a radical new approach to the supply and control of materials.

When we talked about serial accountabilities in Chapter 3, we said that a company really ought to be able to manage with about four, or at a maximum five, serial accountabilities. In that sort of environment we can start to think about running the business Just-in-Time (JIT), because nobody is more than three or four steps away from the customer. Volumes have been written on JIT, hundreds of seminars have been held on the subject, and games have been created to demonstrate the principles. If you've had your head in the sand over the past 10 years, and have missed playing a JIT game, get to a seminar now, because JIT is a key enabler of simplified logistics and systems. How would you react if, the next time you went to the pub and ordered a pint, the person behind the bar said, 'Sorry, you can't have a pint, we only sell beer in barrels.' 'Rubbish', you'd say, 'I only want a pint (or maybe two)'. 'Then you'll have to buy the whole barrel and use up the pints as you want them.' If we aren't prepared to order beer in bulk, why do we continue to allow suppliers to sell us parts like that? The same thing applies to milk. We don't accept delivery of a crate once a month, when all we need is two pints a day. Milk, at least in the UK, is still supplied Just-in-Time, and the trigger for delivery is the empty bottles on the doorstep.

In the world of team-based manufacture, where collapsed lead times have become a reality, we can run the factory much closer to real demand. This allows us to shift from making 80 per cent to forecast and 20 per cent to demand, to 80 per cent to demand and 20 per cent to forecast. Some companies might say that they can never get that close to a perfect world, but it's possible to get much closer than they do now. With reduced serial accountabilities we only have three or four sets of triggers, because we only need to monitor at three or four points. We still have a number of parallel cells to monitor, but serially, there are only three or four trigger points to get a component through to become the final product and into the hands of the customer.

SYNCHRONOUS MANUFACTURING

Most of our discussion on logistics planning and control systems is not concerned with what is going on *inside* the cell, but with what goes on *between* the cells, and between the cells and outside suppliers. Once the people and engineering elements of a cell are in place, we have to support the cell environment with logistics and systems. Think about what we are really trying to do when setting up this serial relationship between cells. Perfection would be to establish such a high degree of synchronicity and pacing between cells, according to the rhythm of the business, that as we complete a component in Cell 1, it goes straight to Cell 2 and is immediately used, and then to Cell 3 where it is immediately used: flowing like water.

Where might you see this balance and synchronicity? Look at a car assembly track. A lot of effort goes into line balancing in car assembly and in assembly processes for products such as washing machines, fridges and dishwashers. Line balancing is making sure that the time and work content on each stage is nearly identical, so that all the work can move down the line on a conveyor simultaneously. This is what I mean by creating 'synchronous' manufacture. With team-based cells, we are trying to get as close as we can to a balanced assembly line. Visible management is important here. If we were to take schoolchildren into a car factory and show them the assembly line, then ask them what was going on, they'd be able to give a fair description. 'The car body shell starts here, it moves down the line, bits are added, and finally a completed vehicle drives off the end.' Simple, yes? But after all the years of experience I've had in manufacturing—the good, the bad and the ugly—there are still many times when I tour a factory based on traditional manufacture, and I'm as puzzled at the end as I was at the beginning about exactly what is going on, after looking at all the convolutions and complications of seemingly unconnected activities everywhere.

Car assembly is very effective at synchronous manufacture, but of course the world it developed from was high volume, low variety ('any colour as long as it's black'), and high demand for the product. But even in the milieu of general manufacturing, and in car assembly plants, we are starting to see some convergence, because brown and white goods manufacturers are starting to have to make just a few of a number of different varieties. Assembly lines are having more of the kind of troubles we see in general manufacturing, and general manufacturing is trying to create more of the flow we get in an assembly line.

In an environment where we are trying to recreate synchronicity, we might have one supply cell, then six component manufacturing cells, a couple of process cells nearby, then five subassembly cells, and maybe six finished product assembly cells (Fig. 7.2). Then, components from any cell could go to any subassembly cell, and subassemblies could be supplied to any final assembly cell, so the logistics issues are many and varied. Nevertheless, we only have five serial accountabilities:

- Supply of materials to point of use
- Make a component
- Make a subassembly
- Make a completed product
- Supply to the customer

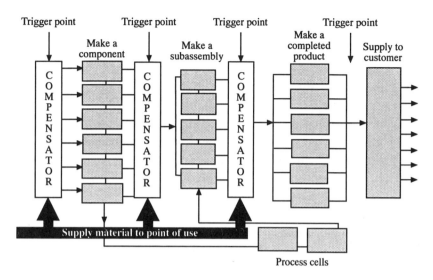

Figure 7.2   Parallel monitoring of serial accountabilities

SINGLE ACCOUNTABILITY TO POINT OF USE

Single accountability to point of use means that the supply team is accountable for delivering all bought-out materials to component, subassembly and final assembly cells as needed. The accountability rests with the supply team, not just for getting material in through the door, but from the supplier to the point of use. In the old days, once it was in stores, it became somebody else's (or nobody's) responsibility. The objective is to set up a JIT system, so that when the team member in the cell holds out his hand, the supply team puts the material into it. Then, if we must have a stores, it becomes the responsibility of the supply team, and this encourages supply to make the task as simple as possible, to avoid being accountable for the overhead costs relating to the stores.

If for some reason a supplier—external, or the previous cell—is unable to respond to requirements on demand, then the supply team has to set up a stores, but it's *their* stores. It does not belong to some other function, for example, production control, so it's an incentive not to have it because the cost is a burden on the company and this is a factor on which performance is measured. Because it's the supply team's burden, they'll be working hard to thin the stores out to the point where they can get rid of it altogether. One way of doing this is to get the suppliers to deliver to the point of use. There are plenty of examples of trackside delivery in white goods/brown goods industries but this same logic starts to become sensible in general manufacturing with single accountability to the point of use.

The team members in the supply team will be responsible for supplier negotiations. They decide what is appropriate, work out supply partnerships, then negotiate JIT supply and delivery to the point of use. Encouraging suppliers to co-operate involves sharing the schedule, sharing information on schedule and costs, and sharing experiences in developing new manufacturing approaches. This means being open with suppliers, and saying to them: 'Come and see what we are doing to improve our manufacturing performance. Visit our factory, talk to our people. To realize the full benefits, we want you to play a part.' This does not mean just giving everything away to the supplier, but actually using information as a lever to get better commitment, to make things sharper and more competitive for both the supplier and the customer. It is a much better approach than staying exactly as you are, but demanding much better cost and delivery performance from them. So just shifting the stores back to the supplier doesn't do any good. It still costs just as much, even though some of the cost may be hidden. Rather, the supply team members should work with suppliers, helping them to get rid of their stores as well, so that they too can be lean and effective.

COMPENSATORS

When you go into McDonald's and look behind the counter, you'll see that there is a little wire rack for each type of burger on the menu. This is a compensator. Each of these racks has a finite capacity. To maintain quality, McDonald's doesn't like to sell a Big Mac more than 10 minutes old, but at the same time they don't want to make burgers that they have to throw away because they are too old. They don't actually make more than a few burgers at a time, triggered by the actual number of customers walking through the door. When the cooks in McDonald's have filled up the little wire rack, they slow down production, and some of them go off to do other tasks which are not on the critical path. When some of the Big Macs are bought and more space created, then they speed up production, always keeping a specific number ready, and throwing away burgers more than 10 minutes old. It always takes the same amount of time to prepare a Big Mac, so at busy times, burgers are produced on a production line, with each person doing one task, cooking the burgers, preparing the buns, putting on the cheese, putting on the relish, etc. At quiet times, one person is responsible for carrying out all the processes, and this slows down the rate of production.

McDonald's has a good idea what the average demand will be, but they don't know what the instantaneous demand is, so they use a compensator (the wire rack) as a trigger to respond to the customers' requirements JIT. The compensator is sized to accommodate the difference between the size of the average demand and size of the instantaneous demand. They do this by working out a forecast for each branch which tells them what the average demand for Big Macs is likely to be on a wet Thursday in April, or a hot Saturday evening in July. They order enough buns, meat patties and other ingredients to allow them to supply to this forecast.

This is also the difference between forecasting push and demand pull. The customers exert a JIT pull on the Big Macs, but the careful forecasting has helped the restaurant to decide how many meat patties to have in the fridge. To take this analogy a bit further, let's suppose that McDonald's has specified preferred varieties of wheat and potatoes for their buns and fries. Clearly, they can't plant potatoes in response to actual customer demand. The farmer plants so many acres of the desired variety of potato long before the customer walks through the door so McDonald's must order their materials to a master planning schedule based on aggregate demand. We've already seen that in each branch, they have a good idea of how many Big Macs will be sold between 11am and 4pm on a wet Thursday, but they don't know exactly at what time each one will be ordered. The aggregate of the demand forecast enables them to place orders for meat, rolls, potatoes, onions, pickle, etc. They will call in quantities from suppliers to meet real demand, but they will have given their suppliers their schedule, explaining that this represents their likely overall requirements, but there will need to be some degree of flexibility. They are saying to the supplier, 'Think about providing 500 pounds of potatoes over a month, but we might need less, or maybe a little more'. They negotiate similar arrangements with the suppliers of meat and buns, pickles, tomato sauce, onions, fruit pies, drinks, arranging each differently, according to need. Each of the many branches of McDonald's will be regularly supplied, perhaps daily. The van from central supplies will have a forecast of daily requirements, plus a little bit to reflect the variability of supply and demand windows. The van driver will top up supplies and remove any time-expired stock.

The McDonald's analogy illustrates two useful techniques we need to apply if we are to get our manufacturing teams to come as close as possible to recreating the synchronicity of an assembly line: using a compensator as the trigger mechanism for demand pull, and at the same time planning material requirements based on forecasts. The compensator's function is to allow for adjustment between the variability in time-scale of supply and demand between two serial cells. A compensator works as a trigger to manufacture more. When it's full, you don't need any more. When it's got space in it, you need some more. Compensators are carefully sized, visible storage areas located right next to the work area. To size a compensator, we first need to identify the variability of the supply window and the variability of the demand window, then allow a slight overlap between the supply window and the demand window, and calculate how big the compensator needs to be to accommodate just enough material to satisfy the identified extremes of supply and demand, recognizing that there is going to be an element of risk (Fig. 7.3). This is not a function of volume but a function of time. So the volume required in the compensator will always remain the same and the size of the compensator, once established, does not need to change.

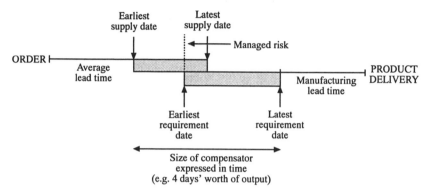

Figure 7.3   Size of the compensator: supply and demand window

Compensators come in all sizes, depending on the type of cell and its requirements. For major subassemblies and assemblies, the compensator will probably contain just one item, for example, one engine. The team is allowed to put one finished product in the output compensator, and to start making another one, using the supplies from the input compensator. But when that is complete, they can't start to make a third product until the space in the output compensator is empty so that they can place the product they have just completed in it. This is the day-to-day manufacturing pull that triggers the physical act of manufacturing.

Using actual demand as the trigger, we create a short chain of serial accountabilities with dramatically reduced lead times, where people are working to actual requirements according to the tempo of the business (Fig. 7.4). This is usually the period of time it takes to get through all the accountabilities once. The tempo of the business could vary from hundreds of products completed in a day (nuts, screws, washers and bolts), to one product per day, to

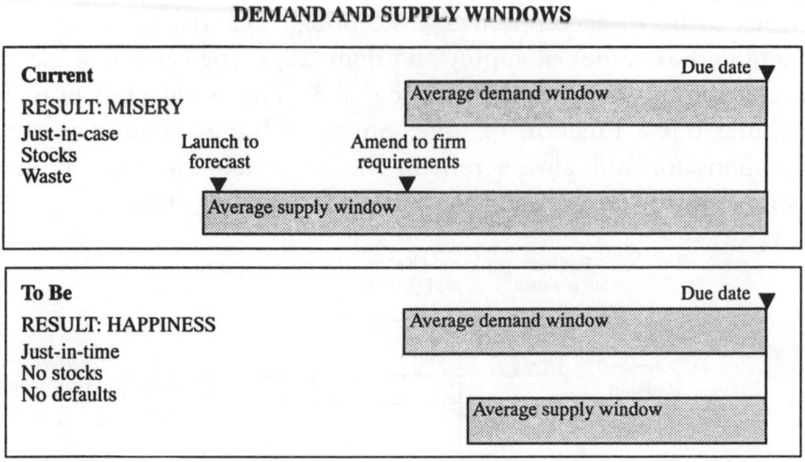

DEMAND AND SUPPLY WINDOWS

Figure 7.4 The key to materials management: making supply lead time shorter than customer's delivery notice

one major product per month or longer (aeroplanes, turbine engines, etc.). Typically, in a business which makes one item per day, the work-to list would represent requirements which are fixed and frozen for a known horizon approximately equal to the period of time it takes to get through the series of accountabilities once. This tells the cells what is actually needed, so they can plan their work, but they are only allowed to ship their work to the next cell according to the availability of space in the compensators.

As with the McDonald's analogy, this allows businesses to manufacture to demand, but plan to forecast. Because we know what demands are being placed, we are able to manufacture to actual JIT demand, based on the space available in the compensator (Fig. 7.5). In an engineering environment, the actual take up of material is generally a little less than forecast. Then we report back actual achievement based on the status in the compensators, because the record of changes in the compensator is a record of what actually happened.

Supermarket shelves are an excellent example of an input compensator. They are loaded with stock, and when gaps appear,

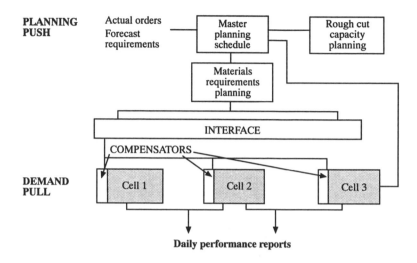

Figure 7.5   Reconciling planning push and demand pull

the staff fill them up from the stock room. Then they use point-of-sale information and bar code scanning at the checkout counter to do their ordering. Until a few years ago there was a continuing argument about whether MRP and JIT were contradictory philosophies. The argument has died down now that they have been shown to be complementary, and that both have their place in manufacturing. Cells and team-based manufacturing make demand pull possible, and allow requirements planning tools to be used for what they are good at, i.e. getting in materials. The cell manufacturing environment makes material supply as simple as possible.

JUST-IN-TIME LOGISTICS: MAKING IT HAPPEN

Gather relevant information

It takes a lot of effort to make supply of materials to the point of use, and the logistics between cells work in the real world, between supplier and customer cells inside the business, and between the business and external suppliers. To size a compensator for each cell and design the way the materials will flow, there is no substitute for going right through each manufacturing component and finding the answers to a whole list of questions:

- What is the preferred manufacturing quantity for the supply cell?
- What is the preferred usage quantity for the customer cell?
- What is the preferred way to deliver the material and in what container?
- What are the required delivery frequencies?
- What are the lead times?
- What are the preferred points of supply?
- What are the preferred points of use?
- What are the forward commitments?
- What is the historic usage?

The answers to the above questions will enable us to design the sort of compensator or logistics support that is most suitable for each individual part. There is no escape. We have to work through all these questions for every component because this is the way we will get as close as possible to the dream of synchronicity.

Make vs buy

The answers to these questions will cause us to start thinking about what we should make in-house, and what we should buy from external suppliers. A company generally has to make the elements relevant to its core business, but it should never let itself become distracted by making things that another specialist company could do better and cheaper. What are we making fasteners for, when there are plenty of companies whose reason for existence is to be competitive at making fasteners? Make vs buy decisions allow a business to focus manufacturing effort on the really significant, core, value adding activities. This makes a major contribution to the overall simplicity we are seeking. Try a simple test: go into the

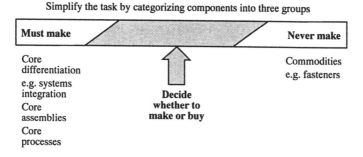

Figure 7.6   Make vs buy decisions

manufacturing stores and pick up any component. If it is not immediately obvious that it is unique to your product, ask yourself why you are making it.

The trick is deciding where to put the arrow between make and buy (Fig. 7.6). First we need to agree what things we *must* make, things which define our core business. If we give these away we'll be giving away competitive advantage. The next task is to decide what items we should never make. Try running through a typical manufacturing report, bearing in mind that the computerized planning system gives exactly the same amount of attention to an engine as it gives to washers and rivets. Highlight the important, core business items; then highlight all the things that should obviously be bought out. (Don't forget that the absence of small bought-out items can hold up the manufacturing process just as much as the big expensive items, and also that *you* are probably your worst supplier for non-core items.) That leaves decisions to be made about the items that don't fall readily into either category. Should we make or buy them? This is where ABC parts classification plays its part.

ABC parts classification
It is possible to assign all parts to one of three categories, as defined below:

A Class   Core to the product, expensive, key to perfor-
          mance and quality. Make in. Buy only if special
          external expertise is required: e.g. aero engines
          bought by the aircraft manufacturer. Unit of
          delivery is one at a time, or a small number,
          definitely not in large batches.

B Class   Medium value, medium volume, machined com-
          ponents, ranging from items which are unique to
          the product to generic items such as large bearings,
          which nevertheless are of fairly high value, so that
          we don't want the stores swilling with them. This is
          the area where designing and sizing compensators,
          and getting parts supplied as needed, will provide
          tremendous benefits.

C Class   Generic, non-specific, high volume supply to
          manufacturing, e.g. nuts, screws, washers, bolts,
          rivets. Control supply of these using a two-bin
          system actually at the point of use. Invite a single
          supplier to take responsibility for all your C Class
          items. The supplier will come round and top up
          the bins as required and send you an invoice. This
          involves building trust, because if they start to give
          you short supply, eventually you'll spot it and they
          will lose their preferred supplier status. (Remem-
          ber that what is a C Class part to you, is the
          supplier's livelihood.)

Supply of parts in kits

Get the supplier to provide parts in kits. In the doors pilot cell at
BAe Hatfield, team members and the supply team worked
together and arranged for parts to be delivered in kit form, with all
the sheet metal work done, so they could concentrate on what they
were good at, actually putting the doors together and making them
work properly, instead of trying to chase parts. If things get really
complicated, start thinking about giving the team a computer to

help manage work planning and supply, but *only* if it really helps.

Make vs buy is all about simplifying manufacturing by concentrating effort on making the parts that really define the company's business. When making fundamental decisions on make vs buy, think back to setting up as a new business. What would have happened then? Incrementally applying capital to the business was very expensive, so no one was going to take the decision to add buildings and machines lightly. In those early days, make vs buy decisions had to be very practical and sensible. Try to get back to that sort of thinking, based on the entrepreneurial flair of the small business. Stick to your knitting. Don't be surprised to find, when talking with suppliers about preferred supplier status and working on a partnership basis, that they will give far better value than if the parts were made in-house. Even if the bought-out and made-in prices are very similar, it is probably better to put non-core parts out with suppliers. Very often I hear the argument, 'We need to make some things in house to use up the capacity and/or to recover overheads', but the question is whether you should really have that capacity in the first place; what is the competitive edge solution? When designing a manufacturing business, we have to draw a line somewhere around a rough percentage of the requirement and say, 'This is the capacity we should have', and for anything beyond that, we'll make sure we have a good network of outside suppliers whose reason for existence is to be good at supplying their specific product.' Much of this is common sense; the question is how far are we willing to take it? The real benefit it brings is simplicity, so that the business can concentrate on what it does best. Well-thought out logistics strategies really do improve manufacturing in terms of cost, responsiveness and competitive advantage.

8

Performance measures and accountability

Implementing major changes in the way we deal with people, engineering and logistics, in team-based cells creates a radically different working environment. The legacy of the design of the manufacturing environment during the early twentieth century had led us to an environment where the emphasis was on labour and machines and their effect on cost. This meant that performance measures placed heavy emphasis on man hours and machine hours, direct to indirect ratios, standard cost variance, etc., which only measure cost after it has been incurred, when it is too late to do anything about it. The trouble with these traditional performance measures is that they concentrate on utilization of manpower and machine tools, which account for only a fraction of total cost, rather than the major contributors to cost: procurement, inventory, quality and overheads. They make little contribution to reducing cost or improving performance, nor do they place accountability for performance with the people who can actually influence results. Nevertheless, production in most industries has been driven by these measures.

In the fragmented world of functional accountability it was not easy to measure real responsiveness to customer needs, and in any case, businesses could generally rely on customers to buy everything they manufactured. Times have changed, and customer satisfaction—the right product, at the right time, at the right quality and for the right price—now has to be the goal of every business. This has meant developing new strategies based on organizing around the customer service chain using teams and cells. Team-based cells require relevant performance measures which foster enthusiasm and empower people to achieve continuous improvement, not just record results. We've discovered that in order to make cells really work we've got to think again about two aspects of measuring performance:

- Creating performance measures that are relevant to the business needs.
- Measuring team performance and rewarding people for their efforts.

We've talked about aligning small team squad solidarity and larger team regimental pride. What we want to do when setting up new performance measures is to get the goals and objectives that we set for the team into alignment with the goals and objectives of the business. Getting this right is one of the four major elements that make team-based manufacturing a success.

TRADITIONAL PERFORMANCE MEASURES

Many people who have worked in manufacturing industry have discovered how the traditional performance measures in business actually encouraged waste and cut across the real goals of the business. Table 8.1 shows how traditional measures prompt actions that lead to results which are contrary to business needs, in much the same way that I described when two colleagues of mine asked me to make the correction of the supplier's fault into a standard operation.

Let's look in more detail at the adverse effects some of the performance measures have on productivity in the business.

Measuring labour utilization and performance related pay

Much time and energy has been expended in measuring what

Table 8.1 Traditional performance measures encourage waste

Measurement	Action	Result
Labour utilization	Supervisor keeps workers busy	Excess inventory, low schedule attainment, piecework anomalies.
Machine utilization	Supervisor maximizes utilization	Excess inventory, raw materials, shortages, reduced responsiveness
Labour reporting	Management focuses on fixed relatively small direct labour cost	Major overhead activities not exposed
Cost centre reporting	Management focuses on cost centre instead of activities	Overlook chance to reduce cost by combining common activities
Purchase price	Purchasing goes for lowest price	Excess inventory, supplier with best overall offering (including quality and delivery) often overlooked
Standard cost overhead absorption WIP	Supervisor over-produces so that overhead absorption exceeds expenses	Excess inventory

percentage of their time the work force spent doing direct labour. This spawned the whole world of work study to establish standard times for jobs. Time cards are used to book on and off jobs and to record actual time compared with credit hours, or standard hours. The odd tenth of a percentage point is pored over and worried about as though it had a great deal of significance. It doesn't matter how much managers encourage supervisors to think about the overall objectives of the business, when their backsides get kicked for three-tenths of a percentage point on machine utilization, they will very quickly realize where they should focus their attention. What's more, no matter how hard we try to measure labour utilization, built in allowances, inaccuracies of estimated times, time wasted waiting for work or shortages, results are rarely accurate and the fog of manufacturing soon descends.

Ordinarily, the standard to which performance was measured would be a 100 per cent ratio of measured standard job time to actual time taken. The time for the job would be measured and people would be expected to be able to turn in performances of 100 per cent consistently. Work study breaks the job down into very small parts and repeatedly observes each part to see how long it takes. Then a rating factor is applied: is the person working fast, at average speed or slowly? A measure of effectiveness of the work is also included. Then allowances for rest periods and personal needs are added on. All this produces a standard time for the job, plus standard allowances. Imagine the bureaucracy of doing all this, collecting the hours available, collecting the hours actually worked, with all the margins for error, and all the mathematics of figuring out the labour performance percentage. It gives you this magical number, labour utilization, which is not really a lot of use to you anyway. That number could vary wildly from less than 100 per cent to well over 100 per cent and the accuracy of the standard times is usually extremely questionable. What an effort. In the event, we have found that the total hours worked can be as little as 40 per cent of time available for work. Nevertheless, production managers pore over these numbers and hand out 'lollipops' or 'whacks across the head' for the movement of a few tenths of a percentage point.

Very often standard hours are also the basis for paying people a piecework rate. Piecework is a powerful motivator, there is no doubt about it, but it is also very crude. There is the issue of inaccurate times, and then basing people's rewards on how well they perform against those times. This creates a situation where you have to put ceilings on people's earnings, otherwise the labour bill goes through the roof, because if people are on piecework, they will maximize production whether the parts are wanted or not. The unions are often the ones to insist on a cap to avoid too much variation in individual's earnings, with consequent jealousy, and the tendency for people to 'cherry pick' jobs, getting the ones that lead to a high income through bonuses. They look for the jobs which they know are good payers because they have nice slack times. They put the jobs in a sequence which will suit their earnings, rather than what the business needs. Standard times are open to all sorts of manipulation and abuse.

Recently I worked with a company which had a cap on earnings because of the inaccuracies in the timing of jobs, and the cap was set at 130 per cent. The workforce consistently achieved better than standard hours without much difficulty. This could have been for one of two reasons. Either the company employed superhuman men and women, or else the standard times were inaccurate. They often stopped working on Thursday afternoon, or Friday morning. When supervisors tried to exert pressure, they replied that they'd achieved their full week's earning already, and there was no point in doing any more for no reward. Then when urgent orders needed completing, the workforce would not co-operate unless they were given overtime, because they'd earned all their money for the week on standard time. Only a dramatic change in culture was going to resolve this company's problems.

So what is the result of focus on labour utilization? It keeps people busy working whether the product is needed or not. Customer service takes lower priority, and the business has plenty of excess raw materials, so you know you've always got something to make. You also end up with shortages, excess inventory and reduced customer service, because the parts that are really needed never get made when everybody is busy making the parts that make the production targets look right and the piecework targets look right.

Machine utilization

This is the brother of labour utilization. Management always seemed to believe that if they kept the machines working all the time everything would be all right and this was OK in the old days when demand exceeded supply. It resulted in measuring machine throughput whether what was produced was needed or not, with high inventory as the consequence. The argument for high machine utilization was put forward with some justification on the basis that machines were expensive to buy and the higher the utilization, the fewer machines would be needed. What actually tended to happen was that average machine utilizations ended up being fairly modest, even though managers treated this as a key factor. In spite of everyone's best efforts, the knock-on effect of large numbers of old machines, organizing manufacturing based on grouping like processes, and the resulting high number of serial accountabilities, shortages, confusion, tool changes, and long set-up times all conspired to drag machine tool utilization down.

Purchasing

Crazy situations developed in purchasing where the focus was always on lowest price only, never on quality or delivery times. Get three quotes: take the lowest, even going to the extreme of getting three quotes to mend the puncture on the factory bike. Buy in bulk because it's cheap. Buying materials in bulk rather than in product sets often meant that we paid for and then stored large quantities of materials that were never *really* needed in the first place. These often considerable 'leftovers' of bar and plate would never be used up. This negated the savings of bulk buying. The best overall supplier, with the best combination of quality, responsiveness and price, would often be overlooked. This true story of purchasing industrial gloves shows what I mean. A heavy job in the factory—moving around manufactured auto body components with sharp edges—required heavy duty gloves for protection. One type of glove cost £2 per pair and lasted 8 weeks. Another glove cost £1 per pair and lasted 2 weeks. Remember the rule: get three quotes and take the lowest. Which glove did the purchasing department buy? You guessed it: the ones costing £1 per pair; and they ended up spending far more than they needed.

IS THE PRODUCT GOOD ENOUGH? THE CUSTOMER WILL DECIDE!

Where were the needs and wishes of the customer in all this? In the old world, the customer was some guy who walked past the end of the gangway once in a blue moon, who had little or nothing to do with day-to-day events in the factory. What we want to do by introducing new performance measures is bring the customer right to the forefront. Is the product good enough? The customer will decide! One hundred per cent customer service means quality assured products delivered when required. We need to gear all our performance measures around this. That brings us to the point of deciding what the objectives of performance measures in team-based cells actually ought to be.

The prime objective of a team-based cell is 100 per cent customer service. Performance measures have to be designed to indicate whether the cell team is achieving this objective (Fig. 8.1).

Figure 8.1   Objectives of cell performance measures

Measures of customer satisfaction are:

- *Achievement of plan* Did the cell complete what the plan indicated it should?
- *Service levels* Was the output delivered to the customer inside the agreed delivery window?
- *Product quality* Is it good enough? The customer will decide (and remember, customers are internal as well as external). If it is not, it does not count as achieving the plan or service levels.
- *Value for money* Does the combination of cost, quality and delivery represent the best overall package that the customer can find?

Another objective of performance measures in a cell environment is reporting to the 'owners' of the business on how well the team is achieving customer satisfaction. Measures that ensure the well-being of the business are:

- Lowest unit cost
- Resources consumed
- Inventory levels

To be effective, the cell team has to have responsibility and accountability for all the costs associated with achieving the targeted performance in these areas.

When we talk about measuring the resources used, why is that not the same as labour utilization? There is a very important difference. With the new performance measures, we are talking about value adding resources, not merely measuring whether people and machines have been kept busy, after the event. The cell team members take responsibility for establishing the resources they need—people, equipment, inventory, etc.—to meet customer service levels. This gives them ownership of the result. In a typical scenario, the team leader has a debate with his 'owner' about what resources he will need to achieve customer service and value for money in the next month's plan. When there is a gap between the two, they work together to decide how to bridge it. To

provide excellent value for money to the customer, the business
can afford to have a given level of resource in the cell. When the
team leader and manager debate how to plan ahead to achieve
production, they are not talking about 2 per cent here or 3 per
cent there, but deciding whether they need nine people or eight,
or perhaps nine people at the start and eight later on. They are
talking about real people and real resources in the cell, rather than
ethereal, inaccurate percentage points aimed at trying to define
whether people have been busy.

Small improvements make a big difference in business profitability

The baseline measure for productivity improvement is *not* the
total number of hours available for work, but the actual number of
productive hours worked, i.e. the hours actually spent making
what is wanted. An improvement in output per person of 30 to 40
per cent can be measured but labour utilization (actual hours
booked divided by standard hours) goes up much less. Why? This
is because the baseline for measuring labour utilization is all the
people available for work. Figure 8.2 shows that very often the
actual time spent in value adding activities is as low as 40 per cent
of the available time. Effective team-based working makes
significant inroads in the gap between 40 per cent and 100 per
cent—wasted time, waiting, shortages, rework, etc.—to the point
where a 10 per cent improvement in labour utilization means that
the team is producing 30 per cent more of wanted output. It is
easy to get 30 per cent improvement on such a small number of
productive hours, and it also makes a substantial difference to the
profitability of the business.

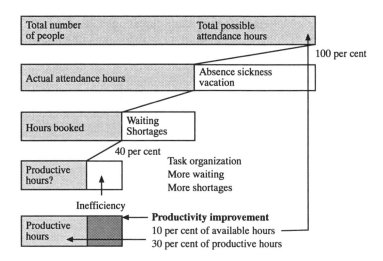

Figure 8.2   The baseline measure for productivity improvement

People might actually clock on for only about 60 to 65 per cent of the total number of hours available for work. They don't book all the hours they are in attendance to actual value adding work, and of the time they do book to productive work, some of it is inefficient. This means that what might be a 10 per cent improvement in efficiency based on total hours available for work is actually closer to a 30 per cent improvement when based on value adding work.

Ask yourself how much it is costing you to keep your current measurement system running. A new process for measuring performance reduces the overheads attributable to this activity by up to half. At BAe Hatfield, the performance measurement team conducted a survey of traditional performance reporting which revealed that they had created a separate organization to measure the organization. Gathering, collating and circulating information on performance was time-consuming and expensive. Ninety-five people were involved in collecting the data required to produce reports and performance charts totalling 100 000 pages a year.

Most of these reports concentrated on schedule and costs and were aimed at keeping senior managers informed. People directly involved in manufacturing rarely prepared or received relevant performance reports so they had no real idea of how they were doing or what they needed to improve. Every time a person punched a clock, it cost £1 in support from the finance department to collect, record and circulate this information. The minimum cost of producing all these reports was calculated at around £2 million a year. All this effort and resource was being consumed without reference to the relevance of the information provided to the people doing the job. Once this was realized, improvements were implemented methodically.

MAKING IT HAPPEN

When team-based manufacturing is up and running, with the new people culture in place, the physical moves complete, and the logistics and systems elements starting to function, it will become obvious that the old performance measures are no longer satisfactory. This is the time to review the business and suggest performance measures which will foster enthusiasm and empower people to achieve continuous improvement. There are five key tasks which must be undertaken in order to create performance measures that are relevant to the business needs:

1. Confirm the key customer needs and business drivers.
2. Agree which performance measures most contribute to meeting these needs and drivers.
3. Involve the teams in developing simple systems for measuring and reporting results.
4. Start to gain acceptance of the new measures from managers and the accounts department.
5. Make links between individual and team performance, motivation, and rewards.

Confirm the key customer needs and business drivers

Most businesses will have a fair idea of the most important customer needs and drivers of their particular business; whether this is cost, quality, speed of delivery, ability to customize or provide variety, etc. The performance measures project team will need to define a methodology for deciding which of these measures are most appropriate to the business, because to make the performance measures process manageable, and to keep costs down, it is vital to limit the number of measures. University research papers, data compiled by engineering research organizations and reviews of companies producing similar products will all help to identify customer needs and business drivers. Having decided on three or four key elements, such as quality, delivery to schedule, and cost, the next step is to design and implement performance measures which help to identify and solve problems in these key areas (Fig. 8.3).

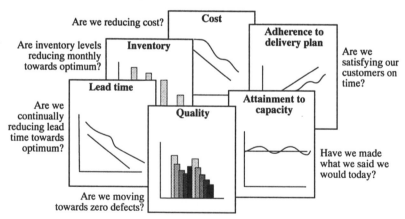

Figure 8.3   Six performance measures which encourage continuous improvement

Agree which performance measures most contribute to meeting the key business drivers

Most businesses will need to have specific accounting measures in place, for example:

Return on capital employed Stock turnover ratio
Sales per employee Debt: equity ratio
Liquidity ratio Earnings per share
Return on sales

Within each team-based cell, measures generally relate to:

- Specific activities
  - Percentage achievement of plan
  - Percentage service levels
  - Percentage quality performance
  - Inventory
- Effective use of resources
  - Materials (waste, WIP), people, costs

Plenty of detailed information which is needed to execute the business can be captured in the cell, but it does not all need to be monitored or controlled at a higher level.

Develop simple systems for measuring and reporting results

The team leader and team members in the cells are the right people to develop systems for measuring performance as they are the ones who will be responsible for keeping the records and achieving the required performance. The performance measures team should work closely with them:

- To make sure their measures accurately record lead time, delivery to schedule, defects, inventory, and costs.
- To develop a system for collating data from all the cell teams to cascade upwards through the business.
- To make sure the teams receive all the business data they need to perform their tasks adequately.

Even if the teams have one or two false starts with measuring performance, and have to revise their systems, it is better to let them own and work the system than to impose one from the outside. The task of creating performance measures shows the team members the true cost of inventory, set-up time, quality problems, etc., and how this affects the business. It is better to start off with simple manual systems at first, to prove that they work, and then to use computers only where they truly make things easier and are clearly seen to add value to the process.

Start to gain acceptance of these new measures from management and accounts

By the time you have come far enough down the road of implementing team-based cell working to be developing new performance measures, everyone immediately involved in the project should understand what is happening, and be enthusiastic and involved. One grey area may be the relationship between performance measures and company accounting. New performance measures can dramatically alter the way the cost base is built up and the way overheads are apportioned. It helps to analyse particular areas of manufacture or support in order to understand the costs incurred and identify opportunities for reducing them, and reducing the need for an area to bear responsibility for costs which are outside the immediate control of its people. However, because it means dispensing with old performance measures such as detailed monitoring of man hours, it represents a major challenge to the whole accounting convention. Senior managers responsible for finance, and all the people in accounts, often accept the principles behind the change, but continue to use the old measurements alongside the new: 'just in case'. This may have to continue until it becomes apparent that everyone's essential information requirements are being satisfied using the new measures. In this way, acceptance of the new measures gradually permeates through the entire business.

Make links between individual and team performance, motivation and rewards

Piecework is a powerful motivator but, as we have seen, it can backfire. Cells, teams and piecework really don't go together. People can't work as a team when one individual gets paid for producing things the other team members don't need. But how can we reward people if we've taken away the motivation of piecework? There are two ways of rewarding people in team-based manufacturing:

1. *Reward the team for meeting targets, achieving plan.* It is possible to work out a bonus scheme which applies equally to all team members of every team, based on achieving customer service, delivery to schedule, continuous reduction in inventory and defect levels, etc., and the information required is already being collected by the team as they monitor business performance.

2. *Reward the individual for depth and breadth of skills.* Flexibility is a key objective in team-based working. A reasonable goal is for 70 per cent of the people to have 70 per cent of the skills required to do the team tasks. In a manufacturing environment this will mean technological skills such as machining, turning, grinding, milling, drilling and basic NC competence. In a support or service environment, each team will identify and define the basic skills requirements. It is the responsibility of the team leader to develop the skills of team members. An effective system is to monitor the breadth and depth of team members' skills using a matrix which is very prominently displayed in the cell area. Figure 8.4 is an example.

The teams set high standards of skill quality and team members have to demonstrate repeatedly their ability to work at the next level, and this has to be documented. Then the team leader will go to the group's manager and say, 'Look, over the last 6 months Bert has consistently demonstrated his ability at the next level of this skill. The evidence is all here in these charts showing productivity,

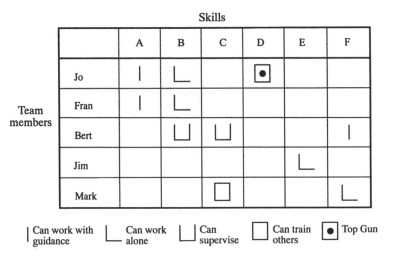

Figure 8.4   Sample skills matrix

quality and customer service. I believe he should be recognized as competent at this level.' Skill broadening and deepening is rewarded by a modest incremental pay increase. Group managers decide the appropriate gap in basic pay, usually the same as exists between the present unskilled and highest skill groups. Then they decide how long it should take individuals to work their way up and this helps determine the incremental pay increase for each step. The most skilled and flexible person in each cell—the top gun—should be clearly rewarded. The skills matrix should be reviewed and perhaps revised once every 2 years, to make sure that people always have new goals to strive for.

A note on performance measures and repetitive strain injury

In context of cells in a high volume manufacturing environment I sometimes hear that team members sustain repetitive strain injury (RSI). People who are doing repetitive tasks under time pressure to perform and achieve team targets, for example, keyboard operators in banks, get repetitive strain injury because the body can't recover and rebuild the injured tissues quickly enough overnight before the same damage is inflicted again the following day. I have a problem with this. I don't believe we can label an activity 'team working' when so much pressure to produce is applied to an individual that they injure themselves. This is not the kind of teaming I have in mind when talking about cells. Cell teams will design the work so that repetitive strain injury is not necessary. Team working is supportive; team members share tasks to ease the burden, or the team redesigns the task to take away the conditions of repetitive strain. I worry when I hear about RSI in banking, where bank clerks are ruled by their computers, which require them to make 13 000 key strokes an hour, or the screen flashes. A good dose of cell teaming in the banking industry is needed so that teams of people can work to achieve a goal and create an appropriate environment. This would alleviate the conditions that cause RSI by a combination of redesigning the task and sharing the burden.

9

Getting started

THEY DIDN'T SAY 'YES' BUT THEY DIDN'T SAY 'NO'

Fidgeting nervously half a dozen managers waited for their colleagues to return from the boardroom. At last they appeared.

'Well, what happened?' was the urgent question.
'It was a bid odd, really. They didn't say "yes", but they didn't say "no"! They just looked at each other, shrugged their shoulders and sort of said they couldn't see why not. They want to see how it goes: so let's get cracking.'

This was how in 1988 a comprehensive programme that completely restructured a British aerospace manufacturing business then employing 1600 people and turning over £60M p.a. got started. Why were they able to persuade the board to support their proposal for restructuring manufacturing? These were the three reasons.

1. They had a plan that showed what had to be done to become fully competitive and how to overcome all the barriers to achieving the goals.
2. The plan was cash-positive so they were not asking for money, but agreement to proceed. Each phase of the restructuring would be paid for in advance by savings in inventory and other excess costs.

3. While developing the plan together, the managers had forged themselves into a powerful team committed to bringing about change and with the competence to achieve this task. Their commitment and competence were plain to see, and the board of directors knew it.

Over the next 2 years, this team went on to realize its plan and create an internationally competitive business with turnover per employee doubled, inventory and lead times down 50 per cent and space requirements halved. As one of the directors remarked, when looking back over their achievements, 'We've got a whole new way of doing things around here'.

How were they able to effect this transition? They used outside help from people who were highly experienced in implementing major change, and they worked together to define the *prescription* for the business, then created the *synthesis* between that and the *process* of implementation (Table 9.1).

Table 9.1 Three essential elements of any change programme

Prescription	Synthesis	Process
Understanding how to achieve the full business potential	Creating and managing the change environment to make sure the benefits are realized	Equipping the people to achieve the prescription

DEVELOPING THE PRESCRIPTION

The process for developing the prescription has three distinct phases, as shown in Fig. 9.1.

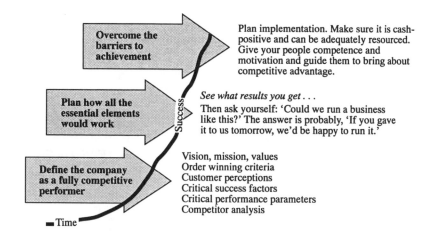

Figure 9.1   Developing the prescription

Defining the company as a fully competitive performer

The first step in developing the prescription for your business is to define what is has to achieve to compete against the upper quartile players in 4 to 5 years. This means setting performance targets and identifying the rate at which you have to improve to get there. The process of doing this is illustrated in Fig. 9.2.

When you look at a range of performance measures—productivity, resource utilization, total value per person employed, stock turn, etc.—and compare them to your upper quartile competitors, it is not enough to compare yourself with upper quartile competition today, since, by the time you have got there they will have moved on. You have to compare yourselves with where they will be in 3 to 4 years' time. This is the size of the task you have to undertake. Usually you find that continuous improvement at the rate of 5 to 8 per cent a year will not be enough because there is a big gap you have to close. This means you will probably need 15 per cent improvement in several areas for 3 to 4 years before you get to a state where continuous improvement is enough. You will find that when you plot your performance against the upper quartile, in some areas you are

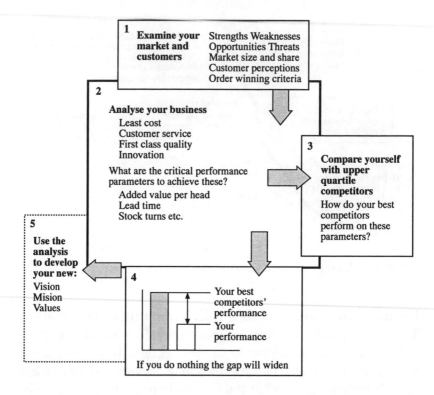

Figure 9.2   Defining your company as a fully competitive performer

quite good, maybe even better than your best competitors, but in others the gap is big. Figure 9.3 shows that, across a range of performances, where companies are good they are quite good, but their average is drawn down because where they are bad they are abysmal.

The task is to bring the worst performance up to where it approaches the best and then to improve on all performance by 5 to 8 per cent a year because by definition your competitors are improving at that rate, otherwise they won't be upper quartile players for very long.

Golfers who play regularly at a particular course will know that if they string together the best score they've ever had on each hole, the overall score will be quite respectable, probably at or near par.

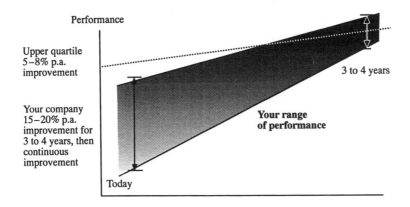

Figure 9.3 Comparison with upper quartile competitors

The logic is that our golfer has the potential to get near to that score consistently with proper coaching and plenty of practice. Applying the same logic to a business, if it can be near world class in some areas, with proper help and practice it has the potential to be just as good in all the other areas. Cells and team-based working are major contributors extending your best developed practice across the entire business. In this way, you can close the gap in all the critical areas between you and your upper quartile competitors.

Defining your business as a fully competitive performer

Take those critical performance parameters for upper quartile competition in 3 to 4 years' time that you have identified as critical to your business and apply them to your business. What does it look like?

- What are the products?
- What are the markets?
- How much turnover per head and how many people?
- How much turnover per unit of space and how much space?
- What stockturns, what inventories and what leadtimes?
- What return on sales and capital?

The results will be startling, with comments like: 'If we didn't have any directs at all we'd still have too many people'. However, the choices are stark! A stake has been hammered into the ground. Go for this level of performance over the next 3 to 4 years or accept second class status and genteel decline.

Planning how all the essential elements will work
The next step is to work out what you will need in place to enable the business to work and be fully competitive in 3 to 4 years.

- How the people will be organized and teamed
- The technology requirements
- The logistics support requirements
- The information system requirements, etc.

This means that you need to suspend today's agenda for a while and be truly visionary. Otherwise you can't get past the difficulties you are having just solving today's problems, never mind looking 3 to 4 years ahead.

Inevitably there are some holes and blanks. But you will build up a vision which has enough information so that you reach a very important point. People will have enough belief in the plans that they will be able to say, 'If you gave me that business, I could run it for you and deliver that sort of performance'. And that is a breakthrough! I've been in meetings where this has happened and it is very profound experience to see people actually go through this realization. Even more important is the fact that once people have accepted that they can do it, all you have left to do is to figure out how to get there.

Overcoming barriers to achievement
Cash flow is always seen as one of the most significant barriers to achievement, so developing a cash-positive plan, or at least a plan that minimizes negative cash flow, is essential. Many a promising project has foundered because of that cash flow problem where in

3 or 4 years' time you are promising the moon, return on investment will be beyond your wildest dreams, but all you can guarantee for tomorrow is pain and misery, negative cash flow and high interest payments on big borrowing. In most businesses I have seen, there has been more than enough cash to pay for restructuring tied up in inventory, land, buildings, under-utilized assets, and poor make vs buy decisions. When preparing a cash-positive strategy, your cash flow curve will show that you save a bit—for example from inventory reduction—and then spend a bit on restructuring (Fig. 9.4). You then save a bit more, perhaps from reducing space, and then spend a bit more.

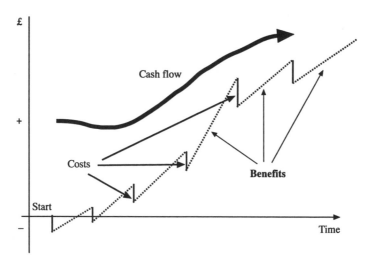

Figure 9.4   Cash-positive project: cash flow

When preparing the business plan, all the cash to pay for restructuring does not have to be taken out of the business in terms of inventory, assets, and make vs buy. Some of it can actually come from growth. If a company gets its plans right and can show that investing in growth is a big benefit, you can actually generate the cash there, and that strategy is also cash positive. And one feeds off the other, team-based manufacture generates growth and growth pays for team-based manufacture. A cash-positive strategy means that you do not have to ask the review board for money, only for permission to proceed.

Synthesis: creating and managing the change environment

The synthesis is the essential link between knowing what you have to do and making it happen. To provide this, the joint team of experienced agents for change and committed managers act as living, breathing examples of the new values and beliefs that are required and transfer them to their people by:

- Personally demonstrating the new standards of behaviour.
- Showing the way forward, based on their in-depth experience of implementation.
- Calming the fears and easing the pain of transition.
- Leading the drive that:
  - Releases the cash to fund the change.
  - Proves that the benefits will be realized.

Only then are people able to go through the process, making the physical changes, and identifying and transferring to their people the competences they needed to bring about the change themselves.

Overcoming the barriers to achieving the vision is a bit like climbing a mountain (Fig. 9.5). You stand at the bottom of the mountain looking up, saying, 'I've never climbed a mountain like that in my life. I'll never get to the top. I'm too fat and flabby'. But all you have to do is take one step forward and you've started! Then as you climb, you begin to see the path snaking away towards the top. Sometimes it disappears into a dip, or doubles back on itself, but then it reappears and you are reasonably confident that it's the same path. Sometimes it will seem to be going in the wrong direction as it goes round the crag that gets in the way, but it will get you there in the end. As long as you have a properly defined implementation plan, you know that if you just keep taking the steps you'll get there in the end. You reach a point

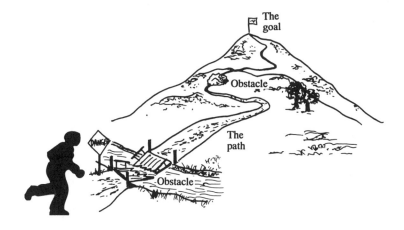

Figure 9.5   Overcoming obstacles to achievement

where the team has taken it on board and they know it's going to be a long hard road but they know where they are going and every step they take is leading them in the right direction and achieving the mission for the business.

The need for management teaming

Preparation of a cash-positive plan that defines the company as fully competitive and shows how to overcome the barriers to achievement is the first essential task in redesigning a business around cells and teaming. It needs a very strong level of management teaming to get agreement of the vision, mission and goals. The problem with senior managers is not that they don't have a vision, because they do, but that they all have their own. This is compounded even further because they all think that their own vision is everybody else's as well. When starting a change project, I imagine all the managers sitting round a table wearing miner's helmets with miner's lamps. The beam from the lamp is their vision, and when we first start, these beams are shining about all over the room, because nobody is looking in the same direction. The process of building a high level of unconscious agreement and understanding of each other's goals among the management team gradually brings all these lights closer together, until they are at least all focusing on the table in front of them, not all exactly in the same spot, but definitely overlapping. The work done by the management team at the start of a project—building vision, fixing the mission, setting direction, deciding where the company needs to go—is fundamental and mustn't be underestimated.

People's attitude towards restructuring the business to introduce team-based manufacturing in cells, usually falls into one of four categories (Fig. 9.6). People who are doing nothing and don't see any reason to are smug. People with plenty of vision, but who are not prepared to undergo any pain to achieve their vision are dreamers. People who only want to squeeze cost out are short-sighted. They go through an awful lot of pain but really aren't any better off at the end of it. People who combine the visionary with the hard and pragmatic are the winners.

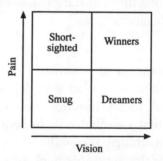

Figure 9.6   Attitudes towards restructuring the business

Winning companies I have worked with as agents for change know where they want to go, why we are there and what role we are to play. Wonderful! They move forward very quickly and they understand what the external people are adding to the project. Short-sighted companies I have worked with are, at the start, in the mire. They've milked the business till it's dry, burnt all the furniture and are starting to rip up the floorboards before they decide they have to do something fundamental. One characteristic of a management team in a company like this is that they long ago stopped making fundamental decisions to improve the business, so as a team they don't know how to make important decisions and they've got to relearn how to do this. What is worse, by this time they often have their backs up against the wall, so the decision they have to take is often 'make or break'. Wouldn't it be far easier to make small, incremental decisions as part of an overall cash-positive business strategy, rather than have to make a huge decision to change direction all at once? When they call in outside professional help, they expect their advisers to solve all their problems, and then resent them for doing it. They are not prepared to acknowledge that they are part of the problem, and as facts start to reveal this they back into a corner spitting and scratching. You start to hear them say things like, 'There's nothing wrong with this business that a few more orders wouldn't fix.' Nothing will change in a company like this until those people are prepared to hold up their hands and say 'I'm part of the problem and I want to be part of the solution.' If only one individual on that board of management did this, he'd really be sticking his neck out. The task is to get them in a position where they can all agree collectively without losing face or giving others the opportunity to attack them.

Outdoor teambuilding

This is where outdoor team activity has a role to play. When a management group which does not have the necessary trust and commitment goes outdoors on a challenging exercise they all want to prove themselves individually; they don't plan on letting any of the others show them up. In reality, the exercises are designed to make sure they become so exhausted that their resistance to change is lowered. 'I don't care, I'll do anything you want, as long as you don't make me go through that again.' Outdoor exercises also create situations of simulated danger where people who may be hostile to each other in the work environment actually have to depend on each other for well-being, almost for survival. When one is hanging off the other's wrist over the edge of a ravine, it truly does start to break down the barriers and encourage trust. Working out of doors with a management team that really is not prepared to admit that there is any problem provides a good spur to recognizing the need for change. It also accelerates the process of bringing everybody up to speed. Taking people away from the day-to-day working environment and using a combination of strangeness and exhaustion to get them to suspend their personal agendas allows the facilitators to help them to focus their attention on fundamental issues. Back in the work environment the shared experiences encourage person to person communication and teambuilding across departmental boundaries.

Getting commitment to change from the local board

When working as agents for change with companies on planning projects, you reach a point where you've beavered away, looked at different ways of doing things, worked with the company's personnel, and now it's time for the team to report its findings to the local board. By this time, the team has designed a strategy, prepared projections of the benefits of cells and teams, and calculated what this will mean to the business. This strategy is usually based on projections of an arithmetical, provable element, and an element which allows for benefits that can't be quantified, but are nevertheless real, and will make the project a worthwhile investment. Most of the review board usually say, 'I will support this project if you can prove to me logically that it is fool-proof and will succeed'. They want to see a report which sets down the dilemma and makes a series of statements with cast-iron logic—for example, you do these things and you get these benefits, you put these machines in and you improve the productivity there—then they will sign off on going through that specific exercise. In this way they are trying to guarantee that there is nothing *they themselves personally* have to do to make the project work, so they can't be blamed if the benefits aren't realized. In truth, it's just a way for them to abrogate their responsibility. They just want to carry on doing what they've always done and let the project work by itself. How many times have I seen this kind of attempt to justify a project!

What happens next is the planning team remodels the project on the basis laid down by the review board and, of course, the results are abysmal. It's not worth while going ahead, because the benefits don't justify the effort and expenditure. Usually at this point, behind closed doors, there is a process that goes something like this. The leader of the local board says to the rest something like this:

> 'Well blow me! I thought we were really going to pull something together to make this project go. If we're not prepared to manage this company to make this happen we might as well pack up our train set and go home. If you lot are not prepared to pitch in and say "I've got something to contribute to this, to make it work", we're wasting our time. I've got to be able to look you in the eye and know you will support me, and you've got to have the same sort of trust that I will support you. If we can't do this, then it's only a matter of time till this company shrinks and probably folds or is sold.'

And this kind of talk from one of their number usually galvanizes the local board into action. A change in attitude takes place that is almost tangible. Suddenly they are all saying, 'Yes, we are going to get those extra benefits. We are going to show people what we can do with this business. We are going to give it the effort it deserves and take some responsibility for the outcome. We are going to drive this through because we do believe it can be that good because we are prepared to work as a team and make it happen.'

That's a major transformation point where the review team actually starts to share the vision, goals and objectives of the business. There are two interesting characteristics of people's attitudes during the time before top management actually buys into the project. During all this time, the outside agents for change talk with the people working on the project, and warn them and try to trigger them off, telegraphing to them what's coming next. 'There's a big project coming up here, it's going to involve all the people in this room and you are gong to have to put a lot of time and energy and commitment into it over many months.' When they finally decide they have to make the project go, and start looking at the actions they have to take, they turn around and moan, 'Look at all this work we have to do. Now look what we've let ourselves in for. Why didn't you *tell* us it was going to involve all this?' And we say, 'But we *did*, we did tell you.' And they are incredulous.

There is a very important characteristic that you'll notice at this stage, this planning phase, while the team is forming itself and setting direction and understanding what the vision and mission is for the business, understanding how it's going to be realized, and how to overcome the barriers, how all the elements are going to work, understanding what the benefits are going to be. It's such an intensive period I often liken it to somebody who is climbing up the roof of a house, and it's damp and slippery and he's just got on a pair of trainers, so he's a bit nervous and concentrating hard, because he has to get to the top. While he's doing that, somebody's standing on the ground shouting, 'You just wait till you get to the top, you just wait till you look over.' His reaction is to say, 'Don't bother me with that. I'm slipping and sliding here. I just want to get to the top of the roof.' And then he does get to the top and looks over ... and says, 'Good grief, why didn't you tell me it was going to be like this?'

The other characteristic of this period is that the people involved reach the 'performing' stage of teaming almost without knowing it. Very often the project team have been working together very closely for several months, sharing the project and starting to build that unconscious agreement about where the business is going. Very strong bonds are formed, and that teaming shows because whenever two team members meet in the corridor and start to talk about the project, they are immediately on common ground and can move forward in their thinking, almost as if they are reading each other's mind about what's going on. When there are individuals who haven't been part of that teaming process, or who haven't been bought into it, conversations about the project on meeting in the corridor are immediately in conflict phase. They start going backwards in time while the participants try to find something they can agree about as a basis for moving forward.

Vision like this is often manifested at the local operating board rather than at the most senior board level, especially in a large company, because those are the people who have had to live with the failures of manufacturing, and who will benefit from the effects of implementing team-based manufacture. They are often being squeezed at both ends so it is often at that level where the vision is strongest at the start. Therefore it's important to have the cash-positive plan which describes the business as a world class performer, shows how all the elements are going to fit into place and work, and how to overcome all the barriers to achievement. When all the team shares this, you're over the top of the roof and ready to go.

The local board has reached this wonderful point where they can look each other in the eye, know what they have to do, and know that they can count on support from each other. What happens next? Then they walk straight into another problem, and it goes something like this. As they've been working together and living and breathing the project, it's gone deep inside. Everybody can reel the numbers off without thinking and individuals know their specialism inside out. Team members can go up to a flip chart and write down all the key facts of the project right out of their heads. The budget? They can just write it down—all of it—because they are so involved. Now for the first time in ages they've welded themselves into a team. They take their proposals along to the board and ask for permission to proceed. Usually, especially in large companies, at this point an army of auditors descends upon them and starts to go through the project with a fine tooth comb, challenging every statement. This happened more often in the days when projects were not designed to be cash-positive, or at least to minimize the impact on cash flow. Anyway, the team recasts the proposal and submits it to the board again. Remember how the senior managers of many stagnant large companies had forgotten how to make decisions. Now they run straight up against this phenomenon. The chief executive has pen poised over the document, ready to sign it, when suddenly, cold feet, and a new question: 'Ah, I'm just not certain about this part here, could you do some more research on it for me please?' Confidence in the local board has been lost, and it's such a momentous decision, affecting the survival of the company. It's so much easier to make a number of smaller incremental decisions than to let the company get into a position where you come to the crunch. I've seen companies take 6 or 8 months re-hashing and dithering over plans, going over and over things they've been through before, because top management were bearing the risks of what they rightly saw as a make or break decision. The operational team had sorted themselves out but the main board just couldn't believe it, they had no evidence other than the plan before them promising so much in the future but costing so much now. One company I know took almost 5 years—during which time their market nearly dwindled away—before they finally made the decision, and then they went ahead and made a brilliant job of implementing their plans and getting the predicted benefits. Another company took 9 months—reworking and reworking the proposal until they had finally brought all the main board members on board—and then they made a commitment.

COMMUNICATING THE VISION TO THE REST OF THE BUSINESS

The local operating board is full of enthusiasm and unconscious agreement, and they finally get main board approval (or at least they didn't say no) and it's time to draw the rest of the workforce into the plans. The problem now is the team seems to assume that everyone else has absorbed by osmosis all the teaming, all the knowledge and all the understanding of where the business is going: of course, this is not true. People on the shop-floor, all the supervisors, the accounts department, purchasing, none of them have any in-depth understanding of what's about to hit them. The team has to start from scratch and sell the project all over again but this time across the entire business.

I have watched the local board go to the people with a presentation that says they are going to do all these things, the road will be hard but everything will then be wonderful ...

> 'Wait a minute! this is the first we've heard of this'.
> 'Why'?
> 'How does all this affect me'?
> 'I have been thinking about this and I've got some ideas'.
> 'Why didn't you ask me first'?
> 'Well, if you think I'm going to help you work myself out of a job, then think again.'

This is the new starting point of the project, with the emphasis on consistent, caring communication. Unless you work hard at getting the communication right, it could inject another delay into the process of change. The Catch 22 is that the local board can't really start selling their plans until they have at least tacit approval to go ahead, but once that approval is given, they should realize that osmosis has not taken place and be ready to put the communication programme into high gear. They have to win trust and show that they deserve it. Trust is won by patience, consistency, honesty and openness. Patience is essential. It's ridiculous to think that trust can be established by decree: 'It's now July 3rd. On August 1st everybody is going to trust each other.' Just imagine the response. Until you demonstrate these traits and win trust, the people are not likely to come along with you wholeheartedly. This is where all the communication issues we discussed in Chapter 5 on people come into play.

PUTTING TOGETHER AN IMPLEMENTATION TEAM

To implement team-based cells, you need a cash-positive plan, and a team of people with responsibility for making the changes. We've usually found that when people try to do this kind of thing part-time, it never even gets off the ground. In larger organizations especially, the managers think they ought to be able to do it themselves. They say, 'All right, we've got to do this. We'll all spend a third of our time on it.' What happens then is, the third starts after people have done everything else they need to during the day to keep the business running: so perhaps they might get round to giving the project some attention at about 3 or 4 o'clock in the afternoon. Do you think people are likely to be at the peak of their energy and creative ability by then? Unlikely. In my experience, within a few weeks the pressure of keeping the business going have wiped the project team right out of existence, and there is rueful acknowledgement that to make change happen, you need a dedicated team of people who can concentrate on understanding team-based manufacturing, identifying all the issues, overcoming the barriers, and really driving change through, making it happen.

The size of the implementation team will vary according to the needs of the business, but a good rule of thumb is one person on the team for every 40–50 people in the business. You can end up with quite a large dedicated team while you are bringing change about, but that is the best way to ensure that you achieve the benefits. This team is usually split into two groups, one concentrating on planning and implementing all of the four elements of cell manufacture and the other driving the cash-positive strategy. In the smaller business the project team will comprise just a few people who do everything: communication, people, teaming, training, workshops, engineering, layout, work-flow, logistics and support, accountability, designing the new performance measures. The important issue is to make sure that the people who will eventually own and operate the cells are involved in the design process; for example, in logistics, the support team must be involved. Therefore the composition of the team is often a mixture of specialists in the management of change, and the eventual core and support team members. This mixed team works on implementing a group of cells, and when they are in place, the core team and support members stay with the cells while the change team moves on to the next group of cells, assembles another operational team, implements that group of cells, and again moves on.

THE PILOT CELL

Your objective is to introduce team-based cells into your business and prove that they will produce the benefits you are seeking. It's usually too big and complex a task to implement all the cells at one go, so you will want to do it progressively. You'll have to do quite a bit of moving about, of machines and people, to get all the processes required for a family of parts co-located and this will probably mean re-layout of most of your operations. This gives the opportunity to free a lot of spare space that you knew you had, and put it to better use, or even sell it as part of your cash positive restructuring plan. Cells are going to be phased in over a period of time. First the structural changes and re-layout will be complete, but you will not be able to say that cells are fully implemented until the teams have gone through all the stages—forming, storming, and norming—to performing. It's not just a question of the physical things but also the people.

Setting up a *pilot cell* is an excellent way to pioneer the process of implementing team-based cells. We have already seen that team-based cells involve quite a few changes to working practices and behaviours. They include the way people communicate and the way performance is measured, and these changes are quite innovative, progressive and far reaching for people who only know the old way of working. At the point where you start, not everyone will have bought into what you are trying to do, and may not

entirely agree with a new way of working. Some issues around
setting up the pilot cell can be structural, involving the unions, and
negotiating changes in working practices with technicians,
managers, the accounts department, etc. This means agreeing
what the practices will be and demonstrating that they are right for
the business. There will be a lot of 'personal agenda' issues, with
accounts and other support departments which have an interest in
maintaining the *status quo*, and can't see much benefit from
change. There is a quote from Machiavelli which keeps cropping
up in management textbooks, so I might as well repeat it here.
The gist of what he said is: change is hard to bring about because
the people who benefit from the *status quo* see all too clearly what
they will lose from change and there will be only lukewarm
support from those who would gain because the benefits are
tentative and in an indefinite future. So the pilot cell is useful for
doing several things:

1. Work through all the issues around working practices, union
   agreements and interfaces with other departments, such as
   accounts. Understand what these issues are, and form the basis
   of agreement for all the subsequent cells. Agree with the
   technicians how they will be organized, what interfaces you will
   set up with accounts, with purchasing, etc., and get permission
   to go ahead from all the people with vested interests.
2. Work out your own methodologies for implementing cells:
   what things do you have to do to get a cell into place and make
   it work. Determine what training cell team members need. Get
   an idea of what the individuals' tasks are, and what their size is,
   when implementing cells. Demonstrate the methodologies.
   These methodologies, refined and improved as you go along,
   will apply to all subsequent cells.
3. Clearly demonstrate the benefits that cells will bring, using the
   pilot cell as proof, showing that it actually delivers reduced lead
   time, improved quality and delivery, flexibility, etc. This gives a
   clear signal to everyone that cells are really going to work.

When you have all the working agreements and methodologies in place you are ready to go and implement all the other cells because you have cracked all the problems on the pilot cell.

Selecting which cell to use as a pilot

How do you know which cell to choose? The natural tendency is to pick the area that's causing the most problems on the theory that making it the pilot cell will crack the problems quickly. I usually try to steer people away from doing that because the area with the most problems will also have the most problems in getting it to work as a cell, and if it fails you will discredit the whole process of cell working. With some experience of cell working under your belt, you can probably tackle the problem area and really make it go, but don't start with the hardest. Choose a cell where the technology issues are not the make or break issues, where the logistics issues are not make or break, but where the benefits will come about through *team working and resolving the people issues*. You want a clear demonstration that the people, working in teams, have brought the inventory down, and not some magical piece of technology. Pick a product where you can't be held to ransom on time. Don't let people pressurize you by saying, 'You've got to get the pilot cell working by a certain deadline, or we are all in the mire.' Pick a product which is not critical, because one thing you have to be prepared to do is take as long as it takes. If vested interests opposed to cell manufacture issue a deadline and you don't meet it, they have a useful rod to hit you with. They can say you've failed and that will make it very difficult to continue, so take as long as it needs to take (I don't mean linger) to resolve each issue and prove the methodology and benefits.

BAe Hatfield used 146 doors as their pilot cell. This was a good choice because technology wasn't an issue. It was a reasonably mature assembly process. Logistics was not an issue because the supplier was already prepared to deliver in kits, and therefore was able to emulate the supply arrangements we wanted for cell manufacture: JIT kit supply. They couldn't be held to ransom on time, because they weren't short of doors. That meant they were able to concentrate on resolving the people issues. When the unions tried to hold up the process, by refusing to let pilot cell team members communicate direct with management, rather than through the union, the managers were able to say, 'That's OK, we're not short of doors, we'll stop making them while we resolve these problems.' When they objected to this the reply was, 'Oh, if you don't want the pilot cell to work, you must not want Hatfield to make doors. OK then, we'll subcontract them. What else don't you want us to make? We'll subcontract that too.' This deflated the opposition to the pilot cell. There was conflict between groups with different vested interests—trade union, middle management, accounts—but eventually we worked through all these issues and got agreement to experiment. Then we were able to use the pilot cell to show that the method really worked and that the benefits came from teaming.

Make sure you set up the pilot cell in an area which is highly visible, near a thoroughfare where many people from different areas have to pass by. Use it to demonstrate how things are going to look physically. Lay out the Kanban squares, refurbish the jigs, etc. Choose a new colour scheme, paint the floor and brighten up the place so that people say, 'We want to work in there!' The magic of a lick of paint: never underestimate it. Give the technicians smart new uniforms or badges, something to distinguish them from people who are not (yet) in team-based cells. This will attract the attention of everyone else in the business, and the pilot cell team members will really enjoy being in the limelight. They will provide just the kind of publicity you need for the new way of working, and the remainder of the cells will be implemented like clockwork.

10

Where do we go from here?

What is the future for cells and teaming in manufacturing—and also in the service sector? It's worth while recalling the many attempts which have already been made to solve the problems caused by the shift in the economic basis of the western world. We've already discussed how **MRP, FMS, CIM,** group technology, etc., were peddled as universal panaceas and all were found wanting because, applied on their own, they failed to provide the poise and agility companies needed to respond to the market. Today, in the mid 1990s, we are talking about cell manufacture and teamworking, how complementary they are, and the impact this can have on manufacturing, and on businesses which provide services.

I do not believe that team-based cell manufacture is another blind alley. The agility, poise and flexibility that cells encourage and the creation of the environment that allows the full potential of the team to be realized must surely mean that the principles of cells and teaming will endure. However, the concept may not be called 'cell manufacture'. I don't think this term will last for long because it is already too restrictive and does not fully describe what we mean. Some new term will emerge to describe the activity of small groups working together, with flexible facilities able to produce a complete family of products or services. Through the 1990s cells and teams will be powerful means of responding to market needs and economic pressures, and the concept will develop and grow to meet the needs of the twenty-first century.

Some things which have already happened will undoubtedly have an impact on manufacturing in the new century. Throughout the 1970s Britain went through constant devaluations of currency to try to remain competitive, while continuing to apply old, ineffective solutions to new problems. Financial deregulation in the 1980s removed the exchange control acts and allowed free movement of capital, and led to the 'Big Bang' on the stockmarkets.

I want to do some crystal ball gazing and look at developments in three areas which will have a profound effect on the way cells and teams will contribute to economic productivity. These are patterns of employment, information technology, and the development of the world economy.

PATTERNS OF EMPLOYMENT

We are already seeing a marked increase in the mobility of labour, which will undoubtedly increase even more. Young people today have no hesitation about travelling and living abroad, and the children of my friends are living all over Europe and North America. People will go to the countries where they see the best opportunities. The single European market and free movement of labour in Europe will allow successful companies to pick the best people from all over Europe and capitalize on the individual strengths of different countries: design flair from Italy, machine tool expertise from Germany, high level conglomerate and stock market management from Britain, adaptability from Spain and strong project commitment from France.

Job tenure

Job tenure is becoming a significant issue. People's employment expectations have been based on having a full-time job between leaving school and retirement, working for a few companies during the course of their careers, tying themselves to each company for a long period. Indeed, many people work for only one company through their entire lives and do substantially the same job. There is a growing trend now for some people—and I am one of them—to try to break this chain (either from choice or from necessity) by changing career, by becoming self-employed, by finding some way to opt out of dependence on only one employer for financial security. Pressures of the market place are changing the patterns of job tenure. If businesses are to be poised to respond quickly to changes in their markets, the roles and tasks that need to be undertaken by the people in the business will vary considerably over a short period and so will the number of people needed. This is starting to break down the old pattern of lifetime employment. Contracts of employment and tying people in to master–servant relationships are much less relevant to business needs now. A trend is emerging for businesses to have a tight core of full-time employees, which varies in size and composition slowly, surrounded by clusters of associates, people who work part-time, or for short periods, providing a particular expertise. This is likely to be a trend for the future. Charles Handy, in *The Age of Unreason*, wrote about the core business being organized with the goal of one-third the number of people being three times as productive and earning twice as much.

This trend leads to another significant change. Because job tenure is no longer secure, people may have a number of radically different careers, requiring different sets of skills, in the course of their working lives. An article in the *Economist* (15 July 1993, page 15) states that the sense of job security that people have always expected (and which has always been illusory) is now disappearing, and individuals will have to get used to the idea of not feeling quite so secure. Just like businesses, individuals will have to be much more poised and agile and ready to go in different directions and this will put greater intellectual demands on them. Unlike, for example, the man I saw interviewed on television some years ago who spent his whole working life welding Mini suspension brackets, ever since the Mini was launched in 1959, and that was the sole use of his skills. What a waste of his talents. What a loss of potential.

In the new world, where businesses have to make the best use of all their people, much more emphasis will be placed on their intellectual capabilities and they will be expected to develop their skills. The parable of the talents says that, if we don't use the skills God has given us, they will be taken away. 'Talents' in this parable deliberately has a double meaning; it can mean money, but it also means skills. The master gave his servants some talents (skills). The servants who went out and used their 'talents' multiplied them, the one who buried his talents in the sand, had them taken away. This is so analogous to the world we live in, because if we don't use our skills, they wither. The horizons of people who stay in one job and use one set of skills all their lives become narrower, whereas people who deliberately choose, or are forced, to change jobs and develop new skills, get wider and wider horizons even though they may feel more insecure initially. The *Economist* goes on to state, 'Western firms assume that tearing up such commitments [to lifetime employment] will generate a burst of entrepreneurial enthusiasm. This is unlikely. Many of these people feel not empowered, but intimidated. This fear is the bluntest of management weapons.' This is why cells and team working have a very important role to play. We want people who, while they feel that they no longer have secure job tenure, can still use their skills effectively; we want to empower them with entrepreneurial enthusiasm. We don't want them to feel stifling fear. We need cells and team working to create empowerment and make that knot in the stomach into a feeling of exciting motivation, not fear. This helps people feel fulfilled and not intimidated.

Unemployment

Unemployment has been increasing steadily in the mature industrial economies since the beginning of the 1990s to the time of writing this book. Let's look at the nature and causes of unemployment and its impact on manufacturing, teamworking and cells. There are two aspects of unemployment I would like to discuss; structural and cyclical.

Structural unemployment is a function of the basic shape of the nation's economy and its fundamental welfare policy. This establishes a threshold income level below which one is better off not working. This unemployment is very hard to shift, requiring unpopular legislation to reduce welfare benefits. In Britain structural unemployment has risen steadily from about 300 000 in the 1950s to about 1 500 000 in the 1990s. Cyclical unemployment is a function of the state of the economy, rising and falling with recession and recovery. For the individual without a job, however, there is only one type of unemployment, that is, total.

There are in the early 1990s over 30 000 000 unemployed people in the European Community. This is starting to look a bit like the start of the first industrial revolution, where displaced farmhands formed a ready pool of resource to fuel the emerging factories in Europe and America. What will be the next revolution that will give these people rewarding jobs?

INFORMATION TECHNOLOGY

Already we are starting to see circumstances where people are 'telecommuting', working in areas remote from the centralized office and using information technology—fax, modem, video conferences—to communicate with their colleagues. The effect of information technology is that people can stay at home in the Lake District, or the Adirondacks, or in Western Australia, or in Samoa, or in Kenya, and be instantly in touch with the rest of the world. Both historically and today, people have wanted to choose where to live and still be able to pursue their careers, and information technology is increasingly making this possible. It also means that branches of a company can be located thousands of miles apart and still maintain instant communication. This benefit also highlights how the differences in culture and time can cause problems. One company I know regularly holds video conferences with American colleagues, and because of the time difference, these tend to start at about 3.00 pm UK time or 10.00 am USA time. Usually, at about 5.00 pm UK time, somebody on the American end of the conference will suggest breaking for lunch and resuming again in an hour, while the people on the UK end want to carry on for another hour, get finished and go home. This is an illustration of some of the problems telecommuting will create: info lag instead of jet lag.

Now that small teams can work remote from one another it is proving beneficial for huge conglomerates to break up into smaller, autonomous units based on the principles of cells and teaming. Take Microsoft as an example. It has a huge central office in California and, until now, its people have all tended to work in the same location. However, they way the world economy is now developing, e.g. the North American Free Trade Association (NAFTA), might make it beneficial to the business to create satellite teams across North America. This is already starting to happen in some companies in the UK. For example, British Telecom is experimenting with having people who provide directory enquiry service work from home using computers linked to the main database and teleconferencing for communication with supervisors. Some of the forecast benefits from having significant numbers of people working from home are a reduction in rush-hour traffic as everyone struggles to get to work on time, and knock-on benefits of reduced fuel consumption and auto-mobile related pollution.

Dispersed small teams working in cells, doing the business, and adding value, will probably emerge first in information-related products. There will be the core business, with dispersed small teams working around it, and even the small teams can be dispersed, with people working at home on their own for much of the time. One difficulty which will have to be overcome by carefully planned communication is the tendency for people to get lonely working on their own all the time. This way of working will be the modern equivalent of cottage industries with home workers and entrepreneurs. It becomes conceivable to imagine the satellite operations becoming more autonomous in their internal

organization, treating the core business more as a customer than an employer. It is but a short step to a core business preferring to help create and work with increasingly independent satellites (Fig. 10.1).

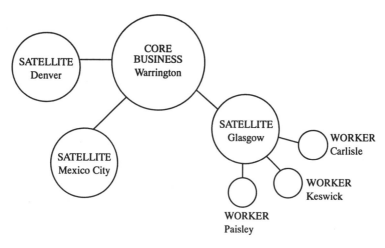

Figure 10.1   Twenty-first century cottage industry

For manufactured products, the size and type of the production facility will depend on the type of product, with the emphasis on keeping them as small and agile as possible. Manufactured products tend to fall into four basic categories, but of course there is some crossing-over of boundaries (Fig. 10.2).

Highly complex, large, expensive products, for example, airplanes, will still have to be assembled in factories. There is no real alternative to the manufacture of the major sections and final assembly in a factory organized around cells and teams. An assembly track for a large airliner needs over 1000 people. The manufacture of the subsystems—switches, cables, etc., and the information technology requirements—can be distributed among satellite companies. For a large capital project like a power station, you will have to bring the people to the site. The only reason for a big factory employing thousands of people will be for the assembly of very large, expensive products. Boeing is now aiming to create

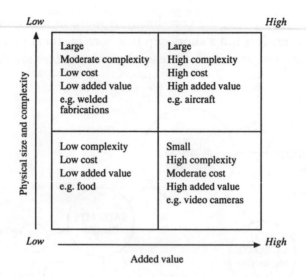

Figure 10.2   Types of manufactured product

separate business units for the manufacture of components. The key business issue for this type of manufacture will be *agility based around cells and teaming, recreating the entrepreneurial flair of the small business inside the larger one, and that is the role for cells in a large business.*

Facilities for producing large, low-cost items such as welded fabrications and castings will be modest in size, perhaps 50–80 people, and *quality will be their key business driver.* For high added value, low complexity products with relatively short life cycles—such as electronics, brown goods and white goods—the key business driver is rapid *product development.* This means optimizing the design and manufacturing process to get your product to market very quickly. PCs are a very good example; 386-based PCs have only been on the market a couple of years and already they've been replaced. The intellectual content of these products is very high, and refinement of simultaneous engineering techniques based on teamworking is likely to continue.

Dispersed teamworking will be very effective for small, low

added value goods such as nuts, screws, bolts and nails, and for the products of craftsmen (e.g. furniture). A furniture business employing a dozen people will source materials from other similar sized businesses, and the key business drivers will be quality, cost and delivery.

Small, low added value, fast moving consumer goods (FMCG) will still be produced in factories, but the key business drivers of those factories are already changing. Power has shifted from the manufacturers into the hands of the retailers; information technology now allows instant recording at the checkout of what products are selling well. The quality superiority of branded goods such as corn flakes, beans, margarine has been largely eroded. Consumers know that many branded goods are now also supplied under own-brand labels to large supermarket chains and large manufacturers of branded goods are beginning to feel the squeeze. Branded goods manufacturers may protest that they don't allow anyone else's label to appear on their products, but consumers' priorities have also changed and they are now discriminating increasingly on value for money rather than brand names. This means that FMCG manufacturers have to compete much more like suppliers to the motor industry who are selected according to these basic criteria in this order: First quality, do you consistently achieve our quality standards? If that's OK, can you consistently deliver? If these two are all right let's talk about what we are going to pay you. Retailers will not be prepared to pay advertising and promotion costs and with open book accounting they will know exactly how a supplier's costs are built up. *The key business drivers for FMCG are becoming the same as those for supplying the motor trade, i.e. quality, service and cost.* Cells and teaming are directly linked to generating improvements in these three areas. Techniques of cells and teaming, such as the use of supermarket shelves as compensators to regulate product flow and re-ordering are already being absorbed into FMCG business. We have already described how McDonald's uses teams and the principles of compensators in its restaurants. So in the future supermarkets and other FMCG suppliers, such as McDonald's, will organize around teams and cells to maximize use of resources, build quality in and focus on customer service.

There are other developments which make the shift away from big, expensive factories possible. Modern methods of transport make it possible to shift products around more quickly, and have reduced the cost of transport. In addition, new technology means that the size of products needed for a particular purpose has been reduced, so they consume less material, are lighter and take up less space when being transported. Calculators are an example of something that has shrunk in size from a table top machine that took two hands to lift, to something that's the size of a credit card. Future developments will mean that the significance of transport as an issue will continue to decrease. Even today we can see that make vs buy decisions tend to encourage the development of satellite businesses with links to a core business. As we have already discussed, the relationship between the dispersed team and the core business is likely to become more like that of customer and supplier. Then the satellites may have to sink or swim on their own, but they can link up with other businesses that need their specialist skills. The needs of the core business will drive the event, but will the change be intimidating or fulfilling for the small spin-off businesses? There is a key role for teaming. The change need not be fearful and intimidating if you get the teaming right. In the same way that good teaming and RSI don't mix, teaming is not compatible with fear and intimidation. If you have fear and intimidation, you haven't got a team.

The decision to break the links with a satellite company is not necessarily voluntary, but the needs of the business can force a company to go this route. For example, when Rolls-Royce crashed in 1971, they had subsidiary operations making components for engines, turbine blades, etc. At the time of the crash the receiver forced them to sell the subsidiaries to other companies. Turbine components were bought by Associated Engineering which is now Turner and Newall (T&N). This spin-off eventually brought benefits to both companies, T&N turbine components now supply their products to a wider range of customers, including Pratt and

Whitney, General Electric, i.e. not just to Rolls-Royce, demonstrating their improved competitiveness.

THE DEVELOPING WORLD ECONOMY

Trading associations

Global competition has led to the emergence of a number of trading associations among countries which see themselves as having common interests. The European Community (EC) and the North American Free Trade Association (NAFTA) have emerged in the West and Japan is now trying to do peacefully what it failed to achieve by war, that is, to create a trading association in South East Asia.

The European Union has created a single European market. At the time of writing Britain has ratified the Maastricht Treaty but opted out of the Social Chapter. The Anglo-Saxon (British and American) view is that the Social Chapter of the Maastricht Treaty is a relic of the past, when expectation of lifetime employment was normal. The Social Chapter as it now stands goes against the grain of changing employment patterns and information technology which will lead to small business units and dispersed teams. Britain's withdrawal from the Exchange Rate Mechanism (ERM) in September 1992 was a measure of the internationalism of the money market and proved that the market is now stronger than governments. Companies will be able to take advantage of this, but at the same time there will be fewer handouts from governments. Whatever the result of Maastricht, and whatever happens with the ERM, the single European Market will have an enormous double-edged impact on markets in the 1990s. It will offer a huge opportunity for companies that are prepared to go out and participate, and plenty of scope for failure for companies that are insular and refuse to speak any language other than their own. Exciting, lively companies will come into the UK from the Continent and suck away the market share of unprogressive businesses.

Across the Atlantic, the North American Free Trade Association (NAFTA) comprises the USA, Canada and Mexico. The biggest impact of NAFTA will be the opening up of Mexico. Mexico can offer a huge low-wage workforce, and plenty of Americans feel threatened by this at the moment. However, the forecasts of the likely long-term effect of NAFTA are really nothing but good. Goods manufactured in Mexico will be cheaper, so demand will be high, more goods will be sold, and the Mexican standard of living will rise, thus producing an even greater demand for goods. NAFTA will encourage dispersed teamworking as companies like Microsoft, in California, disperse and set up satellites where cheap labour is available. Information-based companies are moving out of California fairly quickly now, as they start to realize that they don't *have* to be located there. Routine tasks connected with creating software could be done by relatively cheap labour sources in Mexico. Take the work to where the people are and pay the local going rate. Highly educated, highly paid people will want to move to better surroundings, which makes them candidates for remote working, using information technology. All this is part of the levelling up process, because as work moves to Mexico, the standard of living will rise, followed by wages and prices. Everybody wants to level up rather than level down. First of all you get world class products, and then you get world class prices. Japanese cars are more expensive than American models now and Taiwanese prices are rising steadily.

Commodity prices and the Third World economy

What will happen to commodity prices worldwide? Will they bottom out and start to rise again? What might cause commodity prices to rise again? What will be the impact on teams and cell manufacturing. If we look to the East, we see a quarter of the world's population in China. Already the Chinese economy is growing at over 10 per cent p.a. in the early 1990s. Demand for manufactured products in emerging economies tends to be specific. The *Economist* (24 July 1993) describes the reasons for this:

Because of the fast rise in Asian incomes over the past 20 years, the two greatest opportunities should be about ready to come into their own. The first one is consumer demand. The typical abrupt pattern for consumer goods everywhere is that, for a given item, say a motor cycle, a household buys no motor cycles when its income is below a certain level, and then buys one or more when it surpasses that level. A rise of say 10 per cent in standard income levels will suddenly produce a sevenfold increase in the number of households with the incomes above the threshold for buying motor cycles, and thus produce an explosion in demand. As incomes rise, the cities of Asia are fast becoming a chain of sequentially exploding firecrackers of demand for one consumer good after another.

Motor bikes, fridges, washing machines, vacuum cleaners, televisions, videos, CD players, cars, cameras: will we be able to judge at which income level these things will be wanted? We've seen a sevenfold explosion in demand for products and services in the Philippines, South Korea, Taiwan, Singapore. Add all that together and it's still a drop in the ocean compared to world demand, but imagine that increase in demand in China, with a quarter of the world population, and the size of the markets that will be created. China will start to suck in manufactured products and raw materials in enormous quantities. Now that the Soviet Union has broken up, the economies of North Asia will start to emerge, but it is the surge from China which will pull all the others along. This could turn commodity prices around. Fuel and metal commodity prices have all been depressed, as have foodstuffs, so that we have created mountains of surplus food to keep prices artificially high. As China starts to suck in commodities, all the surpluses which pushed down, commodities prices will start to disappear and prices will start to rise. The heavily indebted Third World countries of Africa and South America tend to be commodity suppliers so you will see a magnifying effect with China as the locomotive which will pull the Third World out of debt and all the other millions of people in Africa, South Asia,

North Asia, and South America will join the bandwagon, earning more and demanding more products.

Factories will have to be built to satisfy these new markets and they will be located near the surge in demand. Infrastructure industries such as steelworks and power stations will grow up in China and throughout the Third World. The Japanese and other industrialized countries will be on hand to supply technical advice but Third World countries will prefer to train local people to manage and run the production process. As we move into the twenty-first century, the issue about marginal increases in income producing a manifold increase in demand will be important. What will happen if the commodity price cycle does change and commodity prices start to rise? Will factories revert to nineteenth and early twentieth century models with high inventory and vertical integration? To understand what could happen, we have to look at the needs that drive the people of the emergent nations.

Cells and teamworking do not have a place in a sweatshop in Southeast Asia, because the workers are much more concerned with having enough food and somewhere to live than they are with job satisfaction and self-fulfilment. I believe we will see Third World economies move rapidly through a cycle of manufacturing that will look vaguely familiar. Emerging factories will be built where there is demand, factories that seem out of date to us will be built and run along the same lines as Western ones in the 1950s. People will have much more in common with the Detroit auto workers of the 1920s than the twenty-first century dispersed teamworkers. In mature post-industrial economies, dispersed working using telecommunications and transport is possible. In emergent Chinese, South-East Asian, South American and African countries we'll see an evolution just like Western countries went through. But in the West, as the industrial revolution progressed, each successive country went through it much faster, and this is how it will be in the Third World economies. The British industrial revolution took a long time because there was no precedent and no source of ready made technology, everything had to be developed from first principles. In America, people were able to draw on existing technology, for example, by taking British locomotive designs and then modifying them to suit their own needs. So I believe we'll see a very rapid cycle, perhaps within half a generation, as the Chinese and the commodity providers progress from factories focusing on labour and machine utilization, to cells and teaming, and then to dispersed working. I think it is inevitable that they will go through this cycle, because the first thing the workers are going to want is money to buy food and pay the rent, then to buy the motor scooter, the radio, the fridge, the hoover, the telephone, all the other things we take for granted in the developed world. There will be a new pool of people becoming available which is better educated than ever before. Then educational systems will take hold and start producing more knowledgeable workers with better skills. These people will be available to think and will contribute new ideas. This could cause a change of emphasis leading to improvement in education and increased recognition for teaching professionals. As people climb higher up the prosperity ladder, they will have more sophisticated needs for personal motivation, and a culture based on cells and teams will become feasible.

Are there enough commodities in the world to meet this dramatically increased demand in the long term? As long as demand outstrips supply, countries will compete for what is available, and the less savoury side of rising commodity prices is the capacity for conflict. When demand rises, where are the raw materials going to come from? Of course the supply of raw materials is not infinite, and steps will have to be taken to locate new sources, to search for substitutes, and to design products which use less raw material. Marginal sources will become profitable again as prices rise. Less productive iron, tin and gold mines will re-open, because it will become economically viable to work them again. Supply can grow in that way but it becomes more and more inefficient.

In the nineteenth and early twentieth centuries large areas of the world had never been explored. There are people living today who were born when Africa was still the 'dark continent'. The pressure for exploration came from a need for raw materials. There are now no parts of the world which have not been seen and mapped by satellites. The last rising commodity price cycle led to the geographical opening up of the world, colonization, the scramble for Africa, and eventual conflict over sources of commodities.

So what's going to be different about the coming cycle of rising commodity prices? To give the consumer the value wanted, you don't need as much raw material as you once did, e.g. calculators are smaller. This has eased the pressure on raw materials. Motor vehicles don't consume as much oil because they are more efficient. But the explosion in demand will still exceed the supply. As information technology makes the world a global village, a colonization approach will be more difficult. One characteristic of earlier colonization was that countries were able to deprive their competitors of information about where they were. Information technology now makes this impossible. Spain tried desperately hard to stop the English from finding out the source of their treasure. But countries can no longer deprive rivals of geographical information so how are they to gain competitive advantage? Temporarily, the Third World will have the advantage of lower wage costs, but as they progress rapidly through the factory development cycle—shipbuilding, steel mills, car makers, electronics, value adding information products—wages will go up until both their wages and their prices equal those in developed economies. Then competition for sources of commodities will arise, and create the opportunity for conflict. We probably won't see conflict between colonial powers on the scale of a world war, but we may well see localized disputes in which the so-called world leaders are powerless, or unwilling, to intervene, and the Bosnia, Serbia, Croatia conflict has been a sad precursor.

CONCLUSION

What will manufacturing have to do worldwide in the 1990s and into the twenty-first century to really bring about a revolution in productivity and profitability? Over the centuries, we have gone through a series of revolutionary steps and each new step has flooded the world with manufactured goods, from cheap everyday metal items in the eighteenth century to a gun and a car for every American in the twentieth century. Fridges, washing machines, videos and camcorders have all been revolutionary steps. Each transition, from making everything at home, to specialists moving into towns, to cottage industries and then factories, has increased the availability of manufactured goods by an order of magnitude. Now we are on the verge of another revolution in manufacturing. We don't see it as step-change because we are living in it, so it seems to be taking a long time to us, but in historical perspective, we are living on the edge of step-change in manufacturing which will again totally transform the availability of manufactured goods throughout the world. World population increases look set to continue and China will become a major consumer, with the consequent increase in requirements for manufactured goods (and there will be enough food for everyone but whether we want to share it is another issue).

Back to my crystal ball: businesses in the twenty-first century can look forward to new employment patterns and widespread use of information technology. The development of the world economy spurred on by China will lead to rapid progression of newly industrialized societies through the development cycle of manufacturing, influenced by modern Japanese manufacturing techniques, then heading quickly for cells and teamwork. I can visualize a world in the late twenty-first century which is a truly global village. A significant portion of the population of the increasingly developed world will work in small, value-adding teams which are fairly autonomous, supplying the wants and needs of their customers. A few large core factories, for big, expensive products like airplanes and ships will still be necessary, as well as moderately sized manufacturing units for smaller products, and small teams feeding them with components and services. Many types of workers will be able to reside anywhere in the world that they choose, so some more remote places of interest might become areas where people choose to live and work, rather than just visit as tourists. However, there will still be people living traditional life-styles in the remotest areas of the world, and there will still be grinding poverty for people who are outside this economic style.

What can we learn from people who were crystal ball gazing in the 1950s. Some of the things that have changed are not what they predicted. For example, they thought kitchens would change, but they have not substantially, because the design and purpose of a kitchen are aesthetic, emotional and human things, not only relating to function. All the things that have changed most since the 1950s are things that are concerned with producing, processing and disseminating information, and I believe that will continue. The houses people want to live in will look pretty much the same, because people want to keep that continuity with the familiar, they want things to be human sized, but the way information is distributed will continue to develop beyond anything we can currently imagine. At the same time, increased competition for sources of commodities will get tangled up with political policy, and we can expect painful localized disputes, similar to the warring Greek city states or the Italian city states in the fifteenth and sixteenth centuries when there was plenty of creativity, intellectual activity and culture, but against a background of petty squabbling. There will be no more global policemen: this has already proved ineffectual and post-industrial economies won't have the will or desire to involve themselves.

In the super-competitive 1990s, which is only a pinprick in the historical perspective of man as a manufacturer, the challenge is to use all the incredibly able brains inside the heads of all the people. Up till now manufacturing has used only a fraction of people's intellectual capabilities. People are not very good at working machines; they are accident-prone, forgetful and tend to get tired or want to go home and do something different. On the other hand, people are the best parallel processors of ideas around, and we only use a fraction of this capability. In the next manufacturing era, we will use the whole of the intellectual capability of a lot fewer people. We have seen how the number of people employed in agriculture has dropped to 2 per cent of the population in mature economies; the same thing seems set to happen in manufacturing. And I wish I knew how it was going to be! Will there be a big revolution in the way we provide support to manufacture? The productivity revolution has not hit the service sector yet. What will happen when it does? Now that we have plenty of capable unemployed people swilling around, something will turn up for them to do, just as the first factories absorbed people displaced from agriculture. What does the future hold? We can only speculate, but team-based cells provide a stepping stone towards the future.

Appendix

Case studies

ALVIS VEHICLES LTD

Coventry
Chris Reed
Operations Director

Context

Alvis Vehicles Ltd designs, assembles and tests light armoured vehicles. In 1993, its major product was a high velocity missile carrier for the British Army, based on the Stormer armoured personnel carrier. A shrinking defence business means fighting hard in the commercial world for every order. This has meant redundancy for 30 per cent of operational staff. Alvis needs a whole new approach to responsiveness, flexibility and quality to win orders in a hard, hard world. The introduction of teamworking is only just starting and both management and staff are working hard to shape the direction. This is reflected in the interview with Chris Reed, the company's young and innovative Operations Director, who is pleased with some of the results but anxious to experience more step-change with the company culture.

Problems

- Old culture transferred to new greenfield site.
- Strong unions steeped in tradition.

- Functional organization with little flexibility and plenty of demarcation.
- Long lead time and high inventory.

Actions
- Reorganization and introduction of five product-based teams with team leaders.
- Used assessment centres to appoint people with leadership skills from the shop-floor.
- Dramatically increased training and development opportunities for all levels of staff.
- Two-way communication through team briefings, newsletters and project rooms.

Results
- Final build lead time reduced from 19 weeks to 11 weeks achieving demanding programme with tight resources.
- More trust between operations management and the workforce.
- More flexibility: fitters and electricians working together and sharing tasks.
- Ownership of the new way of working by all the people has yet to be achieved.
- Disappointing lack of initiative from the shop-floor.
- General understanding of JIT and Kanban, but not much implementation.
- Union presence reduced but not eliminated.

Lessons
- People find it easy to see costs of changing to teamworking.
- Full benefits of teamworking yet to be manifested.
- Manufacturing operations happy with new approach.
- Design, marketing, commercial departments only half convinced.

- Tough going but helped enormously by support from senior managers in other areas.
- Operations management should have given more time and effort in communicating vision, mission and values.

Problems

The need for change　Alvis moved to a greenfield site in 1990, and we brought with us 70 years of engineering tradition and culture, so there was a clear need to change the way we operated to be more in line with what other companies were doing. We had visited Unipart and GEC Large Machines and seen that Alvis Vehicles wasn't keeping pace with other companies in the market place. Then we went through a redundancy, and in the aftermath we had the opportunity to generate change.

Business environment　Alvis had a traditional Midlands manu-facturing structure with the shop-floor tightly categorized into foremen, supervisors and line managers. The whole shop-floor organization worked on traditional methods and approaches, and there was little training. There was a strong union environment with shop steward meetings and union meetings, all run by the shop stewards, with very little communication between shop-floor and management. Working in operations, we didn't feel we had control of the business and I believed that teambuilding and teamworking would be one way of re-establishing this.

When we moved in 1990, Alvis Ltd split into business divisions and in 1992–93 these became three subsidiary limited companies under a small holding company. The outside business environ-ment was also changing: the Berlin Wall was coming down, defence budgets were being cut, and the spares market had virtually been eliminated in certain product lines. The market was very competitive, with fewer export opportunities and reducing British Army requirements. However, Alvis had a good range of products to offer. The Stalwart and the Saracen series were really products of the 1960s. The Scorpion was introduced in the 1970s and a large part of our product support and spares business was based on that. Nearly 4000 vehicles have been built and exported to foreign markets as well as supplied to the British Army. At its peak, Alvis produced as many as 10 vehicles per week over short periods. This reduced significantly to the current volume of about 5-6 vehicles per month (of similar products). Alvis products evolved through upgrades and various modifications and changes. There was no revolution in products coming onto the market. This is an industry in which it has always been very difficult to generate new products.

Functional organization   The old factory was about twice as large as the new one in acreage, with offices dotted about all over the place. The purchasing department and engineering department were in separate buildings, with quite long distances between departments and poor communication. The factory site was 70 years old so maintenance was poor; the general conditions were typical of automated industry of the 1970s and hadn't really changed since then. Everything was laid out by function and located on different floors and levels. Materials flow was a nightmare; we had stores in the basement, parts were moved around too much and inventory was excessive. Unfortunately, we brought much of that culture with us when we moved because it wasn't feasible to sort it out before relocating. We were realistic about bringing old habits to the new environment, and knew there would have to be culture change eventually. However, in a period when business levels were falling, the union representatives felt it was necessary to preserve jobs and maintain demarcations.

Action

Team-based working   We had to put forward a budget to the board in July 1992 showing how the business was going to be run over the next 18 months, so budget preparation started in spring.

We investigated new initiatives at the same time. We were preoccupied by the strength of the union movement at the time and one of my intentions, having seen how Unipart operated, was to reduce the influence of the union movement. That formed a significant part of the strategy. The intention was for teams and team leaders to replace the well-organized union network.

We carried out the task in two phases. The first phase was to reduce head count by about a third of the operational workforce. It was a question of how to handle that in as professional a way as possible, without too much disruption, so as not to demolish the reasonable goodwill that existed between management and unions at the time. The second phase was to generate a new culture based on flexibility and teams.

The redundancy programme   We wanted to restructure how the union operated and this was on the table during the redundancy programme. Because of the scale of the redundancy, we had to put a lot of issues on the back burner, and make compromises which didn't let us drive through all the culture changes we wanted. In the end, we had to let go of changing the way the union operated.

Setting up the teams   The team leaders were appointed in December 1992; the redundancy programme ran till the end of January and the timing, though unavoidable, created some hostility. To decide what teams we needed, we looked at current products and customers, then included the ones we were likely to be involved with in the next 12–18 months. We could readily identify 5 or 6 distinct project areas within the organization, so the concept was to introduce project teams based around these. Up to this point everything had been functional, with foremen for machining, welding, painting, electrical fitting, testing, stores, etc. Because machining provided a service to fabrications, and we had only a few machines, we couldn't really dedicate specific ones to individual projects, so we decided it wasn't applicable to generate a team in that area. We set up a machining team to provide a service, but of all the teams, it's the most similar to the previous function.

Responsibility for production was divided among four other product teams. Fabrication included welding and some processes such as shot peening, metal spraying and painting, all rolled into one team. This team had 24 people, which was too large; the ideal would have been about 12. Mod kits and services included the detail paint shop, the phosphating plant and the coppersmiths. This team also carried out spares and service operations for both Logistics and Aerospace, two of Alvis Vehicles' sister companies. The other teams were vehicle repair and overhaul including development, and production vehicle assembly and test, which was responsible for the assembly of the full vehicle once it had been passed over from fabrication. Both teams now included build and test. Previously the operators who built a vehicle passed it over for testing, and this led to lack of care over problems, shortages, etc. The stores team was added later. It has remained a functional area without particular product orientation.

Assessment and selection Up to the point of introducing a teambuilding process, we had four line managers. One of these was near retirement and one was made redundant and replaced by an engineering manager with project management experience. We made sure these managers were involved in selecting the team leaders. To kick off this process, we declared the 7 existing foremen and supervisors redundant and advertised the new position of team leader. Both ex-foremen and operators from the shop-floor were invited to apply, because this gave foremen an opportunity to avoid redundancy. The 18 applicants all went through a two-part selection process. The results of psychometric and aptitude tests were assessed by the managers and 10 candidates were invited to go forward and attend an assessment centre. We were advertising for 5 team leaders, and thought that candidates who didn't quite make leader would be considered for assistant team leader.

The assessment centre process involved six tasks—some in groups, some individual—a scheduling exercise, one-to-one structured interviews, dealing with a stroppy operator, group discussions: all designed to bring out the characteristics needed by team leaders. Selection went on late into the night and we finally selected four team leaders and three assistant team leaders. Only two of the previous foremen were selected, the rest were straight from the shop-floor. We ran the exercise again to appoint the machining team leader. This process was regarded quite cynically at first by the shop-floor. They found the rate of change difficult to cope with. Not only were they subjecting themselves to the possibility of redundancy through the selection process, but this was also a new way of working which they didn't really know about. In the end, they found the exercises in the assessment centre tough, but felt that the results were fair.

Team leaders had to adapt to a new role. Unlike foremen, they would not be supervisors but were expected to work hands-on as members of the teams; with additional responsibility for integrating and co-ordinating the team activities, developing project schedules, meeting targets, and the welfare, health and safety of the team. As part of the team, leaders felt it difficult to discipline their colleagues so this was still left to the managers.

Communications We held several briefing sessions for the workforce at which we sold team working as the best practice of other competitive manufacturing industries and gave examples. We told them we would provide training both for team leaders and the whole workforce to give them an understanding of best practice ideas, especially JIT and eliminating waste. It wasn't easy to achieve the critical mass necessary to get the whole thing off the ground. It took several training workshops before the message started to percolate through the organization. In all our communications we tried to sell the need to drive out areas of demarcation, to improve two-way communication between the shop-floor and the rest of the company, to solve problems, to improve quality and productivity by involvement and by transferring ownership of the problems into the areas with the necessary expertise, e.g. the shop-floor.

Training and development   We spent about £50K on training in 1993. Compared to some companies, that doesn't sound a lot, but to Alvis, which traditionally spent little on training, it was a significant improvement. We attacked training on several fronts. The line managers had not had a significant amount of exposure to modern manufacturing practices so they each attended a 1-week course in best manufacturing practices. This was followed up by a comprehensive programme of training for the team leaders, since they were regarded as pivotal in this new way of working. They all attended a 2-day seminar followed by a 1-day communication workshop. We also offered NEBSM courses, which were run off-site in conjunction with Jaguar Cars, but only three of the team leaders took this up. This has extended the vision of those attending, opening their minds to new ways of working and new ideas. The links with Jaguar have been fruitful. As part of the training programme we've exchanged visits with GEC Rugby, Rolls-Royce Ansty and Cummings Engines Daventry, as well as paying a return visit to Unipart late in 1992.

Other elements of the training programme included an off-site course in JIT for the team leaders, a 1-day course on set-up reduction and a special course for the stores team leader on stores inventory record accuracy. We also ran teambuilding courses at the Baginton test track site, where there is a training facility. This was a 2-day workshop run by a teambuilding consultant, involving a mixed group of operators and people from other functions such as purchasing and engineering. The group was asked to build a lego 'tank' using traditional Alvis methods, and then to discover for themselves how working in teams to solve problems and make decisions could revolutionize production. To date, we've run eight courses and these have been very powerful in binding together the message of JIT, new ways of working, and the power of a team. Overall, training has worked well with managers and team leaders, but it's been more difficult in other areas and even now we have little outbreaks of cynicism and small pockets of resistance still exist on the shop-floor.

Performance measures We ended up targeting specific reductions in lead time for fighting vehicles. There were bottlenecks on the shop-floor and there were excess inventories in significant areas, so throughput was a problem. At the time of the redundancies a typical throughput time for a vehicle was around 19 weeks from flat armour plate to a vehicle out of the workshop. This was probably not much different to what we achieved at the old Holyhead Road site. It was difficult to determine appropriate inventory levels and identify targets for reduction. In the early days we were more interested in lead time, the number of hours it took to do a job and improving quality.

Results

Introducing team leaders to replace foremen has worked well and has largely been accepted. They are able to add value to the business by contributing to the work hands-on, and are also able to introduce new ideas. The foremen, although they were good at their trade, were not the right vehicle for carrying forward the concept of change. Training for managers has also been a success, and has changed their way of thinking.

People have attended the JIT workshops and various other courses, but there has been a disappointing lack of initiative on the shop-floor to change the way we operate. There have been improvements in housekeeping, as well as more flexibility and less demarcation, with electricians and mechanical fitters working together and exchanging tasks. In other areas where I expected more change, especially in adopting JIT philosophies, maybe the odd Kanban square and the concept of pulling work through the shop floor, change has been difficult to achieve, even in isolated areas. We set up 'presentation rooms' on the shop-floor, one in the old foremen's office, and we've held briefing sessions there. This room was intended as a showcase for charts and team information, but this hasn't happened, so there's still lack of ownership. The feedback from teams has probably not been well organized. We have not been able to capture some suggestions and methods for improvement and this is being changed in 1994. The union presence has been reduced but certainly not eliminated.

Lessons

There are certain areas where we hesitated early on and we've learned that you can never get the situation totally perfect before launching an initiative. That caused us to delay the introduction of essential changes. We were surprised that the shop-floor did not want to take the initiative but waited to be led and there were occasions when we had ideas but we didn't follow them through. The evidence is that they would have been reasonably well received had we done so. For example, we didn't insist that team leaders held regular briefing and feedback sessions, but waited for them to take the initiative. That is being corrected in 1994.

Another failing was that we didn't set firm targets at the start, however unrealistic they might have been; we only came to this later. We knew what we wanted to achieve but it was difficult to quantify this in terms of inventory levels, productivity, etc.

Perhaps we could have taken a tougher line on certain aspects, such as demarcation. We allowed a lot of consultation and discussion since we didn't want to corrupt the team approach. Finding the balance between dictating what should happen and allowing teams to talk things through is quite difficult. We introduced a newsletter in March 1993 and have had two editions since then. It was well received when issued, but its preparation has been quite difficult because people are not willing to contribute articles or suggestions. We realize now that we should have given responsibility for its preparation to the teams.

We haven't been able to get areas outside operations involved or interested in what we are trying to do. We haven't really had full backing: support has tended to be arm's length rather than wholehearted. It's been hard to keep the teaming initiative going at times. When production targets have been missed or teambuilding has almost seemed to get in the way of production, it's been tempting to wonder whether it has been worth the effort, but the answer to that is certainly yes. It's provided us with a theme, a concept for moving forward, and it will undoubtedly form the basis of how we intend to operate in the future. One of the key things with teambuilding is trust, and barriers between management and shop-floor teams have been broken down. That helps new project introduction and improves communication and feedback. One of our key tasks now is to harness the feedback and do something with it.

The verdict of the market-place

The business outlook for the defence industry as a whole is quite dodgy. No one in defence can feel secure. We have a reasonably full order book for most of 1994, but beyond that firm orders are yet to be placed. This picture is being explained and shared among the workforce. As a result of our communications initiative, people are confident that we are telling the truth, and that's coming through quite strongly. Everyone is interested in the long-term future of the business, but the outlook remains difficult. That doesn't stop us from improving manufacturing on the order book we've got.

BAKER PERKINS LTD

Peterborough
Bob Gore
Production Manager 1979–89, Manufacturing Director, 1989–92

Context

Baker Perkins was an early pioneer of cell manufacture, starting in the 1960s. Its manufacturing benefited significantly from cells and applied them profitably to a highly successful range of printing machines that were developed in the 1980s.

Problems
- The potential market and sales growth for the new range of printing machines developed between 1979 and 1983 demanded a 300–400 per cent increase in manufacturing capacity from the same floor space, and at least a 50 per cent reduction in lead time.
- Long set-up times on critical components were adding to the problems.

Action
- Focus on core activities.
- Baker Perkins Printing Machinery Limited extended cell manufacture to 80 per cent of components and assemblies that were critical to performance and customer service.
- The remaining undifferentiated processes, components and product were contracted to preferred suppliers.

Results
- Core component lead times and final assembly lead times were reduced by 4 : 1.
- A fourfold volume increase in printing machine manufacture was achieved from the sale space.

Lessons
- 'Be more aggressive.'
- 'Focus on core products and subcontract the rest out.'
- 'Go for a genuine cell that makes a finished product.'
- *'Although we had probably the most efficient printing press manufacturing plant in the world, we lost the market and we were closed. Knowing and keeping in touch with your markets and customers is vital!'*

Company history

Baker Perkins at Peterborough was a highly successful and profitable business, with markets and operations worldwide. They developed and manufactured a wide range of equipment used mainly in the food processing industry. They also had a printing machinery business producing a range of offset-litho machines for full colour magazine printing. Three separate limited companies were formed in 1985:

Baker Perkins Bakery Ltd
Baker Perkins BCS Ltd (Biscuit, Confectionery and Snack)
Baker Perkins PMC Ltd (Printing Machinery).

Baker Perkins merged with APV in 1987 and the printing business was sold to Rockwell Graphics in early 1989.

Baker Perkins was one of the pioneers of cell manufacture. Their first cell, for manufacturing a family of shaft-like components, became operational in 1967. Over the next 25 years they went on to extend cell manufacture to over 80 per cent of component manufacture and assembly activities on their range of printing machines. Bob Gore describes what happened.

The inspiration for cells

Alan Eldred really started it all. He was Component Manufacturing and Production Engineering Manager and did his degree at Aston University at a time when they were heavily into group technology. When Alan came back into the company on completing his education he was fired up on group technology cells and was looking for an application. The shaft line was the first cell because a lot of our products in Baker Perkins—machinery for confectionery, biscuit, bakery and printing—used lots of small shafts. Alan identified a range of shafts that would fit into a family group. A sufficient number of parts qualified and there was enough work volume to put together a group technology cell with machines that could make shafts from raw material to a completed item. I believe that right from the start we were delivering a complete component in 90 per cent of cases. This was 1967 and 1968.

Actions and results

The shaft cell Right from day 1 the shaft cell was advanced. It has a U-shaped conveyor system which allowed us to advance or hold back shafts. If we put something on the front end of the line we didn't have to keep it in that sequence if our priorities changed. All the shafts followed basically the same route: facing and centring, straightening, turning, grinding, mill and drill. However, if we missed out steps we had the ability to move things around on the conveyors.

We had key machines like CNC lathes and grinders loaded to capacity. The majority of other machines were regarded as secondary operation machines. In most cases these were quite old but they had flexible tooling especially developed for the cell. Some machines were probably 80 per cent idle. However, with flexibility of labour to move around as and when required, a completed product came out of the cell ready for assembly.

We finally ended up with our key operations on DNC (direct numerical control) with a direct link through a file server for the NC programming, but also linked into our business system. A man could come in at the start of the shift, look at the work available to him in priority sequence, decide the most efficient way of tackling it, pull down all his programs (12 programs can be stored on a machine), set up a full shift's work, tell the business system that he'd loaded it, and then, as he finished each job, record its completion through a PC mounted at his machine which automatically loaded it to the next machine in the cell. For cell management, the cell leader was provided with a PC in his office. This was linked to the file server and he controlled his cell by releasing work into the front of the cell. He would access the business system, pull down from the work available and load it into his file server once a day. He controlled how much work went in and when there was an overload he could siphon some of that off and put it out to subcontract.

Before we had the shaft cell it was taking 12 days for each operation, and 6 to 10 weeks to make a complete shaft. With a good cell leader who was prepared to manage what we launched, the average lead time through the shaft cell dropped to about 12 days.

Discs and gears   We used the shaft cell to learn how to apply cell manufacturing. The next two cells followed the same way; we identified other families of parts using the same approach. We identified two more groupings, discs and gears, which were as clear-cut as shafts. We defined a disc as a part having a diameter at least two-and-a-half times its length, plus a maximum length of 15 inches and diameter greater than 3 inches. That threw up a big family. A large percentage of those discs, probably 20–25 per cent went on to have tooth cutting, that is gears and chain wheels, so we created a related cell which would take the output and carry out some special finishing operations, and this was the gear cell. The shaft, disc and gear cells were developed when we were a single company with four divisions manufacturing a wide range of equipment for bakery, biscuit and confectionery and chemical plant, and a relatively small, young business, printing machines.

The printing machine business   In the early 1980s Baker Perkins developed a market-beating range of printing machines called the 'G' series. They sold very well, especially in the USA, and growth was swift and dramatic. A printing press line comprised a line of four to eight printing units and a folder, integrated and managed by a computer-based control system.

We decided that if we were going to produce printing presses really efficiently we needed to extend cell manufacture to making printing cylinders, side frames, gears, eccentric housings and bearings. We determined to be top class at these and to subcontract everything else for JIT supply of kits of components to complete one press, and substantial benefits in lead time reduction were achieved.

Printing machines look pretty standard because every print unit has the same basic components, but there's a lot of variability. Different printing markets produce different sizes of magazines and periodicals. The biggest difference is between A4 in Europe and the old quarto in America. That changes the width and circumference of the cylinder which in turn changes the position of the main bores in the frames, the gears and gear centres. Cylinders, gears and frames were long lead time, high value items. They were customer specific and we had to find a way of making them quickly. Everything else would be made largely for stock or would be supplied as a kit of parts, often by subcontractors.

The cylinder cell   In 1984 we moved cylinder assembly in with cylinder machining to create a genuine cell that took a raw forging right through to a complete assembly, with its gear and its bearings mounted on it, wrapped up and ready to go onto a printing unit. Then we looked at the cell and worked out what we had to do in order to reduce lead time. A cylinder goes through a number of stages. The first stage includes turning the forging, then stainless welding, coating the periphery with stainless steel, turning, grinding, and then an inspection to check quality of welding. The second stage starts with a deep hole bored through the length of the cylinder near the periphery to take the lock-up mechanism, followed by turning of the journals and then a series of complex milling operations which at one time were done on five machines with something like 12 or 14 set ups. What we did was find a machining centre with capacity to do all the second stage operations. Alan Eldred, who specified the process, reduced the set-ups from 14 to 2. The process included automatic probing of the cylinder datums that the NC program worked from and greatly simplified the fixture design to minimize the set-up time.

Working with forging suppliers to reduce lead time and cost   Cylinders are fairly complex and start with forgings costing

£1000 each and weighing between 1000 and 1500 kg. Cylinder circumference ranges from 580 up to 630 mm on the small units and from 1160 to 1260 mm on the larger ones. What our conscientious design and production engineers did was develop a range of individual forgings sized with the cylinders to give us the lowest cylinder cost with minimum machining. However, in many situations we could not order the forgings until we knew what size cylinders we wanted. So we asked ourselves what would happen if, for example, with a family of units like our G14 press, we went to one size of forging—the biggest we could use in length and circumference—and turned that down to suit any cylinder. We were then able to go to our forge master and say, 'We're going to make X number of units this year, with four cylinders per unit.' We gave an advance order for a minimum of say 200 and a maximum of 300, with ability to call them off at 4 days notice. How much the supplier stocked was up to him. We reduced the price from £1000 to £850 per forging, with JIT delivery. We didn't have to worry about forgings any more, but just needed to know how many G14 units we were going to make, looking forward 3 months. We only ever had one press-worth maximum of forgings sitting outside the cylinder shop and we started the first ones within 2 or 3 days and absorbed a whole eight unit press line of 32 forgings in 2 to $2^{1}/_{2}$ weeks. In 1983, when we had a loosely defined cylinder cell we were looking at 15 months from ordering of forging to completing the cylinder. We got that down to a standard time of 8 weeks and we could produce a complete cylinder for a spare in 3 days.

The frame cell Frames are made from big castings, 3 m by $1^{1}/_{2}$ m. We had a plano-mill to do rough milling, an Asquith to do rough boring, and then we used a Burqhardt jig borer, a relatively slow and out-of-date machine, for final boring. We then went back onto the Asquith to do all the drilling and tapping, so we had big bulky frames with a lot of movement and a lot of set ups. It used to take somewhere between 12 and 16 weeks to process enough for one press.

We had to get to a point where we could make frames in no more time than it took to make cylinders, and ideally quicker. However, frames vary not only in size, but are a bit like a Swiss cheese, full of bored, drilled and tapped holes, the position and size of which vary with customer order. We were looking for minimum throughput time for enough frames to make a press and one of the keys to that was set-up time. This was long, because it required lots of adjustment, packing and clamping. We replaced our complex fixturing with a table laid out with eight big magnets and datums for end and side locations. All we had were sheets of aluminium with cut outs to suit each type of frame that was placed on the magnets. In the cut outs we put pole pieces that supported the frame and got the right distribution to miss the main bores. So to set up a frame, we just had to clear off the old set up, put on a new aluminium plate, place the pole piece in the cut outs, slide a frame on, and switch on the magnets. The piece was clamped in position and we could do that through all stages of set up. When we finished, we needed just one big Waldrich Seigen machine from raw casting to a finished frame. Once we got the Waldrich Seigen up and fully operational, lead time dropped to 3 weeks. Process time went down from over 60 hours to $22^1/_2$ hours to complete the machining of a pair of front and rear frames from raw castings. But of course it was an expensive machine requiring capital investment.

The link cell Our next cell was for manufacturing families of components made from profile flame cut and surface ground blanks. It had machining and assembly operations to produce the levers, links and arms used on printing machines. This cell brought together all the many link-type components needed in a set of presses, which meant that they could be made as machine sets rather than as batches scattered through the shop. Using the old method, we could get 30 per cent of what we needed to build a printing unit complete. But the remainder was still scattered all over the shop and pulling together a set of links for one unit was a nightmare. The big advantage of the link cell was that it gave us control. We finished up with a cell with first-class operators, two on days and two on nights. They got to know the complete packages and they could get a complete unit's worth of links through within about $1^1/_2$ weeks. If things were desperate, they could do it in 3 days.

The box cell   Over 3 or 4 years, the folders for printing presses got steadily more complex. They were more flexible, with more remote adjustment, which brought in much more complex folding cylinders and generated a whole new range of components that needed a lot of machining. A common link between these components was that they had a lot of milling, drilling and tapping and some fairly complex shapes had to be generated. These became another family of parts where we could set up a cell with machining centres which could take a raw block and do all the machining in either one or two stages.

Teamworking   As we started to produce more units, floor space became critical. We wanted four units a week and they take up a lot of space so we had to find a way of assembling them more quickly. We could no longer take 12 weeks to produce a unit. We had quite a large team flitting on and off a unit: fitters doing one bit then disappearing, electricians coming on. We had too many people working on a unit, but no one saw the task through from start to test and out of the door. To resolve this, we employed two fitters who stayed with a unit from start to finish. The next thing we recognized was that the assembly shop was organized so that every man had his own workplace with a fixed bench. He'd go back to his own workbench for tea breaks or if he'd forgotten anything. To overcome this we bought portable workbenches to accommodate two fitters and these were taken to the unit. Every team on a unit was like a machine cell. They would call for electricians, coppersmiths, sheet metal workers, or finishing operations on sheet metal work as they needed them. The key was that the two assigned fitters kept everything moving along. As a result the standard lead time dropped to 4 weeks from 12 to 16 weeks. We could build a unit in 2 weeks and the fastest ever was $4^1/_2$ days.

Specialist cells   We also decided to set up a number of cells specializing in making subassemblies like colour register mechanisms, inking systems, oscillating mechanisms, to spread the ink evenly on the rollers. These were fairly complex mechanisms and we achieved a 20 to 25 per cent reduction in process time.

The electronics cell   The 'G12' range of presses was developed in the mid 1980s. They incorporated major advances in the control system, using fibre optics and shifting the emphasis of control even more from metalwork to software. Schematic design had always been done in Peterborough and detailed design in Newcastle, at our specialist control panel unit. As we moved into programmable logic control technology, more of the design was done in Peterborough and communications became a problem, especially with more sophisticated controls using in-house designed printed circuit boards and fibre optic communications. We also had greater volumes, to the point where it was viable to set up a separate unit for programmable logic controls. It was really driven by seeking to eliminate communication problems, to get engineering involved directly with the people building the controls, and to get engineering in one location, where it could work to solve quality problems.

We took on a 20 000 sq ft industrial unit, created a small stores for fragile electronics, with an area for electronics development and testing of printed circuit boards. We installed a number of subassembly stations with an area for testing finished panels and came up with a layout which gave a logical U-shaped workflow. What we didn't realize was that, by accident, we had created a perfect cell, which was fully equipped to do everything from start to finish. It was set up as a flow line, controlling everything from start to finish. The people were co-located in one area with everything they needed and they worked as an increasingly effective team. The work-to list was of good quality and we could actually believe in it. We got JIT deliveries from the control panel building unit. They didn't finish all eight panels needed for a press worth of units and send them for assembly the same day; they could issue two panels, two more 3 days later, and so on: so 8 panels would be launched and fed in over a period of 12 days, in line with assembly build requirements.

Within 4 months of opening the PLC electronics cell, we solved all the major quality problems, so quality improved dramatically. Damage in transit had been a major problem. Working together, the design team discovered the cause and redesigned the control units to prevent this and to make unit assembly much easier. The cell team worked progressively and almost completely eliminated defects. The team saw the job through from start to finish, took on all the tasks, and accepted the need for skills flexibility.

Lessons

Starting again, I would be much more aggressive in focusing on the key components/subassemblies and subcontracting everything else out. Rather than looking for families of components, I'd go for a cell that makes a subassembly which is a finished product, like the cylinder cell. For a complex engineered product with a lot of assembly, the critical thing affecting ability to deliver quality products on time is having a complete kit of parts. Pulling together and delivering kits of parts is a hugely complex problem. Focusing on critical items and subcontracting the rest simplifies in-house management and puts the burden onto the sub-contractor.

Departmental managers, senior production engineers and people in assembly certainly understood the need to be as efficient as possible, and to keep quality as high as possible. Conflict sometimes comes when they see work going out that could have been done in-house; that's a barrier to be overcome. When you get a cell working well and focused, the conflict goes. Try pushing work that doesn't quite fit into a cell and the cell leader will turn round and say, 'Hey! why are you making my life difficult. Stop messing me about!'

The verdict of the market-place

Baker Perkins PMC Ltd was radical in introducing cells and teaming. We got market leadership in a narrow market, giving good profitable volume. Then we started trying to expand, but we didn't make a very good job of developing one particular machine, the G12. In striving to broaden our market, we lost sight of the fact that our bread-and-butter product—the G14—was being caught and overtaken technologically. This put us in a weaker position than we should have been. Our new owner started to realize that some of our products weren't as good as they should have been and that we were no longer as strong in the market-place. Although we had probably the most efficient printing press manufacturing plant in the world, we lost out in the market-place and were closed. Knowing and keeping in touch with your markets and customers is vital! A company can be good at manufacturing, but that doesn't mean a thing if it's a lame product and not in the right market-place.

BRITISH AEROSPACE REGIONAL AIRCRAFT

Hatfield, Hertfordshire
Mike Hodgson
Head of Operations 1987–92

Context

Hatfield was the lead site for manufacture of the BAe 146. Traditional culture: 'We make the 146', was dragging us down. Corporate rationalization plans had put the site's survival under threat.

Problems
- Our costs were too high.
- We were taking too long to build the product.
- We had far too much inventory.
- The problem was 'us'!

Actions
- Reorganization into focused businesses.
- Inventory reduction.
- Cycle time reduction.
- Make vs buy.
- Team-based cell working enabled through people development.

Results
- Lead time for final assembly of aircraft reduced from 20 weeks to 12 weeks.
- Inventory reduced by £124 million in 1 year.
- Pilot cell: passenger and service doors:
  - Lead time down from 16 weeks to 7 weeks.
  - Work in progress down from 82 doors to 16 doors.
  - Delivery conformance: finished sets of doors down from 8 to 3.
  - Quality: defects down from 5 to 1 per cent.

Lessons
- We should have been harder, sooner.
- Despite the improvement, Hatfield closed.
- Developing and empowering people works.

Evolution of the change initiative
During the early 1980s everyone was totally preoccupied with getting the BAe 146 into production so there was not much room

for change. The 146 was manufactured using a traditional manufacturing approach which was reinforced as the task progressed. Building the 146 was very hard work for managers. We got up early for meetings, and shouted and bawled at each other. I used to sit in meetings thinking 'I can't carry on like this until I'm 60'. Nobody was enjoying it. We had some bright people but we didn't know any other way of doing it and had no other skills at our disposal. We were permanently running to meet targets. Nevertheless, we got some results and made the aeroplane, albeit inefficiently.

Actions

The turning point came in 1987 when the production department was incorporated into a larger 'operations' unit and areas such as quality and overall cost (as opposed to just man hours), came under my control. This change was pivotal because it added all sorts of dimensions to the job role which we started to view in terms of how to deploy policy. This got the operations group thinking about new trends in manufacturing and how they were applicable to us. We had already been running team building events for two years and this procedure had proved incredibly valuable for teaming, setting goals at the senior level and gaining executive team commitment. It was a big, powerful tool and we didn't recognize how important it was in those early days.

We managed to put the team development ahead of engineering issues. By gaining commitment to the abstract behavioural issues early on, our progress was more rapid when we turned our attention to the more mechanical, engineering aspects of manufacturing change.

It seems accidental that a group of people came together at Hatfield who saw an opportunity and made it germinate, grow and blossom. We were reading literature and casting about for ways of change. Then we invited two consultancy groups to make presentations showing how they would approach the task of making us world class performers. We didn't know what world class meant then, but we knew it had to be bloody good! Later we established a clear definition of world class which everyone accepted. Our work with consultants proved that change wasn't going to be as easy as we had thought, but we started to get some ideas and most of us were committed to making them work.

The team was a mixed bunch and some were more convinced of the need to change than others. There was also considerable anxiety around the 'what', 'how', and 'effect on me' issues. We discovered that some people can really obstruct reorganization and that change of personnel can be a benefit. Under these circumstances, a number of people left and we were able to reorganize and balance the team. We decided to appoint some younger people and our team building process allowed them to integrate rapidly and apply their energies to the change process. This team created and owned a top level plan, set some goals, and entered the fray by attacking inventory, flow time, quality and cost issues. We used these as the key drivers.

One of the most important things is making a commitment to action. You can only talk for so long, you can do benchmarking trips to see other companies, and hold endless planning meetings, but in the end you have to make a commitment and do something, pull a lever, start to make it happen. In too many companies, managers are strangely reluctant to pull any levers, but repeatedly keep putting off action decisions. This is an issue of 'pressure for change' and several elements need to reach 'critical mass' before people will move. At Hatfield we had a group that wanted to move, and we started with inventory reduction.

Inventory reduction We found we couldn't reduce inventory quickly enough within the line organization because people were too distracted by their daily tasks, so we used a project team approach. Team members worked closely with the functions and this was a great success, with total inventory reduction of £124 million. We started to get some scores on the board by doing focused projects which gave us confidence, and proved to people that we were serious about change.

Quality improvement programme   When a new general manager was appointed, his attitude was not to interfere, but to let us get on with running the factory. However, one of the things he did was probably more powerful than he or we ever realized. He gave his full support to the introduction of a quality improvement programme. The education and development were intensive, and the top team persuaded the general manager to stand up and make a wholehearted commitment to the initiative, saying that he was never going to let us down. Total quality was critical to the success of our change programme. It meant that everyone from top to bottom in the organization set out to solve problems in the same way. The values stressed in quality improvement were particularly important. It established the planks of a cultural change which were reinforced through active participation in quality improvement studies.

Accountability and performance measures   One very important change which we didn't understand fully at the time was the decision to reorganize the site into three separate businesses according to product:

Supply   The manufacture and supply of major assemblies
Final assembly   Aircraft assembly to first flight
Customization   Configuring aircraft to match customer specifications

Breaking the business up like this allowed us to get focus and accountability right, but still we never gave the separate businesses enough financial responsibility. They were accountable for programme, man hours, and quality, but never actually for pounds. The business managers should have been responsible for reporting on the cost of the product, unit cost, purchases, etc. Because the general manager was not part of the process, but simply didn't interfere, we never gained his influence to get top people outside operations, such as the finance director, more than superficially involved. In the end our results were so good that these people came along themselves and wanted to join in. We used to hear comments like, 'It's all right for you guys in operations, you belong to a team! Everything's great in there, but we don't belong to your team.' We took advantage of this, and were close to implementing a system of cell performance measures—whereby the cell team members measured their own key performance indicators—quality, quality improvement, utilization, inventory, flow time, schedule and cost.

Implementing the cells Consolidating the lessons we had learned from flow time and inventory reduction by putting in cell manufacturing was the next major phase. This meant detailed organization change, and that was a huge adjustment. We had no idea how much preparation it was going to take in order to get a single cell in place. In reality, introducing cells was more complex than we anticipated and required a high level of teamwork. This meant assessment, selection and development of the right people, particularly the team leader; communicating a new set of values; and then getting to grips with all the issues of lead time and quality, delegation and performance monitoring. It's a lot to take on board and people can't do it all straight away. To keep track of where we were, we used a matrix with green, amber, and red colour coding, where green was what we had in place, amber was what we were preparing, and red what we hadn't started.

We used a 'layering' technique. We selected the most important issue at the time, cleared it, then selected the next issue and cleared it. By training people and letting them use their new skills, we layered in one level of sophistication at a time and *made sure it was robust and sustainable before moving on.* In too many companies, projects are completed in a hurry and then fall over, and everybody wonders what happened. We never made that mistake at Hatfield; we took as long as we needed to make a thing work, if we didn't get it right we slipped the programme till it did work. We set a very high standard. It took 18 months to plan and install the first cell, and involved clearing many industrial relations and personnel issues and considerable learning on our part. Once the cells were on the conveyor belt, they actually started to get up and running very quickly. We didn't want any 'white line' cells, where somebody painted a white line around an area on the floor and just called it a cell. We had a matrix of all the items that had to be functioning before a cell was worthy of the name. When all the items were checked off the list, then we could truly say we had a functioning cell. Otherwise it was still called a 'development area'. We didn't kid ourselves because we knew that if we did, we wouldn't get results that affected the bottom line and standards for our people to meet would be set too low.

Pilot cell   We used passenger and service door manufacture as a pilot cell to prove the concepts of cell working and to develop planning and implementation methodologies. When we set up the doors pilot cell, we worried about using an ex-foreman as the cell leader. Perhaps he was not the best person, but his selection did give people confidence that they might also be able to get cell leader jobs. We worried about taking away the symbolism of the foreman wearing a white coat. In the end, it all worked and it was very satisfying to see the pilot cell achieving twice the effectiveness of our traditional approach. The team didn't look any busier but measurements proved they were getting through twice as much work. They were now working smarter not faster!

We did make an improvement with every cell we put in, but we were kidding ourselves if we thought we were operating at the sort of performance levels we should have been reaching. I felt that once we had the framework across the factory we would then put pressure on teams to get better performance. There was still much more we could have achieved. Man hours could have been lower, and looking back, we could have moved faster, we felt too comfortable with our achievements on lead time, inventory reduction and quality improvement.

The Cranfield Fellowship   We recognized that we'd never implement such a major change programme without enough people with the right attitudes, knowledge and skills. To make sure we had them, we used assessment centres to pick people from both outside and within the industry who showed potential, and designed a specific Cranfield University Fellowship programme—a 9-week intensive course followed by 9 months of work experience on a relevant project—to bring them up to speed. This was a unique strategic approach which paid dividends. People who attended the fellowship invariably stayed with the company long after their training was complete. We empowered these young people and gave them real jobs where they could actually do something. Cranfield provided accelerated learning, it didn't give them the in-depth education that comes from gaining a further degree, but it equipped people and gave them enough confidence to go out and implement change.

We were meticulous in our selection process for the Cranfield Fellows. The operations executives acted as the assessors so they had ownership of the decisions made about the people selected for training. They couldn't take an 'us and them' attitude towards the young people because they had been responsible for selecting them. I'm very much a believer in aligned learning and I think it's critical if you are going to spend the company's money to get the trainees to work on projects in the plant and stay close to the business all the time they are being educated. This means they make a real contribution and have credibility when they are assigned a permanent role. Cranfield really came off.

Getting people to support the change   We were always very open about what we were doing. There was as much honesty as there could be; we admitted that jobs would go, and showed that there was no option. We set up a 'control room' where we displayed information about what we were doing to improve and monitored our achievements. Everyone had access to this room, which remained the focal point for the change project for 4 years. As development progressed, the general manager did a series of briefings and the operations executives ran road shows, using Lego models of the new plant to show where cells would be, and identifying the skills and competences each team would need. Our quality control manager was an ex-shop steward and he was a perfect barometer of how the shop-floor would react to any communication and was able to pinpoint the really awkward questions that would be asked so we were able to prepare answers to them. It was useful to have somebody who could keep our feet on the ground.

We got the involvement of the shop-floor by taking them on awareness visits to other companies, such as Rolls-Royce, IBM, Royal Ordnance and Nissan so they could see the new way of working in action. Then the Works Convenor, other shop stewards and managers undertook a benchmarking study tour to the USA. After the first few cells were functioning, people on the shop-floor were proud to tell visitors to the Hatfield site about their success and this was an important motivational issue. One of the lessons I've learned is how important it is to be consistent in communicating the message. At Hatfield, we kept faith with the objectives. Our communications were absolutely consistent and in the end we gained credibility, not by what we said, but by what we did.

Empowering the people At Hatfield we practised empowerment, putting responsibility for actions and results back into the factory, to the point where I no longer needed to know where anything was in the factory or whether an aeroplane was going to fly next week (previously I always felt obliged to know). I left that to the people in charge. My real role was concentrating on process improvements. I felt very uncomfortable about it at first, but when I got used to it I understood that making the primary level responsible for quality and output is the most powerful thing you can ever do. Managers who empower their people can suffer during cultural transition because their colleagues who don't understand what they're doing see them as weak managers. This attitude has to shift, because it makes the wrong attitudes self-perpetuating. It is reinforced in 'unreformed' companies where managers promote people in their own mould. *I see my role now as holding an umbrella over my key people, to shield them from criticism, so that they can get on with creative thinking and management of change.* I have to 'keep the rain off them' so they can get on with the job. Plenty of people talk about empowerment but can't practice it. It's a buzzword so it just trips off their lips but they have no idea how to make it happen. Teaching people a mechanism almost by rote such as our total quality initiative at Hatfield, which they then practice, helps to get these ideas accepted. It gave us a framework to work in, with simple rules.

Getting overheads out   We didn't have any pressures which were forcing us, so we used a slow approach to taking labour out, and we only did it at the end, once we'd switched on the capability for the organization to run successfully without those people. We felt that an aggressive reduction at the same time as initial cell implementation would have caused a backlash of non-co-operation. In any event, large numbers were being lost with the closure of final assembly at Hatfield. When we had all the capability available at primary level, we began to hold planning meetings where we debated how to get the surplus people out. To plot the operation, we set up a T-card manning board with the names of all employees and managed the redundancies, giving people all the advice and assistance we could about getting another job.

A piece of unfinished work   And then it was all over ... the whole site was scheduled for closure. If we'd had another 18 months we'd have pulled all those people out and the business would have looked scintillating. That's why I feel Hatfield was a piece of unfinished work. Sometimes I wonder if it would have turned out differently if we'd attacked it the other way around, getting the people and overheads out first and then driving in the improvements. In retrospect, when the consultants at Hatfield told us we had about 650 people too many for the business, we might have taken an immediate cut, to show we meant business. We were too gentlemanly, too slow in biting the bullet on some of those issues, and that is something I would do differently now. Perhaps we indulged rather too much in the total process and the excellence of every aspect of change. I think we could have had more of a financial edge; we could have been sharper and harder in our approach. Our presentation of product cost was weak in that factory product cost was burdened with overall project infrastructure. Identifying the activity based cost would have been helpful to illustrate and interpret.

Results

It might seem like all the good things that we did at Hatfield went up in a puff of smoke and disappeared in the wind, but that simply is not true. Many of the people involved have moved on to other jobs and are applying their considerable expertise in new roles, within the company on the 146 aircraft production at Woodford and with BAe Airbus at Filton, Manchester and Chester, as well as other industries altogether, or indeed as consultants. BAe has always been prone to the 'not invented here' syndrome, but the dispersal of so many talented people around the company who have the philosophy of cells, teaming, total quality and continuous improvement embedded in them is helping to dispel that attitude and there are many case studies of operational detail that are relevant.

Judging by the number of times participants are still asked to speak about the project, people are starting to realize that they never really appreciated just what an achievement Hatfield was in this industry, how far ahead it was. Even Boeing has initiated its development of contemporary practice by establishing a manufacturing cell making aircraft doors. The business climate caused by recession has made change imperative. Many of the approaches taken at Hatfield are providing useful case studies. There is not an operations director in the company who doesn't recognize and appreciate the value of contemporary manufacturing methods, but the challenge lies in making it happen.

Mike Hodgson is now Head of Manufacturing Engineering at British Aerospace, Chester.

BRITISH AEROSPACE REGIONAL AIRCRAFT LTD

Woodford
Pre-Equipped Wing Section
Matthew Holmes
MSc Project: March 1992–August 1993

Context
The opportunity to apply the principles of cells and teams as part of an MSc course.

Problems
- Shortages
- Lack of production engineering support
- Long lead times
- Poor quality
- Poor motivation of operators

Actions
- Dedicated logistics and production engineering support for the cell.
- Break down the traditional barriers between supervisor and operators.
- Communication to generate enthusiasm and improve motivation.
- Team agreement on performance measures and targets to be achieved.

Results
- Lead time down from 12 weeks to 3 weeks.
- Scrap and rework down 70 per cent.
- Number of sets in progress halved.
  (Labour hours per set down approximately 40 per cent)
- No significant capital expenditure

Lessons

- Motivation and willingness to take responsibility increased when people worked in teams.
- People saw for themselves how dedicated logistics and engineering support improved results.
- Cost benefits were not quantified, owing to so many complex factors in the business.
- Problems with one major supplier were difficult to overcome.

Situation

British Aerospace Regional Aircraft's Woodford site carries out final assembly of 146 Regional Jet Aircraft. Wings for the aircraft arrive in sets from Textron in Nashville, Tennessee, with electrical looms, air, de-icing and hydraulic systems already installed. The task of the pre-equipped wing section is to prepare the wings for final assembly and perform basic function checks. On the leading edge, the team fit the pylons and the shoulder cowls to hold the engines and connect all the services between the shoulder cowl and the wing. On the trailing edge, they fit the flap tracks and the carriages, the flap, the spoilers and the ailerons and do the initial rigging of these flying control surfaces. Matthew Holmes became the Supervisor of this Section in March 1992. He was studying the principles of cells and teaming as part of an MSc course at Warwick University and took the opportunity to apply as many of them as possible in his new role. This case study shows what one person can achieve *with no significant capital expenditure* by working through a series of initiatives aimed at motivating people, making them accountable for their own actions and giving them the power to influence results.

Actions and results

The starting point   When I took on the pre-equipped wing section, it comprised a group of 25 operators, 2 inspectors, a night shift of 8 and, later, 3 electricians. The section was taking up to 12 weeks to equip one wing set. Often, shortages meant that the set was taken for wing join up to the aircraft before it was complete. The group of 30 people were often working on seven sets of wings at one time, one or two sets in the section, and the rest already fitted to the aircraft before they were complete.

Parts supply Because parts supply was handled centrally, it was difficult to identify what parts were *really* wanted, and which would seriously hold up production if we didn't receive them. Progress chasers split their work by type; basic operations, handwritten orders, rejects, etc., rather than by area, e.g. pre-equipped wings. As a result, no one person had a comprehensive list of shortages for the pre-equipped wing section.

Production engineering support The production engineering team of five or six people answered queries for the whole track. They used a simple method of prioritizing their work: the next aircraft to go into final assembly was always the most important. Therefore, queries from the pre-equipped wing section were rarely answered unless they were holding up production. Replies to requests for repair or planning queries regularly took 2 or 3 weeks. We had two problems here. First, jobs were stopped until they became critical, and this demotivated the workers, because they never seemed to be able to finish what they started. Then suddenly we'd get an answer and everything would be urgent again. Second, as it took 2 or 3 weeks to get an answer to a production related query, we never had any incentive for 'what-if' thinking, because we knew we would never have any access to development advice from production engineers.

Quality Rejects and scrap were high. The operators were scrapping 5 or 6 items a day. Their attitude was 'Nobody seems to care if I get it wrong, so it must not matter if I do.' Some were small things like brackets incorrectly drilled, but also bolts or subassemblies, scrapped either because they had been wrong on receipt or they had been damaged in assembly. Requests for replacement parts were processed very slowly. In addition, snags highlighted by inspectors after completion meant taking people off the section to do repairs on wings which had been attached to aircraft. The people who caused the snags were not necessarily the ones who were asked to repair them, so nobody was learning how to eliminate the same snags next time.

Motivation Production engineers had the power to grant requests for repair, and to hold up operators' work when design queries weren't answered. Operators felt that there was no reason why they should worry about quality or lead time when production engineers weren't giving them the support they felt they were entitled to have.

Performance monitoring The only official information available for the pre-equipped wing section was labour-hours booked against each set of wings. There were no details about the number of snags, number of concessions, number of engineering queries, etc.

Diagnosis Two areas were causing the most problems: parts supply and production engineering support. All the other problems—quality, lead time, even motivation—could be traced back to these root causes. The principles of cells and teaming were needed to help people feel responsible for improving performance so that we could achieve lead time and quality targets. But a team-based cell wouldn't work unless the operators felt they were getting the right support, both from their manager and from other areas. I wanted people to treat work in the same way they might treat playing football in the park on Saturday, and to put a bit of effort into achieving some results. I realized that I couldn't just go straight to this. My first task was to break down the traditional barrier between supervisor and operators, to generate some enthusiasm, and to make sure the right support was available.

Getting the right support To solve some of the basic support problems, I decided it was essential to bring a production engineer and a procurement person under the umbrella of the section, which was not yet ready to be called a cell. The progress chasers' manager readily agreed to try dedicating the services of one progress chaser to the section for a while, to see how it worked. It was more difficult to get the full-time services of a production engineer. Eventually, a production engineer who was not very happy in his job was transferred to the section. In his new role, he was able to demonstrate his true capabilities.

When the section was getting improved support from specialists in its problem areas, results started to improve almost immediately. One progress chaser focused on the pre-equipped wing section and was able to get an overview of its needs, to identify major shortages and how to tackle them. Having the instant advice of the production engineer began to cut into unproductive waiting time and thus reduce lead time. This provided a good foundation to start the real work of teambuilding, because people could see they would get the support they needed.

Creating the team At this point, the section became a cell, and the group split naturally into two teams, one of 10 people and one of 15. The team of 15 later increased to 25 as more work was taken on, and this was really too many for effective teaming. Teambuilding activities progressed on two levels, a formal weekly team briefing, then individual conversations.

Performance targets Operators had always been wary of performance targets, because they thought they would be continually asked to meet objectives that were unattainable. Without setting targets, we decided to start monitoring the number of snags, concessions, engineering queries, etc., just to get an idea of what was happening. The statistics displayed on the section's noticeboard showed that teamworking was leading to improvements anyway, even without a concerted effort at achieving targets. I finally got round to raising the issue of targets by asking the team what they thought they could reasonably achieve, not by telling them what they were required to achieve. We then had discussions among ourselves, without any nastiness or shouting, to decide what targets we felt capable of achieving. Everybody agreed that 3 weeks was a reasonable lead time to complete a wingset. The results achieved over a 9-month period are shown in Table A.1. The team is still working to sort out a problem with a major supplier who delivers 90 per cent of items on the critical path about 1 week late in a 3-week build cycle.

Table A.1   Achievement of performance targets

	Starting point	Target	Achievement
Lead time	12 weeks	3 weeks	3 weeks*
Scrap and rework		Down 50%	Down 70%
Number of sets in			
progress	7		3 or 4
(Labour hours	2500	1700	1500)

*When the major supplier is not a week late.

Labour hours had to be handled carefully because operators were very sensitive about anything they thought might reduce their overtime. You can lose the friendship of even your closest allies if for one moment they think you are taking overtime away from them. So I monitored these, but kept the results to myself.

There were a number of intangible benefits as well. Everyone felt more motivated. When I walked onto the section I could tell that people felt more happy to be there. We certainly established a team identity. We now have an official pre-equipped wing noticeboard, and an 'unofficial' pre-equipped wing noticeboard situated right next to the lockers. I wanted to encourage people to use the official noticeboard for everything, but people were reluctant to put messages, announcements about pub crawls, cars for sale, and cartoons on the same board as programme bar charts, performance targets and achievements.

Lessons
I was unable to quantify the cost benefits as a result of this project because there are so many complex factors in the business. We reduced work in progress from seven wing sets to three or four, and this would be a cost benefit if we weren't tied into a contract with the wing supplier, who delivers them more frequently than we need them. We could only meet our lead time target occasionally, when our major supplier actually delivered on time, instead of 1 week late. There is more work to do on resolving this problem.

BRITISH NUCLEAR FUELS LTD— GRAPHITE MACHINE SHOP

Lillyhall, Cumbria
Ken Jackson
Assistant Chief Engineer 1981-83

This case study takes us away from the mainstream of cell manufacture. It goes back 10 years to review an early example of implementing step-change. It gives an intriguing viewpoint on how teamworking helped to set new benchmarks in project management performance and methodologies.

Context
In the early 1980s BNFL needed to relocate its graphite machine shop to release the site for the construction of THORP. At the same time, an upsurge in graphite fuel element requirements for the Advanced Gas-cooled Reactor (AGR) programme was forecast.

Problems

- Big site culture.
- Out-of-date manufacturing technology.
- Pressure to vacate the old site to a tight timescale.

Actions

- Graphite machine shop relocated to a new site 18 miles away.
- Up-to-date manufacturing technology introduced.
- Closely knit project team.
- Training and development to get the best out of the people who worked in the new facility.

Results

- New facility operational in 21 months from the start of planning, on time and to budget.
- Met operational goal of achieving a fourfold increase in capability to manufacture AGR components with the same human resources.
- Small site culture with teamworking and flexibility created.
- Achieved Just-in-Time customer service, although JIT was not then part of the vocabulary.

Lessons

- *Project management teaming*: 'A step-change in the way we managed projects.'
- *Culture change*: 'Only years later did we realize that we had put in place the building blocks for what we now call cells and teamworking.'
- *Software*: 'Plenty of people can write computer code, but only the customer can truly describe what he wants the system to do.'

Project scope

Graphite is a key component in nuclear fuel elements. The very first Windscale piles were graphite moderated air-cooled reactors and they used huge quantities of graphite blocks which were manufactured in a machine shop on the Sellafield site. The land occupied by the original graphite machine shop was needed for THORP and for the vitrification plant that serves both THORP and the Magnox plant. BNFL had bought an old Courtaulds factory at Lillyhall and the first move in the construction of THORP was to move the graphite machine shop there. This was one of Ken Jackson's first tasks as Assistant Chief Engineer. He describes the key aspects of the project.

The graphite shop makes a range of products which are used in different types of nuclear reactor, and also at BNFL's Springfields foundry, and we thought some of these products would be in demand for 20 years or more, while some seemed to be nearly at the end of their product life. We decided to stick with what we'd got for products that were nearly out of date, but to make a step-change in technology on the new products. We asked consultants to suggest what technology we should use in a new shop and, of the options presented to us, we decided to take the most radical in terms of investing in new technology and making a step-change in productivity. Given the necessity of moving, we decided to start with a clean sheet of paper and come up with the optimum solution for graphite machining.

Actions

Building a project team   Cell manufacturing was not part of anyone's vocabulary in 1981. At that time the job was viewed purely as a production engineering task, but nevertheless there were some issues around people, team roles, assessment and selection, performance monitoring, and information systems which we had to deal with. My approach was to draw in experienced people from outside. We weren't production engineers so we went to the market-place to bring in some innovative thinking. Our objective was to bring together the best of our graphite machining experience with the best in production engineering. We weren't going to get a ready-made team so we had to find people with expertise and create one. As the project developed, I noticed that there was a gap in our team which I had to fill. We didn't have any process engineering experience, yet there was quite a significant services element to this project, e.g. ventilation systems, dust extraction, boiler plant, water treatment plant. This taught me not to be satisfied with just the obvious mix of skills but to identify a whole range of requirements.

Getting the people to accept the change   Moving the factory and the people 18 miles up the road meant that we had to get the people to accept this change. To do this we tried to get them involved as much as we could. The first step was to get the people who worked in that machine shop to realize that technology had moved on and the working environment would be radically different. Some had been there since the shop first opened, for example the shop steward, who still had his notebook going right back to the 1940s and constantly referred to it during negotiations. We tried to get people out of the workplace to visit other factories and talk to the workforce where they were using new technology, to get them to regard it as an opportunity rather than a threat. Our approach was to open people's eyes, show them the art of the possible, and then draw them into the team and give them a chance to input their experience. We were lucky because work was expanding and nobody was going to be made redundant.

Total quality management   We had recognized the importance of quality control for many years. Throughout BNFL, we were making the transition away from reliance on inspection to measuring quality all the way through the process; today this is called total quality management (TQM). At this point we were halfway between quality control and quality assurance and the methods we chose for the graphite shop typified this. We were beginning to appreciate that we could get more out of in-line measurement than simple quality control. For example, we could get statistical process control information and begin to trigger action to correct trends towards 'off spec' products before we actually produced them. The new measures must have been successful because I have never heard a complaint about the quality of the products since commissioning was completed. This is not to say there haven't been any, but we can be fairly comfortable that they have never been significant enough for our external customers, Nuclear Electric and Scottish Nuclear, to register concern. I think that is quite a tribute to the people in the graphite machine shop.

Software systems   The greatest difficulty we had was with the software systems. All the mechanical equipment was set up and tested off-site before installation and the task of machining graphite was well within our grasp, so getting the mechanical engineering systems working went well, though it was a time of intense activity with plenty of teaming between the production engineers and the BNFL employees. However, we had trouble getting the information systems working and it lasted a long time. This was in the early days of MRPII systems and plenty of other companies were having trouble implementing them as well. Compared with other systems available at the time, the one we chose proved not to be as flexible and easy to adapt as we had all thought. I learned plenty about computer software, and realized that experts were not nearly so expert as I thought they were, or even they thought they were. The computer information systems in the graphite machine shop were a bit of an afterthought and I don't think we really understood them. It is essential to define the logic behind any software system. What is it trying to do, what is its function? Plenty of people can write computer code, but only the customer can truly describe what he wants the system to do.

We are certainly able to make a much better job of specifying computer systems and software systems as a result of that experience. Now, with every project we take great care to be very detailed about our applications description. We have been able to develop a methodology and a language for describing the functionality of control systems and have actually sold this methodology outside BNFL because it is so effective.

Project management approach   My approach to project management has always been based on getting the best out of people. Most things are possible, and we should not be afraid to do things in a different way. The people have to drive the project, not the other way around. This approach has three key elements:

1. *Involvement.* A project only succeeds if everyone *believes* it is going to succeed. That means getting people to buy into what is going to happen, so that they want it to happen, and it's not something that's imposed on them. This means building a team so that everyone is committed to the wider objectives of the project, even though they still have individual objectives.

2. *Strong leadership.* There always has to be an element of authoritarianism in project management, or what some would call leadership. Having built the team and built the concept, nevertheless, people have got to understand that they are required to work to the programme. The programme is a statement of what is expected, what must be *made* to happen, rather than a statement of what we'd rather like to happen if nothing else gets in the way. That is an important piece of psychology. People have to take the project plan as something that *will* be achieved, not as something which somebody in a back room has come up with as an ideal situation that could conceivably happen.

3. *Empowerment.* When the programme has been designed and the commitment of the team gained, people need to have the freedom to deliver what they are supposed to deliver. That means delegating authority and not expecting to be personally involved in every decision. At the same time, when the need arises, the manager has to be prepared to grab hold of the situation, take charge and make decisions, always walking a fine line between empowering people to do things, because that is

what gets the best out of them, and being ready to intervene if things are going off course.

Justification of expenditure Our reason for moving was unrelated to graphite production. We could have just moved all the machines from Sellafield to Lillyhall and the cost would have been little more than removal and fitting out the Lillyhall building with a ventilation system. However, what drove us to invest was getting a payback in increased productivity and improved rate of return on capital employed. This prompted the decision to use technology to manufacture components for AGRs, which at that time we thought had a big future, rather than equipment associated with Magnox reactors, which we thought were being phased out

Managing time and cost Time and cost are related, so completing the project on time obviously helped to keep it within budget. There is a good chance of achieving budget (as long as the estimate of cost was realistic in the first place) by being on time. If it's late there is a very high possibility of overspending as well. That's the glib answer, but there's more to it. You must do the thinking before you start spending. This means:

- Defining the process up front, being clear in your mind about what you want to achieve and how you are going to achieve it.
- Defining stages and identifying review points before the start.
- Specifying the approval mechanism for moving onto the next stage.
- Going for absolute minimum change of plans during the project.

It is usually possible to build a factory once within the time and budget allowed, but if you find you have to do it one-and-a-half times or even twice, because of changes, you are in trouble.

Cash flows from decisions to spend and controlling the decision-making process is the only way to control the final cost of the project. We've learned to plan and control the rate at which we become committed to spending money. Every project needs to have three plans running in parallel, for time, commitment to spend money and resources. There is a lot of benefit in setting these three plans out alongside each other when making decisions. Only by keeping to all three plans can you have any hope of success.

Training and development   Most people on the project had been involved in running the graphite shop, many for their whole working lives. The first thing we did was send them on some straightforward project management courses. With hindsight, perhaps the most significant feature was that every individual who was to work at the new shop was trained in elements of his or her new role. No one was expected to move from one place to the other without being trained. The training process gave people an opportunity to form their own views on whether they wanted to be involved. There were a few who felt that they wouldn't be able to make the change, and they were relocated on the Sellafield site. We tried to take the fear out of new technology by arranging for people to see it in action at other companies, and we set up special courses at the local college on subjects such as keyboard skills, using computers, and inspection technique. Back in the 1980s this was pretty new and we didn't have any fancy names for it. The manufacturers of the new machines trained the people in how to use them and one group spent a lot of time travelling around visiting our suppliers.

Organization structure   At Sellafield, the graphite machine shop manager was one of many at the same level. Because the graphite machine shop was outside the Sellafield site, a much flatter, less formal structure was possible. This comprised the site manager, factory manager, 2 or 3 foremen and the workforce, a total of about 80 people. We were able to create a different culture at Lillyhall, even though this project predated formal flexible working agreements within BNFL. We blundered into teamwork by the way we arranged the machinery, just by doing it in the most logical way. We recognized that traditional demarcations were not appropriate to this new equipment. I can remember many hours of debate with the shop stewards because labour was divided into skilled and semi-skilled, each group represented by a different branch of the union and different shop stewards. Our biggest industrial relations challenge was to get them to accept more flexibility and we did manage to get through that without any formal agreement.

Examples of culture change

1. *Just-in-Time.* We had a number of production lines, and a production line represented a team of people, but at that time we wouldn't have dreamed of calling them cells because the word wasn't in our vocabulary. Nevertheless, the people knew that their job was to keep the product going to the end of the line and they had all the materials and authority they needed to make a particular product. Only years later did we realize that we had put the building blocks in place for what we now call cells and teamworking. In the new culture, an individual's job was not just to machine the third groove on the outside of the sleeve, but to contribute to the final product, and that was a fundamental change from what we had done before. We made a big effort to reduce work in progress and to get away from the old culture of overcoming all your production problems by having huge buffer stocks between operations. We were going to a Just-in-Time (JIT) philosophy within the production line, and that phrase wasn't in our vocabulary at the time either. (In another context, I find myself trying to get people to realize that JIT on its own is not the answer to everything, because sometimes it turns out to be 'just too late'.) In the graphite machine shop environment JIT certainly was right. Getting it accepted meant culture change, and we had to overcome tremendous resistance, particularly in the transfer of the old Magnox lines where we were taking the old machinery with us but trying to apply a new mentality. Dissuading people from

hoarding pallets of work-in-progress was a big fight, so we physically designed thc line to make sure there was not enough space.

2. *Canteen management.* However radical we thought we'd been, I realize we could have gone further. You think you are pushing the frontiers of people, organization and technology, but with hindsight you always regret not having gone further. In the heat of a project, when you have to take decisions, you always think, 'Have I gone far enough? If I go any further will the whole thing collapse?' Canteen management is an example. This may seem like a triviality but we wasted much management effort deciding who should run the canteen. It was a real nuisance trying to maintain the industrial relations between a group of people trying to machine graphite, and the canteen workers and management. We had set up a nice ring-fenced project on a new greenfield site, with teambuilding and a new way of working, then imported some of the old culture by letting the canteen management do the catering. Now I wish we'd not let that happen. The reason why it happened was that, like everybody else, I had my mind on machining graphite and didn't really think broadly enough about the totality of the culture, about the influence that one culture could have on another. It is a matter of regret that I allowed some of the old culture to creep in. We could and should have put the catering out to tender. In fact, in later years, when it came to arranging catering for THORP, that's exactly what we did. As it happened, the Sellafield catering department won the contract, but we made them compete for the job and what a change in attitude this produced among the same people in the same department. When faced with the challenge, they set out to win, and they did, and they are doing a good job.

3. *Purchasing and contracts.* I think the people who were most influenced by this project were in purchasing and contracts. We asked a centralized BNFL bureaucracy to work on the graphite project in a totally different way—one which was quite outside their previous experience—and they were changed

people because of it. I remember talking to one quite senior person in the contracts department when we were trying to decide where to place the main equipment contracts. As part of the final tender evaluation process, I said to him, 'What we'll do now is take a trip round all the tenderers and see their factories.' He said, 'Why?' I asked, 'Don't we want to go and assess their capabilities on the ground?' He said, 'What for? We've got the tenders in. I'll produce a report and we'll take the cheapest.' I said, 'Oh, no we won't. What we'll do is visit each one, interview the factory manager, inspect the workshop and take a view on whether he is competent or not.' He agreed, and went with me, and afterwards he said, 'This has been an eye-opener for me. I've worked in the BNFL contracts department for years and I've never, ever been to an equipment manufacturer.' In the past, it had not been part of the process to go out and have a look. He had managed the purchase of all sorts of equipment over 25 years. He'd never been asked to visit a supplier; clearly it had never occurred to him to go or that there could be reasons why the cheapest tender wasn't necessarily the best one.

Implementation timescales   The whole project took 21 months from planning to start up of the factory. Design, construction and procurement of new technology probably took 18 months. The actual transfer of the workforce and some existing equipment which was needed went very quickly. For the Magnox components, it was a matter of days from closing down at Sellafield to being in production again at Lillyhall. To get up to full production took only a few weeks. The implementation was extremely rapid and set benchmarks about how fast people could get a task done if they really wanted to. The whole project was on a fast track and went extremely rapidly. This was a tribute to the workforce who knew what was expected of them because they were involved in the planning process.

Results

The overall objectives we set ourselves were achieved and after the usual commissioning struggles, the plant worked. The structure of the project and the way we handled it was a success, and I remember it as a step-change in the way BNFL managed projects. The training of the people and their acceptance of the new culture was also successful. With the benefit of hindsight, we could have put more effort into improving the efficiency of the machines in the Magnox line, despite what we thought about their having a relatively short life. Sticking with old technology on graphite for Magnox reactors was probably a mistake. Magnox reactors continue to run and run and we'll still need to make components for them at least until the end of the century, i.e. nearly 20 years after the new graphite shop started running. If we'd known then what we know now we'd have updated the technology for all of the components. The computer control of the in-line inspection equipment was very successful but we didn't make a good job of the information systems and it would be interesting to go back now, after 10 years, and see how well they are working. It was a success from the local community point of view. This was a move into a different constituency. It was only a few miles up the road but in political terms it was quite important and that is an ongoing benefit to BNFL. The existence of BNFL facilities outside the area around Sellafield is quite helpful to us. It is an exceptionally clean facility considering that it handles graphite.

Because the AGR programme was curtailed the production requirement for graphite sleeves has reduced but the machine shop is still running. The arguments go on now about the cost. The rate of production, particularly on AGR sleeves, is lower than planned so the unit cost is higher than it should have been. Our internal customer, the fuel division, is always asking the question, 'Should we close down Lillyhall and go elsewhere?'

Ken Jackson went on to become Project Director for THORP, and is now Director, Engineering Group, British Nuclear Fuels plc.

BRITISH NUCLEAR FUELS LTD.–THORP

Sellafield, Cumbria
Brian Watson
Senior Commissioning Manager, THORP

Context
One of Europe's biggest engineering and construction projects, subject to public scrutiny. Built to reprocess the Thermal Oxide Fuel from UK and overseas facilities on long-term contracts and designed to take reprocessing technology into a new era of safety and efficiency.

Problems
- Large numbers of people to be recruited for commissioning and running the plant.
- The need to get these people working effectively to complete commissioning on time and be ready to run THORP securely and profitably.

Actions
- Involvement of all the people in designing and implementing flexible teamworking.
- Building ownership of vision, mission and values.
- Assessment centres to select key people.
- Total Quality Management (TQM) to compliment teambuilding.

Results
- Commissioning on time and to budget.
- 'We have been able to build a new way of working'.
- Commitment and initiative maintained during the uncertainty over start up in 1993.

ng task, broadly defined the operating tasks, and
the full range of skills we would need—mechanical
rocess engineers, fitters, electricians, etc.—then drew
job specifications for every role. We knew we also
le who were capable of working in teams, and some
leadership qualities, so we took the job specifications
technical expertise and relevant experience; we also
ersonality factors. Would the applicants be team
hat were their team roles? We developed assessment
help us select people with the right technical skills,
and personality factors for each defined role: manager,
r and team member. Every person employed as a
f the permanent operating staff of THORP went
e of these assessment centres. We wanted people with
chnical skills and experience so that they would stay,
th the sort of personality that meant we would be happy
stay.

it people to work in the plant, we tried to tie in as many
sting labour force as possible. Every person on the
ite attended a presentation about THORP. We thought
ge was so important that every single presentation was
a senior manager and we had to make presentations to
50 or more from morning till night for weeks. We were
ul to tell people that if they wanted to come to THORP
dn't work in the old ways they were used to because we
bring in the permanent BNFL industrial labour that we
uiting on a flexible basis. Our presentation clearly stated
nly wanted people to apply for jobs on THORP who:

ted to do the job
ted to contribute to the team
e prepared to be flexible
e prepared to offer and accept constructive criticism
e prepared to be trained in new skills, and to take on new
onsibility
e prepared to train others

Lessons

- Performance measures are important. 'We are still working on defining effective performance measures for our operators.'
- Involvement of all the people in solving problems has paid dividends.

Company history

THORP, BNFL's new THermal Oxide Reprocessing Plant at Sellafield, Cumbria, reprocesses irradiated oxide fuel from the UK's Advanced Gas-cooled Reactors (AGRs) and from Light Water Reactors (LWRs) both in the UK and overseas. Uranium and plutonium, which are valuable and can be recycled, make up 97 per cent by weight of the irradiated fuel. The remaining 3 per cent is made up of fission by-products. Both the irradiated fuel and the products of reprocessing are highly radioactive and must be handled according to internationally agreed safety regulations established by the International Commission on Radiological Protection (ICRP) and the National Radiological Protection Board (NRPB). THORP has been designed as the company's flagship, to take reprocessing technology into a new era of safety and efficiency.

THORP is also one of Europe's largest and most complex engineering projects. In size, complexity and cost—as well as the public controversy surrounding it—it is comparable only to the Channel Tunnel. Its success has depended on contributions from many disciplines: applied sciences (chemistry, physics and mathematics); architecture and design; engineering (civil, mechanical, electrical and production); and every aspect of computer technology; but most of all on the elusive skill of management, i.e. getting the best out of people. As construction was nearing completion, Brian Watson was appointed THORP's Senior Commissioning Manager and took on a dual role:

- Commissioning activities to get the plant up and running.
- Getting the right people to run THORP on board, organized

and motivated, and getting them to understand what they had to do.

'For me,' he says, 'the key word for achieving both these tasks is *involvement*.' He continues the story.

As construction was progressively completed and commissioning began, we wanted to build up a large team of people to handle commissioning and within this group to have a core team who would eventually run THORP. We wanted to set the scene for a new way of working and needed a team of competent, motivated people who were willing to work flexibly together to solve problems. We saw the introduction of flexible working as one of the key issues, and many of our actions were geared towards achieving this.

The original personnel plan gave us about 2 years to get THORP up and running. Then when permission to start was delayed we had to find some way to stay confident, to maintain morale and motivation, and that meant making sure the teams were absolutely fastened in on what they were doing.

Actions and results

The core management team   One of the things that we were really nervous about was how we would get people with the right qualities to bring onto the job. We started out by quite deliberately targeting individual people already working at Sellafield, who we knew, who we wanted, who we knew could do the job, and we started this process and very quietly just kept chasing them. The other divisions on site were very helpful and supportive of this process. Getting together this core team of managers was the first step.

Deciding how many people we needed to commission and run THORP   In 1989, this core team did an exercise to support the Commercial Department with the objective of analysing how

---

THORP would be run and
commissioning was comple
number wrong. THORP
Sellafield site, but all under
scale factors to see how man
each process in THORP. In
the operating numbers and u
operating costs would be. W
people we would need to co
these numbers in mind we be

Job roles and recruitment   H
us and split the job up into ser
at how we would build up the r
a large and very successful exer
of job roles and recruitment
extensively just within the Sella
management and commissionin
qualified people in other parts
went to BNFL's Risley site on
presentations to audiences of 1
talk to us afterwards. In this way,
to transfer permanently and fo
come on a temporary basis until

We wanted to cast our net a
company as well as inside, so we
went barnstorming right across th
rising steadily at the time and w
recruit in a harsh economic climat
applicants and then our people had
those we considered most suitable.
the people involved that, almost
delighted with the people we even

We went to a lot of trouble to
wanted, and that is another reason
up such a cohesive team for

---

commission
established
engineers,
up detailed
wanted peo
people with
further than
included
players? W
centres to
experience
team leade
member
through on
the right t
and also w
for them t

To recr
of the ex
Sellafield
the messa
fronted by
groups of
very caref
they coul
wanted to
were recr
that we o

- Wan
- Wan
- Wer
- Wer
- Wer
- Wer
- resp
- Wer

- Were prepared to get their hands dirty
- Were prepared to do jobs they didn't like as well as ones they did
- Were prepared to meet a major challenge and a tight programme

The response to these presentations was encouraging and produced benefits on several levels:

1. They encouraged a large number of people to apply for jobs on THORP.
2. They kept people across the entire site informed of what was happening on THORP.
3. Even people who didn't choose to apply for a job were made aware that the company was looking at a new way of working.

Teambuilding, training and development   When the Oxide Fuel Division and THORP Construction Division merged in 1990 to form THORP Division, people were very committed to a team approach to dealing with the job. One of the first things the Project Director did was to create a team out of the new people who were working together. At the first meeting, he said, 'I want this group of people to get themselves organized in a sensible way because we've got a major workload to deal with here.' At the time, three senior managers had divided up the workload between them, but he said three people were not enough. He wanted five, so he appointed two more and sent us all on a Coverdale course with instructions to sort ourselves out. We arrived at the first course suspicious of each other. Suddenly three people were having to give up work to the other two (it wasn't work we minded giving away, it was prestige) and there was 'blood on the walls'. At the end of that course we all knew what teaming was about. By the end of the course, we were successful at working and planning in leaderless groups and transferring what we'd learned back to work.

We were so impressed with that exercise that we thought it would be a fine thing in terms of setting milestones for divisional development, if we took all THORP Division's employees—

whether staff, industrial, manager, supervisor or worker—through a basic 1 week training course on teambuilding and a structured approach to task management. Over the past $2^1/_2$ years about 1400 permanent BNFL staff have attended the course.

It was very important that people should not think that the training consultants were just off-loading their message to our workforce. Divisional management had to show that they were totally committed to the process. We decided to take primarily volunteers, and also people who showed they had the right skills, and give them more detailed training in how to run workshops. Twenty people have been trained to run the workshops and, working jointly with the consultants, we are spreading the teaming message throughout the workforce.

Problem-solving workshops   About 18 months ago we really had a watershed in making progress as we were starting to bring large numbers of permanent staff into the plant. We took all the senior managers off the job for 2 days to attend a workshop at a hotel in Windermere. The objective was to identify what we thought were the five key issues that were going to inhibit progress unless we solved them. The issues we came up with were:

1. How to introduce flexible working into THORP.
2. How to establish the working arrangements to run the plant, things like control of clocking, overtime, changing room arrangements, etc.
3. How to establish a large and fully integrated commissioning programme.
4. How to devise an integrated training and recruitment policy, with emphasis on training.
5. How to establish the most effective organization structure to operate THORP.

As a result of that workshop we decided to set up a project team with a project manager for each issue, and to address the tasks in a structured way. The introduction of flexible working turned out to be a key issue. At the same time, we were introducing total quality management (TQM) into the business and TQM and teambuilding fit together beautifully; it really was a lovely merger. In TQM we were analysing where we were, deciding what we wanted to do to improve things, and then bringing teamwork into play to achieve those improvements using a structured approach.

Introducing flexible working The issue that had the most impact was flexibility. Despite the fact that we had told everybody coming to work at THORP that we'd have to achieve things that hadn't been achieved before, to be fair, we didn't know how to make that happen. We tried to define flexible working by a simple illustration. We said:

> Why not go about your work at work in the same way you would go about it at home? Suppose you are a trained fitter. At home, if you've got to put a plug on a lamp, you'll just do it. If you've got to strip wallpaper off the walls and repaint the woodwork, you won't go and get somebody else to do it, just because you are only trained as a fitter. So why not work in the same way at work. And to help you do that, if you are doing something new, all we want to do is blur and remove the demarcations that exist between people now, but *not* by moving the demarcations to somewhere else. Let's not think demarcations at all, but let's think how individuals can co-operate, work together and train each other, and how we should remove these boundaries between you.

This was good enough for people to grab hold of. It was something that the workforce wanted. The trade unions had been saying to managers for a long time: 'This can't be the right way to work. Why are we always in confrontation? Why do you always ask us to show our passes at the gate, take our brains off, hang them on the perimeter fence, and not collect them again till we go home?' So there was tremendous commitment to flexible working.

We asked the project manager working on the flexibility issue to form a team with members selected from across the entire workforce—management, team leaders, shop-floor people—who would steer the introduction of flexible working. Their specific remit was first to find out what simple steps we could take to get started.

Team formation   One of the things the flexibility team decided that we had to do early on was to form this large phalanx of people into properly structured teams of mixed skills and disciplines. To do this, we looked at an area of the plant and analysed the work activities that had to be undertaken in it, and the skills the people would need to undertake those tasks. This enabled us to specify what skills the team needed to look after that area, e.g. fitting skills, electrical engineering skills, instrument skills, process skills. In my experience, this approach was unique for the Sellafield site, because we were not the least bit interested in functional management; we were only interested in what skills we needed to do the job in a particular area. We selected team leaders to look after these teams by extensive use of assessment centres. One of the real changes we found in setting up teams was that a person who had been used to supervising fitters would suddenly find himself in charge not only of fitters, but process operatives and instrument mechanics, and he might find himself with not only a maintenance responsibility but also a major operational responsibility. The people we selected had to have the appropriate teaming and leadership potential.

Some people were disappointed to find that they weren't appointed team leaders, and others were delighted to be put into a team leader position when they hadn't expected it. That was quite hard and gave us some motivational difficulties. We had a group of people who were very motivated, saw a real future for themselves, knew exactly where they were headed, and another group who were confident they had a future, but wondered where it was going to be. We overcame this with one-to-one counselling for people who were nervous. We just took the time out, opened up the office doors, and said, 'Look, if you're worried, we're here. Come in and talk.' We tried to give them assurance that we would be careful that they were put into jobs they understood, which were big enough for them to prove themselves and show that they could grow. This was quite important and enabled us to jump over that hurdle.

Keeping the unions involved The whole plant is unionized. We've got extensive shop steward coverage in the plant, and we've got tremendous trade union and shop steward commitment to taking THORP forward. We felt that it was extremely important to be able to make progress on these issues in THORP, so we involved the site-wide conveners and staff representatives at a very early stage, told them exactly what we wanted to do and gave them a chance to talk to us, tell us their opinions and express their fears. Then right at the start of the Coverdale training programme, we ran a session for staff-side representatives, conveners, and senior shop stewards, to give them a chance to sample the way we intended the management to work. We told them that's what we'd like them to participate in, and they were suspicious, but they agreed. It said to the rest of the site that the conveners and senior shop stewards had committed themselves to this because they had agreed to take part. It sent out a hell of a signal to the rest of the site: 'These guys mean business!' They mean business to the extent that they are prepared to involve everybody who is affected by these different ways of working and that is powerful.

Flexibility co-ordinators Flexible working was a key issue and it was clear to us early on, and despite what we'd done on teamwork training, despite what we'd done to form mixed discipline teams, that we had to do something else. People didn't know how to go about sitting down as mixed discipline teams and deciding where flexibility could be employed in teamworking. They didn't know, having identified those areas of teamworking, how to get management and trade union agreement to work in that way. They didn't know how to estimate whether they were really identifying efficiencies or not. We decided to do two things immediately and then follow them up. First we got a group of volunteers, from whatever part of the workforce wanted to volunteer, to advise people on how to make progress. Some volunteers were shop stewards, others were from the shop-floor, team leaders, managers, engineers, or process people. We called them flexibility co-ordinators and ran a workshop for 25–30 of them, which enabled them to:

- Get some understanding of the site-wide formal agreements on flexibility.
- Develop ideas on how local agreements might be formulated and formally agreed.
- Formulate some views on what their role as flexibility co-ordinators should be, and what it shouldn't be.

We wanted flexibility co-ordinators to provide additional help to the process, but not to infringe on the role of line managers and team leaders. Then we kept calling the group back together, to show the rest of the workforce that they were there to help; to identify them as the individuals who could give practical advice. The flexibility co-ordinators have been variously used across the plant, according to the levels of commitment in each area.

Flexibility workshops Another important concept was our decision to take some key people, predominantly team leaders, middle line managers and shop stewards, supported by co-ordinators, conveners and senior managers, into a 'flexibility workshop'. Its purpose was to provide information and help people to understand how they should go about sitting down in teams, identifying genuine areas where flexibility would provide benefits, and forming agreements which would get those flexibilities functioning. The THORP team developed all these workshops in house; we decided what the purpose should be, we decided what the programme should be and we used Coverdale purely as a consultancy service.

Teamwork and involvement in safety The safety case for what we are doing is enormous. Some key parts of that safety case refer to things that people must do or *must not* do. Traditionally, in generating a safety case we have delivered these as rules to the workforce. This time we're doing something a bit different. We're saying that the safety case provides information. It says some important things about the way we operate the plant, and some are things we must or must not do. We want the workforce to take that information and sort out how they are going to demonstrate to the world at large that they are working within the safety case. So then they have responsibility. There are some rules, like 'Thou must wash down the inside of the in-cell cave once a week.' We won't tell them how to do that, but ask them please to think about it as a team, decide how they are going to prove to the regulatory bodies that they've done it, and to decide what information, equipment, etc., they need to be able to do it. The act of organization will get their commitment to undertaking that activity in a thoroughly desirable and auditable fashion, but they will have decided how to do it themselves and so own the results.

Lessons

Performance measures   We've set up a group within THORP Division to start formulating performance measures. It's been extremely difficult to do this up to now because commissioning is such a dynamic activity and we've been growing in manpower at such a rate, and we've been doing so many diverse things that, to be frank, I don't know what you would measure. The only measures we have right now are manpower and efficiency levels. Back in 1989 we estimated what the manpower requirements would be and what efficiency levels we would have to achieve for that manpower to run the plant. We'll know soon whether we can run the plant with those numbers and we'll know whether we've achieved those efficiencies. So we have some degree of measure of success just now, but we are only starting to identify ongoing measures.

Rewards When it comes to deciding on rewards, we're in a strange position in THORP because, despite the fact that we are an island site, and it's a new plant, our workforce is still substantially subject to site-wide agreements. The agreements that have been formally struck on flexible working across the site incorporate THORP and these are site-wide mechanisms that determine the rewards that come from the implementation of flexible working. We do have an opportunity in THORP to move forward more quickly than the rest of the site. We have a workforce that have been picked to do that, and are committed to doing that, but in moving forward more quickly they are subject to the constraints of the rest of the site in terms of rewards. This is not a problem at the moment, but it might become one.

Sixteen divisional cultural vision statements We had a wide range of change initiatives in place and at the same time we were trying to set up organization structures in a different way, not by developing hierarchies, but by making sure we had only the management layers we needed to do the job efficiently. We felt this could be very confusing to people who hadn't had the chance to become thoroughly steeped in the new way of working because they would not understand just how well all these things interlocked. It was important to underpin this by setting ourselves some values which people could look at and say, 'Well if that's a value we think it actually works and is being applied properly', or alternatively, 'Well, if that's the value, it's not working'. We asked the Director of THORP to participate as a group member, not as a group leader, in a project to develop some value statements. The group, as usual, comprised members from the shop-floor and right across the whole management structure. It devised 16 short, sharp, snappy value statements, for example, managers must have an 'open door' policy. We then developed a technique called the 'Bounce' which enables people to look at those 16 statements and decide whether they buy into them or not, by analysing whether what we were currently doing was consistent or inconsistent with these value statements. Where there was inconsistency, it allowed us to develop continuous improvement tasks, and to change the way that we worked.

Now and again we've been faced with a ticklish management decision, which might affect a substantial number of people. Having taken that decision, in a number of instances we've pulled out the 16 value statements and measured the decision against them. If it has not been consistent with our values, we have had to ask ourselves if it was the right decision. If one of the values is having an open door policy, and I say I've got one, but every time someone comes to see me I'm not available, I will quickly find an action coming up in my diary to change that. We think that's significant and it applies right through the whole factory.

Morale Morale has to be put into context against the situation over discharge authorizations by Her Majesty's Inspectorate of Pollutions (HMIP). Up until HMIP delayed granting a discharge authorization, morale was very high because everyone felt we had achieved a major challenge and we could see a big future in front of us with exciting new ways of working. Commissioning is usually a very motivating time anyway, as people see the plant start to come to life. Morale is very mixed now: there are big plus points and big minus points. The job of commissioning THORP is still a tremendous motivator for people. People still believe that THORP must be allowed to start. They think, 'When it does start, we'll be effective, we'll be efficient, we'll make money. We'll be the company's flagship; we'll be something for the workforce and the company to be proud of.' And that keeps people surprisingly well motivated. But over the last 6 months in particular, the continuous gruelling pressure from the lack of a decision on whether THORP should start, does without doubt undermine everybody. In the current circumstances the morale is about as good as anybody could reasonably expect, but it's not what it could be. When the decision to start is made*, I think

---

*A high court ruling in March 1994 removed the final barrier to THORP start up and was welcomed enthusiastically by the workforce.

there will be a gigantic release. The benefits could be awesome in terms of what people would then want to achieve. The situation challenges people's beliefs. Will all that fine work they've done over 15 years of design and development, 9 or 10 years of building and 3 or 4 years of commissioning be allowed to go to waste? Having said that, we do understand the dilemma. That's the funny side, we really do understand the dilemma and the pressures; we understand that it's the nature of our business to be in the goldfish bowl. Questions are asked about this business that aren't asked about any other. We are trying to keep people very focused on driving forward against the programme and ignoring what people outside are saying. Our best answer will be to get THORP ready to go, and to be sure that we work in a different way.

Achievements What we have achieved until now is a little different because most large firms which have created major change have had to do it or die. We have been able to build a new way of working on a greenfield site. As a result of all that work, the site-wide initiatives, people have an enormous amount of commitment and the teams in the plants have started to generate significant agreements on flexible ways of working together. We are 2 or 3 years down the path now, and looking back, it could have all gone wrong; it could have been one of those 'flavour of the month' things, but it isn't. We've put in a lot of tools and building blocks and have tried always to behave in a manner that's consistent with the ideals we've set for ourselves. We've worked very hard at making sure the message is consistent.

Teamworking really has enabled us to build the skill levels by suspending previous ways of working; going back to first principles and working according to common sense. All we are doing here is the application of common sense; it's the sort of thing you do at home, in the street, with your family and friends. I think we see identifying ongoing performance measures as one of the major challenges for the next 2 years, because we don't want to stand still and become blasé about what we have achieved. We really do want to try to achieve continuous improvement.

GEC ALSTHOM LARGE MACHINES LTD

Rugby, Warwickshire
Charles M. Paterson
General Works Manager

Context
In 1987 the issue was survival with a capital 'S'. We were up against the wall and the message was change or die!

Problems
- Large old site.
- Medium sized company with a big company bureaucracy.
- Out of date culture.
- Losing money.

Actions
- Radical business restructuring.
- Cells and teamwork.
- Major teambuilding and culture change programme.
- Make vs buy, focus on core capabilities.

Results
- Business transformed.
- Sales doubled with stable people numbers.
- Lead time down 50 per cent.
- Inventory down 25 per cent.
- Overheads down 25 per cent.
- Winner of 1992 IMechE Manufacturing Effectiveness Award.

Lessons
- Be prepared to take the blinkers off and rethink from the ground up.

- We have to be changing and improving faster than our competition or we are dead!
- The area we underestimated was getting our people to accept culture change.

Company history
GEC Alsthom Large Machines Ltd specializes in the design and manufacture of large bespoke electric motors and generators. The company inhabits a large site that dates back to the early years of the century when it was occupied by BTH (British Thompson Houston). At the end of the 1950s there were 13 000 to 14 000 people working there. In 1988, at the start of this restructuring project, most of the buildings were still standing and a large boiler house provided heat and power for the whole site, but occupancy had dropped to about 1500 people. Clearly, the volume of business and the market situation could not support that type of infrastructure, so it was urgent to find ways of taking out fixed cost. At the same time, the company took the opportunity to review its product strategy and examine trends in the world market to identify what sort of targets it would have to achieve to be a leader in future years. Charles Paterson says, 'We knew we had to adapt the techniques usually associated with high volume manufacture, such as cells and teaming, just-in-time techniques, total quality management and design for manufacture, to make them suitable for a low volume bespoke manufacturing environment.' He continues the story.

Problems
The company was in a situation where it had become uncompetitive at a time when world markets were becoming ever more demanding. We knew that we had to do something radical or die. Basically, we were trying to achieve three specific targets:

- Halve the area of occupancy

- Increase sales turnover by well over 50 per cent
- Reduce the number of employees by about a third.

Of course, we knew that achieving these would also result in tremendous cost reduction.

Actions

Project planning We prepared a plan which left no area of the business untouched; it was a radical, major restructuring. The plan stated how much money we were going to spend, and specified what the turnover and number of employees should be at the end of the project. Head count reduction and a significant increase in turnover were part of the strategy, and we knew that if we couldn't show how we were going to achieve these things, the project 'wasn't a goer'. We recognized that the required turnover would increase with inflation, but we first set it as a figure in 1988 monetary values.

Project management At the start, the project was handled by a team comprising fairly senior managers and other people in the business. They were withdrawn from their normal day-to-day activities and appointed to that team full time to ensure that they weren't distracted by other duties. Clearly, there were some senior people we couldn't afford to release for that work. This team planned the physical changes. Then, about half way through the physical change project, we set up the 'world class' team. This comprised some very bright, well-qualified young men, blended with some experienced people who had been in the business a long time. They launched a massive training programme which involved every employee in the business and it was really through this team that we brought about the cultural change.

Financing the restructuring The business was to finance the investment through savings achieved. We had a very tight target

for the project timescale and it had to be self-financing as well. As
we went along there were phasing difficulties with the financing
because obviously we had to spend some money before we could
get the payback, but overall the investment programme of £27
million was self-financing.

Physical change   We had decided to make physical reorganization the driving force for the project so the dramatic culture
change needed for cells, teambuilding and systems changes rode
in on the back of the physical change. We were on a very tight
timescale and realized that if the physical changes removed the
space in which all the work in progress was cluttered then people
couldn't find space for work in progress. So physical change acted
as a driver to make sure that some of our other objectives were
achieved.

Culture change   It was self-evident that the business was
struggling and we put out the message that GEC Alsthom Large
Machines had to do things that everybody else in the world was
doing, but we had to do them even better. Everyone knew that
people in Japan or Taiwan were into flexibility and lean
manufacturing, and if we couldn't make the same changes the
business wouldn't last. So it was very simple: change so that we
equal the best in the world and survive, or stay where we were and
die. That was a very powerful message.

The area that we seem to have underestimated, and it always is
underestimated, was in getting people to accept this cultural
change. This was particularly difficult here because over a number
of years, with a business that was in trouble, there had been a
number of initiatives to try and pull it back, and these tended to
become 9-day wonders. When we launched the world class
programme, there was a degree of cynicism: 'Here we go, this is
the flavour of the week.' To get through that, I tried to convince
people that if we could make this work, their quality of life was
going to be better. For supervisors: less hassle, less aggravation; for
people on the shop-floor: better planned work, and a better

understanding of what they were doing and why. Everyone would know what the objectives of the business were and have more job security. Once people started to see that things were better, we could breed success on the success that we'd had.

We put in a tremendous amount of effort on communication and training. We designed a business game to demonstrate to all our employees the philosophy of JIT. That game was played by everybody in the business, and has even been sold to other companies. However, cultural change doesn't come easy and to be absolutely frank I think we are still struggling with it today. We had to come from a long way back: we didn't start with a greenfield site like Nissan or Toyota. They don't have to struggle with culture change because their people have no preconceived ideas. We had a business that went back to the turn of the century, so changing people's ideas and getting them to do things differently has been a real challenge.

Filling key roles   We found that we had to define key roles in two different ways. One key role was as an influencer of people. When implementing change, it's difficult to get disciples of the new culture in the right places. Sometimes the most influential person in a particular area bubbles to the surface and turns out to be the shop steward. We had to find out which people had influence, and it was not always management. The situation arises in some work areas where everybody believes that if Joe says it's all right, it must be all right so they all follow. We made a big effort to identify these people, bring them forward and use them as trainers. We used all our own people as trainers: some supervisors, some production engineers, and some shop-floor people. Our objective was to make these influencers the trainers, getting them to stand up and train the people in our philosophy.

The other key role was based on personality as well as skills. We used a variety of psychometric tests when selecting people to fill key business roles and examined personality profiles before making appointments. We wanted to know two things:

1. Is this person's personality likely to help him or her to be successful in the business in the way that we want?
2. Are we putting people in who will lead from the front, get the best out of other people and build teams?

This took a lot of very careful work and we didn't get it right all the time, but when you are doing something as radical as what we've been doing—*something pioneering*—if you are right more than half the time you are well off, and you learn from your experiences.

The majority of our cell supervisors are graduate engineers with some experience, rather than traditional foremen who came up through the shop-floor, having served an apprenticeship. There has been a subtle shift and we are continuing with that because cell supervisors are now being trained and encouraged to become 'managing directors' of their own mini-businesses so their role is changing. The whole process of world class performance is a path, not a destination, and programme generates change at an increasing rate in response to changes in the world market. No one can afford to stand still and we are now bringing in cultural changes that we never envisaged 12 to 18 months ago.

Measuring and rewarding performance   Changes in these areas were quite dramatic because we had to throw out a lot of the traditional measures in the business and substitute them with measures which encouraged people to achieve the things that we felt were important in the new business situation, in the new culture. That brought some major problems for the management team because we had to carry on reporting traditional measures to our head office and our performance continued to be measured by those traditional measures. However, in-house these traditional measures could often be in conflict with the things that we were trying to do. Perhaps the most glaring example of this is in overhead recovery. We had to achieve overhead recovery budgets and, of course, to achieve these, the philosophy was to keep everybody gainfully employed for the maximum amount of time. Gainfully employed could in fact mean making things in bigger batches than we needed, doing things earlier than needed, and putting things in stock or having them lying around as work in progress for a long time. The whole emphasis was on keeping the direct worker employed for the maximum number of hours. Our new philosophy meant making one-offs at the time the customer required them. This meant reducing stock and WIP, and reducing throughput times, so if we had a facility which didn't need to run in order to meet customer requirements, it didn't run. We went through quite a long period of agony while overhead recovery went through a loop because we were no longer keeping people employed producing stock and WIP which might well be required (but we were producing it too early), to a situation where if a machine didn't need to run, for whatever reason, it didn't run. We tried to keep the person gainfully employed doing something else, which itself led on to the need for flexibility. Flexibility became one of our key measures. This was an extremely difficult time because the traditional financial results went through a loop before we actually started getting benefits in the other areas. Once we started getting benefits in these other areas people could see that the process was working and that the bottom line was coming right. Then life became easier, but we certainly went through hell for 12–18 months.

Before the project started we had individual bonus systems for shop-floor operators. When we created cells and teams, we changed to a cell bonus system which included all the direct workers, plus all the people who contributed to the success of the cell. This included crane drivers, store keepers, inspectors, people who traditionally had not been included in a bonus scheme. That scheme lived for about 2 years, but when cultural change began to take hold it reinforced the need to reduce stock, WIP and batch sizes, and to produce one-offs, doing things when the customer needed them. This led to improved flexibility, so we were moving people between activities much more often. If we had an underload in one area and an overload in another we moved people across trade union barriers, and occasionally across skill barriers, giving them training and putting them onto the activities that were overloaded. Now, in some cases they were not as quick or as proficient as the people who had been doing that job for a long time, so the cell bonus scheme began to fall over. It was working against us in reinforcing this new culture. In the end, it fell into disrepute because some cells stopped making bonus. It was only the fabrication cell that continued to make bonus targets for quite a long time after everybody else had stopped achieving them, so in the end we had to unplug the scheme. Now there is no bonus system in the company.

Logistics and systems   One of the philosophies behind the project was to reduce non-value-adding activities. Reducing the size of the factory had the knock-on effect of reducing material handling by cutting down the distance parts and materials had to travel. In the case of generator pole assembly, the distance travelled had gone down by 94 per cent, from 3000 metres to 184 metres. We are still changing and developing today, because nothing can stand still. Take our Kanban system on small machines. We put in Kanban 1 during the initial programme. We then went to Kanban 2 and Kanban $2^1/_2$. Today we've got Kanban 3 and I still don't think that's completely right. There will probably be a Kanban $3^1/_2$ in another 6 months.

Systems is probably an area where we weren't as successful as we would have liked, so we've just launched another team of capable, well-qualified senior people to look at business systems requirements for the next decade. The new team looking at systems is having ideas we never even thought about when we did programme renewal and cultural change. We are setting up an electronic mail network so a lot of statistics in the business which have traditionally circulated on paper will be distributed electronically, with emphasis on eliminating non-value-adding activities. I now have a PC and have been trained in Word Perfect and Lotus 123, so that I can make use of this information. This will be another cultural change on the systems front. We are going to have a system with about 200 PCs on a network and this is a much more profound change than switching from mainframe to distributed.

Make vs buy   Identifying our core competences was a significant element of the programme. Many operations which were not central to the business were being carried out in large, sophisticated facilities with high overheads when they could have been done more efficiently virtually in backstreet garages. We examined this and drew up a set of rules which, in effect, knocked the bottom end of the business out. For example, the first rule we made was that we would buy in any item less than 50 mm in diameter. We stopped making gaskets and bought them in. We struck up a supplier partnership for all the fasteners we used. A company comes onto the site every week and fills up the bins on the shop-floor with all the industrial fasteners and certain other things that we use on a regular basis. They tell us how many they've used to replenish the system and we pay the bill at the end of the month. We know that they are not likely to take advantage of the situation because we would eventually find out.

Design for manufacture   We want to concentrate core activities on site, but have an outside manufacturer fabricate and machine our terminal box bodies. One of the issues highlighted in the first make vs buy exercise was whether we should now get our supplier to provide us with an assembled terminal box. We carried out an exercise in which we trained everybody in the techniques of design for manufacture, using the Smallpeice Trust in Leamington Spa. We hope that people are now living and breathing design for manufacture, modular design and standardization. Our second make vs buy exercise looked more at modular construction and design for manufacture. In the machine shop, the two main bays have all the large sophisticated machine tools which are core to our business. In the annexes, we have small lathes, milling, and grinding machines. We are now shutting the annexes down, taking all the people who drove those small machines and retraining them on the larger, more sophisticated machines, with a view to increasing the shifting in those core activities. This will give us more value adding. We now realize we are in a state of continuous change, treading a path rather than reaching a destination, setting a continual, renewable mission, and improving faster than our competition.

Results

GEC Alsthom Large Machines achieved all the business objectives set at the start of its 5-year restructuring programme. Throughout the programme, production was not only maintained, but increased, so that all the supporting investment could be funded from company resources. In 1991, the company was highly commended in the UK Energy Award Scheme for a 40 per cent saving in annual energy consumption. In 1992, it won the Manufacturing Effectiveness Award, organized by the Institution of Mechanical Engineers, against competition from 46 UK companies. The key achievements of the project are listed below:

150 per cent increase in exports	New noise test facility
92 per cent increase in sales per employee	New Cycloconverter test facility
50 per cent reduction in cycle time	New products
40 per cent reduction in energy use	Full CADCAM introduced
40 per cent reduction in occupied space	Improved environment and site layout
25 per cent reduction in inventories	
25 per cent reduction in overheads	

Once the company started down this path it found that it was on an upward spiral of continuous improvement. Now it is leaping forward again in other ways that were never really conceived in the original plan, as a result of developments over the last couple of years. In some areas the business is as good as the best, in other areas it still has to make improvements, and the competition aren't standing still either. GEC Alsthom Large Machines has to run very hard to keep ahead of them.

Lessons

Charles Paterson concludes, 'The results were certainly worth the effort, because there is no doubt in my mind that this is a very competitive market. There is a surplus of capacity around the world; everybody is undercutting everybody else to try and fill their factories, and if we hadn't restructured around cells and teams, we wouldn't be here. That is undisputable.'

Personally, I've learned that you have to be prepared to rethink everything—from the foundations up—at any time. If somebody comes into your office with a suggestion and asks, 'Have you ever thought about that?', the glib answer is: 'No, I haven't and it wouldn't work anyway because ... .' Then you pat them on the head and off they go and that's another good idea killed. You've really got to take the blinkers off and give everything serious consideration because sometimes what may seem to be a silly suggestion is something that in a modified form could bring about major benefit. Nothing is written in tablets of stone. Everything can be changed. We have to be changing and improving faster than our competition, and if we aren't doing that we're dead.

McDONALD'S RESTAURANTS LTD

World-wide locations
Andrew Corcoran
Regional Marketing Manager

This case study resulted from our belief that the principles of cells and teaming were just as applicable in other industries as in manufacturing. We believe that the way McDonald's restaurants operate clearly illustrates how JIT scheduling can be applied and integrated with planning. Our observations of McDonald's in action and our interview with Andrew Corcoran, who recently moved into his present position from Restaurant Manager, show that they operate their restaurants as team-based cells in the fullest sense, fulfilling all of our criteria for people, process engineering, logistics and performance measures. We believe Andrew Corcoran's comments are thought provoking and challenging. There are lessons we can all learn from the way McDonald's has approached team-based manufacturing and JIT supply.

Context
McDonald's is the world-wide market leader in fast foods because of high quality, cleanliness and value with fast, friendly and efficient service.

Problem
Keeping market leadership means challenges for McDonald's with:

- Supply leadtime.
- Product shelf life and wastage.
- Quality of product and service.
- Motivating production staff.
- Capacity planning.

Actions
- Putting people first.
  - Teamworking
  - Career planning
  - Training and development
- Just-in-Time production.
  - Cooked product stock control
  - Line scheduling
  - Production on demand
  - Global logistics planning

Results

- In 1993 there were 13 000 restaurants world-wide in 63 countries.
- McDonald's restaurants now have approximately 12 per cent of the quick-serve restaurant market or 73 per cent of the burger house market.
- McDonald's leadership in fast food has been attributed to the corporation's underlying philosophy of quality, service, cleanliness and value.
- The key feature of McDonald's success is the fast, friendly and efficient service that they provide.

Andrew Corcoran explains what happens when people are placed as the most important ingredient in a company's business strategy.

Problems

Our management policies have been developed to make sure that we keep our customers happy. Some of the things that could go wrong are:

- Supply lead time. Because supply is handled centrally, shortages mean lost orders and disgruntled customers.
- Product. Bad management can lead to high wastage, because the product can only be stored for 10 minutes.
- Quality. Poor service usually means customers lost to Burger King.
- Production staff: Since many employees are young (under 21) and work part-time, maintaining their motivation and loyalty can be a problem.
- Capacity planning. Resources have to be planned 24 hours before they are needed.

Actions

Putting people first In our appraisals of personnel, we say that people—both customers and employees—are the most important ingredient at McDonald's. Putting people first and keeping the workforce happy is the basis of our customer service because unhappy workers aren't going to produce happy customers. Most staff members are reasonable and if the people in the organization are happy and motivated, then the business will move forward. They'll find sales leads, identify opportunities, keep their people happy. Therefore, McDonald's recognizes the need to invest in training, for everyone from crew members to senior management.

Career structure   Staff can come into the business with degree qualifications as trainee managers, or as crew members who work their way up. Probably 60 per cent of our people do the latter. For example, the president of the McDonald's Corporation in the UK started as a part-time crew person while he was at college in the USA and came across to help open the first McDonald's in Woolwich in 1974. If someone joins at the age of 16 it would probably take until they were 22 to become a reasonable restaurant manager, and someone starting at 18 could manage a restaurant by the age of 24. The next step is to go on to area manager and then progress through middle management to regional manager. This approach allows us to take advantage of the growing number of formally educated people at higher levels in the organization, to reward employees at all levels appropriately and to allow some room for initiative at the lower levels in the organization. Managers are taught to make sure good decisions are being made and *not* make all the decisions themselves. We're fortunate that this type of culture has been created by the people who set up our business.

Training and development of managers   McDonald's probably has three or four major training courses on the way through to restaurant management. They include subjects such as stock control, forecasting and human resources. Managers are judged on their ability to run the restaurant as if it were their own business, so a lot of things are thrown into the melting pot: ability to market the product, ability to look after crew people, ability to train; all things affect profitability, so maximizing food output and minimizing wastage is just one of those things. However, a higher wastage figure could be right for some businesses, especially at the beginning of a restaurant's life, when managers may well need to keep plenty of food there until they know what the sales pattern is going to be. This way they won't get dissatisfied customers, since the product will be there for every customer who enters the restaurant. It's more difficult to manage a drive-thru' restaurant, because we can't see the customers driving in. For example, it takes approximately 5 minutes to produce a filet-o-fish™. If two cars arrive at the serving hatch and the second one wants three filets-o-fish, although it takes the same time to cook three as one, and this branch normally only sells three or four an hour, the production caller might make a decision to keep three in stock, knowing that each customer who drives through will be served without waiting. When the manager gets to know the trading pattern of a new restaurant, he or she will be able to decide on the best levels of cooked products to hold in stock. Managers get this expertise by a combination of training and experience.

Training the grill teams A big part of the managers' training programme is spent on how to train grill teams. We train people in a specific function, so it's always quite regimented. When it's quiet, they do other things. Once they can do a task to a required level, they move on to the next one, gradually building up a bank of knowledge, and this governs what job they are given to do. Two newish crew people might be assigned to cook filet-o-fish, pie and chicken products, even though one experienced person could do it alone. On the other hand, the manager has the option of putting one experienced person to train two new employees on the hamburger section. If the manager is short of experienced people that day, he or she may decide to have two inexperienced people cooking while the experienced staff member does a key task. The manager has to balance business needs and staff levels to make sure that he gets in the maximum amount of training, so we don't allow a situation where on one shift everyone is experienced and on another they're all inexperienced. By getting the right mix, we can bring inexperienced people through at a rapid pace to a really good performance and increased productivity for the business. This allows the manager to review hiring requirements, maybe giving full-time employees more sociable hours, because there is less need for them to work in the evenings as part-time people become more experienced.

Every year in September we have a natural changeover of staff as some move on to higher education and some come into sixth-form colleges. We need to overlap incoming and outgoing staff to keep the business running smoothly. If we hire good people in September and train them well, they're ready for the busy Christmas period. They can have time off college to earn Christmas money and also cover our busier periods. After Christmas they have less time because of exams and that allows our full-time staff more work.

Product mix   A printout from the till gives a breakdown on how many products we've sold in a given period or in each hour. We never get a perfect situation where we can use historical data to predict the future to the nearest 10 minutes, because we can't predict how many customers will come in. But we can estimate during each hour whether we are going to sell, say, 60 or 70 Big Macs™. We are thus able to determine that we need to keep 6 in the buffer store for every 10-minute cycle. We'd probably use 4 as a minimum stock level, so if someone buys 2, we'd make 4 to bring it up to 6.

Finished product stock control   We keep a buffer stock of products, which the manager sizes using 'minimum level' charts. The restaurant manager has 'minimum level' charts for French fries and the holding of French fries and other products, but some gut feeling will also be brought into play. For example, if the restaurant expects to turn over about £500 per hour, it would be necessary to have 6 Big Macs in production at all times, but we never keep any product for more than 10 minutes, so these have to be sold within that time or thrown away.

Although we may have to throw 4 of the 6 in stock away because they are outside their shelf-time, 6 has been established as the requirement which gives the best interaction between the customer flow and product waste. Obviously we want to keep wastage as low as possible but we also want to keep the quality for the customer as high as possible. To McDonald's, quality isn't just the product by itself, but also the way we serve. We need to serve customers quickly, especially at lunchtime since people with short lunch hours are not prepared to wait for service. It's therefore a question of balancing all the activities of the business in order to minimize waste.

Line scheduling We refer to the person who requests the product as the 'production caller'. These people build up information through experience and knowledge of what sells when. At lunch times we will sell more Big Macs, because male customers tend to buy Big Macs more than female customers. In the afternoon, there will be fewer Big Macs, since customers tend to be more family-oriented: mothers with children order lighter products, such as a McChicken Sandwich™. During holidays we sell more hamburgers and cheeseburgers at lunchtime because of the greater numbers of younger children, who are more likely to eat the hamburger products. Production callers aren't part-time workers, but experienced people who've been with us for some time because it's quite a skilled position. This person is the lynch pin in the process, whose ability governs whether a restaurant either spends or saves hundreds of pounds each week. The success of our operation depends on the production caller's knowledge of the volume of business the restaurant will be doing through the day, and what kind of day it is, e.g. holiday, school term, weekday or weekend. They learn their skill through a combination of training and sales analysis, with some intuition based on experience thrown in.

The production caller asks for one of four specific modes of production, which vary the speed at which the products can be produced. The production caller and manager have to calculate which of the production modes they need to use for each £1000 of sales. Therefore, one of the requirements for being a manager is that you have to pass a mathematics exam as part of your training. Obviously, restaurants vary and they have to know the circumstances of the area they serve. Once they understand that, it's usually very easy for them to say, 'Right, I need this method now and I'll step up to that method when I need to.' In very quiet periods they just ask for each product as it's needed. This is especially true after about 8 pm or 9 pm in a city-centre restaurant, when customers who come in aren't in a great rush so we have got time to prepare, and they get the hottest, freshest possible food (not that 10 minutes preparation is a long time).

Even having done it myself, it's difficult to explain how a manager could survey a certain group of customers, maybe even regular customers, walking through the door, and just know what product he needs to put down the line to satisfy those customers. However, it still takes 10 minutes to produce a product. Once he or she has satisfied a particular group of customers, they go back to the levels required by what we call the 'product mix'.

Varying the speed of production depending on demand The quality of the products is not affected when we vary the cycle time by varying the method of production, because the time taken to produce each product remains constant. We have clamshell-style grills and we can cook just a few or a run of up to 12 pieces of meat on each one. We can put 12 pieces of meat down the line, wait, and when the meat is cooked, remove those 12 pieces of meat, and place the tray with the 12 Big Macs into the waiting area. Then we can begin the cycle again by putting the next 12 pieces down the line.

To increase production, we can put 12 pieces of meat down the line and, when the first batch is half-way through the production process, start another batch of 12 down the line. When the second batch is half-way through the process, you can then remove the first batch (Kanban), and place it on a tray in the waiting area. An even faster method of production is to put a batch of 12 down the line with 2 people using the same grill. We can speed the line up by adding more people to the product line during the busier hours. We can also open up another grill area in order to reduce cycle time. Some restaurants have two, some have three and some have four grill areas, depending on the volume of business, and managers balance supply and demand by moving staff around. They achieve this by using a positioning guide (capacity chart), which decrees the number of people needed for a given number of customers. It also allows them to calculate the number of grill positions and cooking specification areas that will need to open.

Raw material stock control   Managers control inventory by doing volume projections. Restaurant managers carry out a number of monthly volume projections for ordering raw material. This part of the ordering procedure is computerized to balance the usage per £1000 with the orders. The computer automatically sets the date for an order; therefore the manager has to check the due date of each order. If managers decide to increase the order quantity of raw material because of a promotion, they would fail if they neglected to change the projections. We have to do a monthly projection for ordering purposes, but the weekly and daily projections are optional. Naturally, the monthly projections are more accurate than the weekly and daily projections. If a manager estimates that for £3000 of Big Macs two bags of lettuce are required, from the projections the computer will say that this amount of lettuce is needed for that delivery period.

   With a restaurant that's been trading for some time, it is possible to construct a trend profile from historical data of what was sold and other relevant information, such as dates of school holidays. However, in the case of a new restaurant, in order to build a projection of sales, we tend to look at similar restaurants in areas with similar demographic profiles and then estimate what sales we think we may get. This is how the restaurant manager will deal with staffing and stocking, by projecting likely volumes from what's happened in the past. I suppose in industry a similar situation would be that if a dealership is ordering 100 Ford cars a week, then that's what Ford would base its business plans on. But if they have a new product such as the Mondeo coming out, with lots of TV advertising, sales are going to jump; and this means that Ford will need more nuts and bolts. That's the way it works in our restaurants.

I'd be foolish to say we don't run out of stock, because we do. However, it's very rare. An automatic stock buffer is built into the ordering system. A restaurant manager would probably have a 2-day buffer level for safety. We are allowed to keep bread buns for 4 days before throwing them away, so if in 2 days we'd use 20 trays, i.e. 600 buns, we'd never go below that: that would be our stock level.

A first-in first-out system ensures that the product is used within its shelf life. However, sometimes, the manager estimates incorrectly, or the weather turns sunny and we sell lots of milk shakes when we hadn't considered this possibility. We may increase our milk shake order quantity in the summer in anticipation of good weather, but instead it rains for 2 days; so we have to throw the milk shakes away. Things like this happen, but we aim to minimize the effect through use of buffer stock levels and through recalculating the projections and the requirements every time the order is done, making sure to check it before pressing the computer button and committing ourselves to it. The computer has given us the statistical information and we hope that the experience of the managers will enable them to alter their projections appropriately, based on other factors such as a marketing promotion.

Global logistics   Our ethos is based on getting supplies locally as much as possible. When investing in local infrastructures we try to take our supplies from that country using internal company suppliers. However, we use a central distribution agency, Golden West Foods. They co-ordinate the orders from all the restaurants and they too have projections for the hamburgers and buns which they keep in their warehouses for the restaurants to call off.

Performance measures   Restaurant managers are measured on various things based around maximizing sales and optimizing profits. Control of the food costs, which is basically the raw food you take in, is important: the ideal situation is to turn all your input of raw material into sales or employee meals. Wastage of raw material is monitored weekly and analysed. If we've wasted milk cartons every week, or even just this week, we look at why this has happened, and if our buffer stock is 20 and should be 10 then we make it 10. We also record production waste, and the amount we've thrown away once it's been cooked. If we're throwing away too many hamburgers, for instance, we could reduce our 'minimum level' charts or decide that this week we should break wastage down hourly, which may show that we're not cooking enough at lunchtime but we're throwing product away during the rest of the day. In that case, we could raise the level of stocked cooked products during the lunch hour and reduce the level of stock during the rest of the day. This would bring supply into balance with demand and minimize wastage.

Results

Ray Kroc bought McDonald's outright in 1961 at a price of $2.7m; 1974 heralded the opening of the 3000th McDonald's restaurant, and the first one in the UK. There are now 13 000 McDonald's restaurant in 63 countries, employing over 22 million people. It is estimated that more than 100 McDonald's hamburgers a second are sold world-wide, which constitutes a turnover of approximately $18bn a year. In 1993 there were 490 restaurants in the UK with a turnover of approximately £570m and an increase of 35 restaurants per year planned. McDonald's is constantly changing with regard to development and innovation. New items, like fat-free burgers and (more recently) pizza, are always being added to the menu. Restaurant designs and customer service techniques are constantly under review.

Index